# ETERNAL COMPANIONS

# ETERNAL COMPANIONS

Edited by Douglas E. Brinley
and Daniel K Judd

BOOKCRAFT
Salt Lake City, Utah

Library of Congress Catalog Card Number: 95-60340

ISBN 0-88494-972-9

Fifth Printing, 1999

Printed in the United States of America

# CONTENTS

# INTRODUCTION

After a particularly stressful visit with a couple one day, I [Doug Brinley] came out shaking my head. I wondered to myself, "What would Carlfred [Dr. Carlfred Broderick], or Dan [Dr. Daniel Judd] or Dick [Dr. Richard Chidester], or Charlie [Dr. Charles Beckert] do to help this couple?"

I went down the hall to visit with Dan Judd about this particular problem, and we kicked around some ideas that might be of help. It became obvious to us that the gospel contained the answer to the couple's dilemma, and that their problems were not dissimilar to those of many other LDS couples who were not applying the principles of the gospel to their marriage relationships. The more we thought about it the more we decided it might be a great service to the Saints if we were to ask a number of professional marriage counselors each to write a chapter detailing their "best counsel" to Latter-day Saints that would help them to work through their marital problems and also enrich and strengthen their relationships. We were anxious to include also any preventive maintenance ideas they might be willing to share.

We went through a list of those we knew who had been involved in a great deal of counseling or who had taught others in an educational setting how to improve marriage and family relations. Our request to each of them was simply this: "Will you put in one chapter what you consider your very best ideas or counsel to help Latter-day Saint couples improve and strengthen their marriage relationship?" We did not want to limit them or assign topics to them, but wanted them to simply reflect on their own experiences in working with Latter-day Saint couples and to share their techniques and approaches.

This book is the result of that request. It comes from individuals who have spent countless hours listening to LDS couples and assisting them to enrich, change, refurbish, and restructure their relationships. They have assisted others to gain an eternal perspective of the gospel, improve their relationship skills, soften hearts, make essential changes that are in harmony with gospel principles, and thus build a marriage worthy of an eternal duration.

A wide range of ideas and many years of practical experience are behind the wisdom presented herein. These men and women are committed to the Restoration, faithful Latter-day Saints anxious to help couples in the Church to attain better and stronger companion relationships. Their wisdom and collective experiences will bless the lives of all who read this volume.

The premise of this book is the concept expressed by President Gordon B. Hinckley in an October 1990 general conference address:

> Strong family life comes of strong and clear religious understanding of who we are and why we are here, and of what we may eternally become. Strong family life comes of the perception that each of us is a child of God, born with a divine birthright, and with a great and significant potential. Strong family life comes of parents who love and respect one another, and who love and respect and nurture their children in the ways of the Lord. These are undergirding principles of our teachings as a church. To the degree that we observe these teachings we build strong families whose generations will strengthen the nation. ("Mormon Should Mean 'More Good,' " *Ensign*, November 1990, p. 54.)

We think you who read this book will find within it the keys to improve your marriage, to cultivate a more long-range marital perspective, and to develop an effective philosophy of living happily with each other, along with numerous practical means to enrich your relationship. That is our purpose.

A separate treatment of this subject for Latter-day Saints is justified because theirs is the only church that teaches the principle of eternal marriage, the doctrine that family relationships can continue beyond this life. This doctrine stems from an understanding of the atonement of Christ, which guarantees that all mankind, both male and female, will be resurrected; and once resurrected, a person cannot again die (see D&C 138:17; Alma 11:45). Being then unable to die, yet retaining either the male or female traits and attributes of premortal and mortal life, would one not be desirous to continue the family relationships begun in this life? Such a wonderful post-resurrection relationship is possible when a man and a woman are married in mortality, or by proxy after death, by priesthood authority (the authority derived from an eternal being rather than from a mortal power), and keep the covenants they make at the time of their marriage. Would they want their relationship to cease simply because of physical death—a condition Adam and Eve brought about millennia ago? The mission of Jesus Christ was undertaken to restore us to conditions of immortality lost through the fall of our first parents.

The only time married couples who have married in the temple and been faithful to their covenants with God will be separated ever again is during the brief span when one spouse moves on to the spirit world ahead of the other—there to await the arrival of the spouse. Elder Bruce R. McConkie explained:

> We have the power to perform a marriage, and we can do it so that the man and the woman become husband and wife here and now and—if they keep the covenant there and then made—they will *remain husband and wife in the spirit world* and will come up in glory and dominion with kingdoms and exaltation in the resurrection, being husband and wife and having eternal life. . . . That is our potential; that is within our possible realm of achievement. ("Celestial Marriage," in *1977 Devotional Speeches of the Year* [Provo, Utah: Brigham Young University Press, 1978], p. 172, emphasis added.)

To continue beyond this life an eternal marriage relationship begun here requires that we build as solid and righteous a companionship in this present existence as our mortal life span permits. The careless or indifferent, if unrepentant, cannot expect to extend their marriage into the next life, for "what doth it profit a man if a gift is bestowed upon him, and he receive not the gift? Behold, he rejoices not in that which is given unto him, neither rejoices in him who is the giver of the gift." (D&C 88:33.)

If two married people do not like each other in this life, does it seem reasonable that death will change their minds and nature so that they will want to be married forever? Though the Lord may be patient with us in our early years of marriage as we learn to adjust to each other and establish our fledgling union, as we age and mature together we should be able to work out any kinks in our relationship.

The gospel theory is: *the longer we are married, the stronger our marital bond.* After all, exaltation—the goal we all seek as Latter-day Saints—is the eventual perfection not only of the individual but also of the marriage relationship. Hence as Latter-day Saints we have an interest in organizing and perfecting our family units.

To that end we hope the counsel in this book will help couples to enjoy the great privileges inherent in marriage and parenthood.

DOUGLAS E. BRINLEY
DANIEL K JUDD

# 1

# REMEMBER THE SIMPLE THINGS

## H. Burke Peterson

*F*or several years I had the great blessing of interviewing, and when appropriate restoring former blessings to, men and women who had earlier been excommunicated from the Church for serious offenses. In time they had found their way back into the waters of baptism and were now anxious to be restored to full fellowship.

Through that experience I learned some valuable lessons that I would like to share with you, insights that have come after numerous interviews with individuals as I sought to know their true feelings. I came to know of the events in their lives that brought them to the point where they finally lost their membership in the Lord's earthly kingdom.

I noted that by far the great majority of those who needed to be disciplined came out of a troubled marital situation. Now, I am not suggesting that all troubled marriages end with one or both parties being involved in Church discipline. I am just saying that it is my observation that most serious sins seem to be associated with marriages that are not going well.

I sought to learn how and why each one lost his or her membership, in the hope that their lives had changed in ways that would preclude their involvement in a similar situation again. In every case I found that trouble began with what each at first thought was a "small, insignificant" event. Perhaps it was lunch with a secretary, a ride home with a colleague, or a little flirtation with an associate that got them started. In their minds no single event at the time it occurred

was thought to be major, but when left unchecked it became cumula-
tive, and the seeds of temptation were planted, nurtured, and finally
blossomed into serious sins. The Lord's counsel as to good causes—
"Out of small things proceedeth that which is great" (D&C 64:33)—
works for bad ones too. The whisperings of the Spirit to stop or
change directions went unheeded, and soon these seemingly innocent
acts grew into an avalanche from which the participants could not escape. Finally their sins became of such a nature that the individuals
could no longer retain their Church membership. Broken hearts,
shattered marriages, and damaged children were the consequences of
their sins.

Through the atonement of Jesus Christ and the principle of repentance, they now sought forgiveness and a restitution. In seeking
relief from their torment they saw a brighter day dawning. The
chance to be cleansed of past mistakes was uppermost in their minds.
The gospel provided new perspective for them. And, what was always
interesting, they could now see clearly that the lessons they had been
taught from childhood to adulthood were directed to help them avoid
the very transgressions in which they had become enmeshed.

I have learned that there are many things that matter in maintaining a healthy marriage. However, there are only a few things that
*matter most.* Not that other things are unimportant, but when a few
basic elements are in place a tone and pattern are set which allow
everything else to fall into line. After many years of observation and
interviews I have come to understand that *the quality of a marriage
rests on the strength of each marriage partner's faith and testimony in the
Savior and his mission.* That is paramount. Helaman taught his sons,
"It is upon the rock of our Redeemer, who is Christ, the Son of God,
that ye must build your foundation; that when the devil shall send
forth his mighty winds, yea, his shafts in the whirlwind, yea, when all
his hail and his mighty storm shall beat upon you, it shall have no
power over you" (Helaman 5:12). No doubt some of these storms will
become quite severe in our lives, but they will not sweep us away to
destruction if our foundation is built on this rock.

These experiences have led me to see the importance of proper
guidance by parents from childhood on, with a father and mother who
care about their children and who take the time to express their love
in simple ways from the earliest stages of life. The relationship between parent and child seems to be a significant prelude to the quality

of the relationship each child will have with his or her eventual spouse. Because of parental mistakes some will have to work harder to develop a happy adult alliance, but with an understanding spouse and a firm desire to live gospel principles they can be successful.

It is not unusual to find that one marriage partner is more in tune with spiritual powers than the other, and that such individuals are anxiously hoping their companions will make some sweeping changes (sometimes they demand them) in a short period of time. However, traits and character deficiencies are usually developed over a lifetime of habit. For most of us, one sweep of the hand is not sufficient to bring about permanent change. Most of us do not change quickly without a change of heart. It takes time—even in a safe teaching and learning environment with a patient, cheerful, and therapeutic spouse—to change personality and character traits imbedded in us since our infancy. Patience is an essential virtue in marriage.

Sometimes differences in spiritual values and maturity do not become evident until the partners have been married for a while, and most often they come to the fore with the advent of children. I suppose the blossoms from the "flower of love" hide our real thorns. We are pretty good at masking negative personality traits during the dating stage. Thus it may come either as a sudden shock or as a gradual realization by one partner that the spouse does not have the spiritual strength that partner anticipated before the ceremony took place.

When this occurs—and what two people, after all, are spiritual equals at the time of marriage?—an immature marriage partner may be impatient with a spouse, not realizing that love, devotion, selflessness, strong faith and testimony, and relationship skills may require time to develop. Too often a marriage partner who seeks a transformation in the spouse tries to manipulate that change, only to find to his or her rude awakening that *matters of the heart*—love, trust, devotion, and faith—*cannot be forced.*

However, there are things we can do in marriage to prepare our hearts to feel an immense love for—and commitment to—each other; essential attributes and personal sensitivities that can be acquired with a little effort. It has been my experience, as Nephi and Jacob taught, that the formula to come unto Christ is rather simple. But in our modern, sophisticated age, we have a tendency to "look beyond the mark" and think that answers to our problems must be more complex than they really are (see 1 Nephi 17:41; Jacob 4:14). Let me share a few examples of things that couples can do to ensure that continued feelings of love and mutual devotion grow and blossom over the course of the marriage.

1. *Look for the good in each other.* Couples would do well to focus on the good things a spouse does and each regularly (daily, I hope) make mention of what he or she appreciates and values about the other. This must not be contrived or phony, and in most instances a brief mention is all that's needed. It is far better and easier to encourage another to correct a fault or an inconsistency in his or her personality when we look for the good rather than pointing out faults. Most of us are aware of the things we do wrong.

I personally have a hard time with people who say they believe in constructive criticism. My experience does not lead me to believe there is such a thing. My point of view is that criticism has a connotation that does not come from above. I think it is important to note that *correction* is different from *criticism*. The Lord discussed correction in his revelation to the Prophet Joseph Smith (see D&C 121:43). He emphasized that any corrections are to be performed when "moved upon by the Holy Ghost." If we are inspired to chastise, however, the Lord insists that there be "an increase of love toward him whom thou hast reproved, lest he esteem thee to be his enemy" (D&C 121:43).

Criticism is more judgment-oriented than correction, and most of us do not have sufficient knowledge to be critical of others—especially of a spouse and children who are still growing and developing as we are.

2. *Remember that we all come to marriage from different backgrounds.* I think we need to keep in mind that as marriage partners we are products of wherever we've been and whatever we've come from in our lives before marriage. Again, judging someone else's background has little place in marriage. Somewhere I read that all men and women have a target they would like to hit—a target of good, positive things. They would like to do better and be better than they actually are. They aim at the bull's-eye, but seldom, if ever, do they hit it directly; and those of us who think we know best judge them by what they hit rather than by what they are aiming at. In a marriage relationship should we not spend more time building each other up? When you think about it, don't you function better when you are encouraged (knowing that it wasn't your best, you could have done bet-

ter, and next time you will); what you need is an understanding response, rather than being castigated and chastised?

The Lord counseled that we should pray for each other, speak well of each other, and build each other up in positive ways (see D&C 108:7–8). Consider your own patriarchal blessing. Does the Lord, who *is* perfect, criticize you for what you are not doing, or does he indicate your potential and extend blessings to you if you will live for the promises made to you? True, he may caution and warn of danger in our mortal weakness, but he wants us to know of the great blessings that can be ours if we will use our agency to conform to the principles of the gospel and the whisperings of the Spirit of the Lord.

3. *Improve communication between spouses.* Every married couple can improve their communication skills, sharing hearts with each other and really hearing what the companion is saying. Every couple needs to take time to examine their communication patterns to realize that *how* they communicate is as important as *what* words they use. If every couple were humble enough to ask if they are meeting each other's needs, they could make improvements long before things got out of control. I know of situations in which couples who have had difficulty communicating have used a few simple exercises by which to help a partner learn from the other better ways to share feelings and improve techniques.

4. *Eliminate selfishness, the great curse of our day.* We find many places in the revelations where promises of great blessings are given to those who will develop the selfless attitude and bearing of the Savior. We should constantly keep in mind that self*less*ness is Christlike while self*ish*ness is satanic. Thus we should express and show our appreciation every day to our spouse, both verbally and by simple acts that ease the companion's burdens. There are many things we can do for each other on a day-to-day basis that are service oriented. A good neck-rub, for example, is usually therapeutic, and an occasional flower or surprise can work wonders on a wife's heart. Love messages are not conditional on the extent of our bank balance.

5. *Don't neglect individual prayer and praying as a couple.* An important and simple principle that builds strong marital bonds is prayer. Individual prayer is needed to gain personal inspiration in your own marital stewardship, and the two of you need to call down the blessings of heaven upon your own relationship and to assist you as parents. Though this sounds simple, it has been my experience that

many couples have a hard time developing the "habit" of prayer, and if something upsets either one they are prone to stop. There is great value in a couple kneeling together (why not hold hands?), pleading both morning and night with Heavenly Father to assist them in their marriage and family responsibilities. Both need help and strength from a divine source if they are to be equal to their great family roles.

Though before their temple marriage nearly every couple receives counsel to pray together, many don't follow that wise counsel. If one or both have served missions, this practice should be automatic! Pray for understanding, patience, and added strength for you to become effective marriage partners. Prayer softens hearts. Don't neglect praying for your spouse too; it is difficult to be angry with someone who is the subject of sincere prayer.

6. *Read scriptures individually and together.* It makes a healthy contribution to the marriage when marriage partners spend a few minutes each day drinking from the scriptural well. It does not have to be a lengthy period, but every day would be ideal. What we are talking about here is the undergirding principle of a happy marriage—increased faith and testimony in the Lord and Savior, Jesus Christ, and in his gospel. Too often we falter when we lack background knowledge, and we lack the Spirit that will come into our lives when we immerse ourselves in the words of the Lord. Worldly influences can harden our hearts so easily. We counter that influence with the words and counsel of the Lord through his prophets.

The scriptures bring us back to the realities of life and renew our long-range perspective. It is the scriptures that bring us the eternal scope of our premortal, mortal, and postmortal lives, which reveals more clearly the reasons behind God's commandments to us. Thus our obedience becomes more certain and heartfelt. Alma recorded, "God gave unto [Adam and Eve] commandments, after having made known unto them the plan of redemption" (Alma 12:32). As it was with Adam and Eve, so it is with each of us. When we understand the plan of salvation as recorded in the scriptural records, we increase the likelihood that we will treat each other in a more Christlike way because we see the purpose of our marriage and family life in an eternal framework.

Until we come to understand that we are part of God's eternal plan and know for ourselves what we ought to do and why we ought to do it, we find ourselves groping in the dark. Scriptures strengthen our spiritual sensitivities and open the way for more effective marriage relationships.

7. *Follow the counsel of living prophets.* I remember that in April 1993 President Gordon B. Hinckley, in some wise counsel to the General Authorities, advised us to keep our lives and teachings simple. He assured us that most things would fall into place if we would do the following four things: (1) pray daily; (2) read from the revelations, particularly the Book of Mormon and the New Testament (so that we are familiar with the Savior's life and teachings); (3) attend sacrament meetings weekly, sincerely renewing our covenants; and (4) pay tithing. Then, he promised us, marriages will be happier, young men and young women—our sons and daughters—will marry in the temple, and more young men (and young sisters as they desire) will go into the mission field better prepared to be successful missionaries.

I think it really is that simple. In my experience in working with marriage problems, I've found that if couples will follow the basic pattern President Hinckley mentioned (which, by the way, is the essence of Moroni's counsel in Moroni 6:4–6), they will be able to put the most important particulars of life in proper priority.

Even though both marriage partners may not be equal spiritually, if one of them will give his or her best effort, good will result. And who knows but what in time "the unbelieving husband [will be] sanctified by the wife, [or] the unbelieving wife [will be] sanctified by the husband" (D&C 74:1)? That is my hope for all. We have the tendency to complicate our lives with the sophistication and learning of our day. When we follow simple, basic gospel principles, and give heed to what we may think are "little things" in our lives, we can build the kind of relationship that brings true joy and happiness and eventual exaltation in the kingdom of our Father.

*In the October 1993 general conference, Elder* **H. Burke Peterson** *was made an Emeritus General Authority. His first calling as a General Authority was that of First Counselor in the Presiding Bishopric, where he served from April 1972 until April 1985. He was then called to the First Quorum of the Seventy. He was the Jordan River Temple president from May 1985 until September 1987. He has served as an Area President for the North America Southwest and North America*

Central Areas and in the Temple Department of the Church. He has a master's degree in civil engineering. He served as a naval officer in the Seabees during World War II. He has been a bishop, stake president, and Regional Representative in the Phoenix, Arizona, area. He and his wife, Brookie Cardon, are the parents of five married daughters.

# 2

# SURVIVING ETERNAL MARRIAGE

## Carlfred B. Broderick

*I* was having lunch with two old friends. One, a Protestant minister, ran one of the campus religious centers; the other was on the faculty of the Law School. The conversation drifted to the topic of the recent epidemic of lawyer-bashing jokes. Among the more elaborate examples offered (by the minister, in this case) was the following:

A very-much-in-love young couple were on their way to the wedding chapel to be united in marriage. When only a few dozen yards from their destination they were hit and killed by a truck whose brakes had failed.

At the pearly gates Saint Peter offered to grant them the standard righteous-desire-of-their-hearts (which, at least in jokes, seems to be guaranteed to the righteous dead prior to moving into their respective heavenly mansions). He was taken aback, however, when they insisted in a single voice that they had only one desire, and that was to complete the wedding ceremony they had been so rudely and unjustly cheated out of. St. Peter tried to explain that this was a highly irregular—even improper—request. There was no marrying or giving in marriage in heaven . . . it just wasn't done. But they were adamant and persistent. This was all they wanted. Heaven wouldn't be heaven unless they could be together, and so forth. Finally, St. Peter said, "O.K., O.K., I'll check into it and see what I can do, but this may take some doing and some time, so be patient."

But they were not patient. Every day they checked two or three times to see if any progress had been made toward granting their desire.

Each time Peter said, "I'm working on it, I'm working on it." Finally after three seemingly endless weeks of unrequited longing, the good news came. It had been arranged.

The ceremony was lovely, but simple; just the minister, the young couple, and St. Peter and one other angel as witnesses. Afterwards they set up housekeeping in their own heavenly love-nest.

But things did not go well. Small disappointments and disagreements escalated into major quarrels. Major quarrels escalated into knock-down, drag-out fights. After only a few weeks they returned to St. Peter demanding a divorce.

"A divorce!" he said, "after all the trouble I went to get you married!" "Believe me," said the man, "it wouldn't be heaven if I had to live with this shrew for eternity!" "I demand my rights to personal privacy and peace," said the woman, "and I don't get a moment of either with this monster. I demand a divorce!"

St. Peter looked at them for a long moment. "You really don't know what you're asking," he said, shaking his head wearily. "It took me three weeks to find a minister up here. Do you have any idea how long it would take me to find a lawyer?"

It was a clever joke on three counts. It zinged the minister who told it; it double-zinged the lawyer; and even more slyly, it triple-zinged the third member of the group, who was known to be an advocate of the doctrine of eternal marriage. The point scored all too painfully. How often have I heard those very words from couples who had been sealed for time and all eternity in the temples of our God (closer to the "pearly gates" than the storyteller could imagine)! "It just wouldn't be the celestial kingdom if I had to be tied to this miserable person for all eternity." Secular divorce rates stabilized at an all-time high in about 1979. Divorce rates for temple marriages, traditionally several times lower than secular rates, have continued to climb, gradually narrowing the gap that separates the two. The current survival rate for temple marriages is not overly impressive.

Often I have asked myself why this is so. Latter-day Saints know the principles of eternal unity. I am persuaded that there is no principle of successful marital life that I could share with good LDS couples that would be new to them. In fact, any principle that purported to be true and crucial to successful living which was new to them should be immediately suspect. The laws governing marital satisfaction are but special applications of the laws of the gospel, and every good Latter-day Saint learned them in Primary (or, in the case of converts, in the six missionary discussions and the Gospel Principles classes on Sundays). The problem seems to come in making the special applications from the general gospel principles to the specific marital situation.

The point was illustrated vividly in an experience with a colleague. He is Jewish and one of the finest family therapists I know. I have referred close friends and relatives to him with good results. One day a woman called me to see if she could make an appointment to bring in her family for some counseling. Their problem was a rebellious teenager and an escalating power struggle between the girl and her parents that was getting out of hand.

Without minimizing the seriousness of this type of problem, it must be acknowledged that it is a common bread-and-butter sort of issue for family therapists. They deal with various versions of it every week. Both research and common observation have shown that when teenagers get into trouble it is generally a case of too little supervision and too few consequences for breaking family rules, or, equally often, a case of too many rigid rules and overly strict and intrusive enforcement leading to rebellion. In the first case the therapist works with the family to set up a more structured home environment. In the second case the therapist works with the family to unwind the system a little.

This family who called appeared to be of the second type. As it happened, they lived on the opposite side of Los Angeles from me and quite near my good Jewish colleague. I suggested that they might wish to save themselves the long drive and trust their problem to this excellent clinician. They agreed that this was a sensible suggestion and started to work with him.

After only a couple of weeks I got a call from my friend. "Carl, I need some help with this couple you referred to me."

"What's the problem? They probably just need to loosen up the parental iron fist a little."

"Of course. If they don't, this kid is about to run away from home or attempt suicide or do something else drastic. But, Carl, every time I suggest any movement in the direction of loosening up they patiently explain to me that I just don't understand their religious obligations as Mormon parents to keep this kid in line. Frankly, I don't know how to deal with this. I don't want to attack their religious beliefs, but the situation is explosive."

I thought a moment and then said: "Here's what you do. First, tell them that since you have started working with them on their problems you have developed a real curiosity about the Mormon religion. This will serve to get their attention. Then say that there is one issue that keeps coming up when you ask about it that has you mystified. You keep hearing about some 'war in heaven,' but you can never quite figure out what it is about."

"That's it? I just ask them to explain this 'war in heaven'?"

"That's it."

"Carl, what's the war in heaven?"

"It doesn't matter; just do what I said, and let me know how it goes."

A few days later he called: "Carl, I can't believe it. I did what you said and it was like magic."

"So tell me about the session."

"Well, as you suggested, I told them that since I started working with them I had become sort of interested in the Mormon religion. You wouldn't believe the response. Even the rebellious teenage kid promised to give me a copy of some book on the Church with the family picture in the front. Then I said there was just one thing that kind of confused me about their beliefs. I kept hearing about some war in heaven. What was this war in heaven? Well, the mom in this family didn't as much as take a minute to collect her thoughts. In seconds she had launched into some story about a council in heaven and two plans, and she gets about three minutes into it and she stops cold in her tracks and gives me a funny look and says, 'All right, Doctor, you've made your point.' From that point on they were like putty in my hands. It was like magic. Carl, what is this war in heaven?"

Of course, there was no magic. This good LDS woman simply had the unnerving experience of explaining Satan's plan to an "investigator" and in the midst of her explanation recognizing it as substantially identical with her own version of responsible Mormon parenting as she had outlined it to him the week before. She understood the gospel principle fully. She just had been blinded to its applicability to her everyday challenges as a parent.

In the remainder of this article I should like to share three gospel-derived, inter-related marital survival principles that may be labeled collectively The Law of the Harvest. They apply with equal force to temple marriages or to any other kind, but my concern here is with the potential eternal union. When these principles are observed, husband-wife relationships prosper; when they are ignored, the relationships wither and die, and in that process become toxic to the souls of the participants.

## The Law of the Harvest
### Principle 1: Water, Feed, and Fertilize

The first principle related to the law of the harvest is this: *Marital relationships, like all living things, require regular nourishment in order to thrive.* This point is vividly illustrated by a series of studies on the impact of pregnancy and childbirth on marital morale. One set of investigators tracked marital morale among a group of couples over the first five years of their marriage. They noted that among those who had no children over the five-year span there was a slow but steady decline in the enthusiasm the couple had for the marriage. This effect had been observed in other studies and seems to be the normal result of the often unrealistic expectations many couples bring with them to marriage being challenged by the complexities of actual marital experience.

Couples who had a child during this five-year span also experienced this expected decline, but in addition suffered a precipitous drop-off in marital morale during the pregnancy and the early infancy of the child. After the first few months of parenthood the marital morale recovered in some degree, but it never regained the level of those who had no child over the same span of months.

Some of the couples had not just one but two children during the period of the study. These suffered the same loss of marital morale as others during the pregnancy and the early infancy of their first child, and then a similar drop with the second child. The recovery from this second dip fell short of the level achieved by those with only one child (let alone the level maintained by those with none).

You can readily appreciate that this finding might be unnerving to someone like my wife and me, who have had eight children. If the pattern found in this study held for all eight pregnancies and early infancies our marital morale should have been doomed to end up in some emotional sub-basement.

The good news is that it doesn't have to be that way. Other studies have shown that some couples manage to inoculate themselves against the loss experienced by most couples in these circumstances. Those who manage to avoid the dip are likely to have three characteristics that set them apart from others:

*First,* they jointly planned and wanted the baby. Studies show that about half of all babies come as the result of failed contraception. Such babies can be cherished also, but the advantage, both for the child and for the marital relationship, is with the anxiously antici-pated and warmly welcomed child.

*Second,* in these happier couples the husband is very much more likely to have been involved in the pregnancy, the delivery, and the care of the newborn. He is the type who informs himself about fetal development at each stage of the pregnancy and proudly exhibits sonograms to his friends; he is very likely to have attended Lamaze classes and coached his wife through the challenges of the labor and delivery processes; he is available to give the baby its first postpartum bath and is active in its care from that point forward.

*Third,* these couples do not get so wrapped up in the process of becoming parents that they forget to be marital partners; they plan and protect time for being alone with each other. It may not be pos-sible to achieve this as easily or as often as before the baby compli-cated their lives, but they manage it regularly and reliably. These oc-casions are the pillars that support the roof of their marital morale structure. As any architect knows, supports do not need to be placed right next to each other to do the job, but if they are spaced too far apart the roof will surely sag.

Of course, this principle not only applies to couples coping with becoming parents but is operational also at every other point in the marital relationship. If couples hope to maintain a vital, bountiful re-lationship, they understand that they must protect it and nourish it regularly. Part of this is refusing to let other important life tasks (the children, the job, demanding parents, or Church assignments) crowd out the prime relationship. They structure their time and energy so that significant segments of their life are shared and so that the pillars of their relationship do not stand too far apart.

## The Law of the Harvest
## Principle 2: Weed, Weed, Weed

One of the disturbing features of gardens and of relationships is that if you only take thought to nourish the crop you may yet lose the harvest because of weeds. I know many a couple who spend a great deal of time together in shared activities but the result is toxic because the nature of the interaction is noxious. Three of the most common and destructive marital weeds I observe among those with temple marriages are these: (1) well-rationalized mismanagement of anger and disappointment; (2) well-intended but toxic and erosive criticism; and (3) unacknowledged, nonverbal "meta-messages" that challenge or demean the partner.

1. *Mismanaged anger and disappointment.* It is not possible for any couple to live together for any extended period without each of the partners experiencing irritation and disappointment. But some styles for handling these natural feelings are particularly harmful, not only to the quality of the relationship but also to the individual spirits of the partners. In the classic case, one partner may acknowledge (almost with pride) that he or she has a "short fuse" or a "hot temper." Probably it has been shaped and legitimized by generations of forbears who were fine people but who also had hot tempers. From time to time, as irritations reach some critical point, there comes the characteristic explosion of unkind and often all but unforgivably hurtful words and actions. Afterwards the person feels much relieved and in a mood to forget the whole thing. Perhaps, if the reaction of the spouse is extremely negative, there may be promises never to do it again. But, of course, the promise is not kept.

It would not be uncommon for the partner with this destructive, self-indulgent addiction to be married to a spouse who is afflicted with the equal and opposite addiction, the "slow-burning, self-pitying resentment-hoarding" that never lets go of a hurt and sours both the relationship and the character of the hoarder. Those who have experienced either or both of these styles can testify that they are weeds, indeed, and can choke out many a loving seed that might otherwise thrive.

2. *Toxic but well-intended criticism.* A bright and worthy young doctor married an equally bright and worthy (and, judging by her wedding pictures, very beautiful) young woman in the temple. That night, the magic, long-awaited intimate moment came when, as he put it, he unwrapped the package to see just what he had bought. The first, loving, romantic, never-to-be-forgotten words out of his mouth were: "You know, honey, you could lose a few pounds."

It should be noted that this intense young physician gave high priority to physical fitness in his own life. His food intake was meticulously monitored as to both balance and amount. He ran six miles before breakfast every morning. He would doubtless have sunk like a rock in the Great Salt Lake. His comment was well-intended. Yet some readers, at least, will not be surprised to learn that despite an enormous amount of well-intended—and knowledgeable—guidance, effort, and supervision on his part, by the time I saw them in therapy eleven years later, far from having lost the original "few pounds" this woman had ballooned up to over three hundred pounds. How could this have happened? Especially, how could it have happened given the remarkable good fortune of having a bona fide M.D. weight expert in your own home who was willing to invest any amount of energy or money to help?

If this seems perplexing to you, ask your spouse to explain the dynamics of it.

I do not want to leave the impression that this pattern of toxic but well-intended criticism is a characteristic peculiar to virtuous LDS men. In fact, based on my clinical observation, I would wager that most of the world records are held by faithful, loving, competent, helpful LDS women. The righteous desire of their hearts is to help their foot-dragging patriarchs become the priesthood leaders in their homes that they could and should be, but are not. Often the results of their unflagging efforts are as impressive as our young doctor's, and as disappointing and perplexing.

Studies have shown that the optimal diet for a happy marriage provides a ratio of nine positives (non-demanding touches, kind words, compliments, up-beat comments) for one negative (criticisms, complaints, reminders, accusations, requests, demanding touches). Would you care to guess the national average? Various studies put it at about seven negatives for every three positives. My guess is that this is about the average for temple marriages also, although I know of no research on this matter on this population. In any case, most would agree that there is room for improvement in the ratio of positives to negatives in most "celestial-kingdom-bound" relationships.

3. *Unacknowledged "meta-messages" that challenge or belittle the partner.* Students of human communication have pointed out that every exchange of messages contains two parts: the "message," which contains the manifest content of the communication, and the "meta-message," which is carried in the *way* the message is presented—the tone of voice, the inflection, the body language—and which *defines*

*the relationship* between the sender and the receiver. A comfortable, symmetrical, straight-across exchange may indicate an egalitarian relationship. On the other hand, if the meta-message is judgmental or arrogant it communicates that the sender feels the receiver is inferior; or if it is worshipful, that the receiver is felt to be superior; if it is well-defended and suspicious, the receiver is defined as dangerous and untrustworthy; if open and loving, as safe and trusted.

Because meta-messages are rarely put into words, they are hard to pin down. Frequently the sender denies any intention of sending such a message and may not even acknowledge to himself the feelings they reveal to the sensitive receiver. But never doubt that relationships thrive or waste away based on the impacts of these relationship-defining exchanges.

Again, the findings of a long-term study of marital success and failure come to mind. In this case the investigators had newly married couples participate in a "hot debate" on some subject that they disagreed on. This debate was video-taped, and the individuals were also monitored for blood pressure, pulse, and palm sweat. The exercise was repeated every year for five years in one study and nine in another. By the end of that time a certain number had already separated or divorced.

The investigators were interested in seeing whether they could identify a "debate" pattern that predicted eventual failure. Surprisingly, the most damaging pattern was *not* the symmetrical hot debate, despite the yelling that sometimes occurred. The key to these couples' survival was that the *meta-message* even in these relative free-for-alls was "we are equals." The most damaging pattern was a vicious cycle that involved the wife trying to get the husband involved in the discussion and his stone-walling her. One can debate who was the more at fault, him for his stubborn refusal to cooperate or her for her dogged persistence and pursuit. The more relevant point is that the *meta-message* exchanged by these couples was "we are competitors for control of this relationship." Independent of the content of the quarrel, the style was a power struggle. In contests of will, relationships are often the losers.

The same study also produced another finding that was pertinent to our discussion. Couples filled out questionnaires before they did the "hot debate" exercise. The single item that best predicted survival over the whole five- or nine-year course of the study was this:

"Husband voluntarily and cheerfully participates in housework." I routinely ask audiences of LDS couples why on earth this item should have this remarkable predictive power. Is getting the housework done expeditiously really the key to marital survival? Of course the answer they give me is that it is the relational message in the "voluntarily and cheerfully" part of the question that is the key. The meta-message from the husband to the wife is validating, loving, and egalitarian. One woman came up after the discussion to confess that although she had been reluctant to bring it up in front of all the other couples, for her, "voluntary and cheerful participation in housework" was foreplay.

I cannot sufficiently emphasize the point that we are not typically conscious of the messages we send. My children have pointed out to me a couple of truly embarrassing defects in my own meta-message repertoire. I have always prided myself on my tolerance of other people's opinions that differed from my own. "Let them believe how, where, or what they may" is my motto. I have often bragged that my children were encouraged to think through issues on their own and we could then discuss alternative views calmly and with mutual respect. As evidence, I have often noted that in the 1992 U.S. presidential elections various members of my family passionately endorsed and voted for each of the three major candidates.

But not too many months ago I was interrupted in the midst of such a brag by one of my children noting that it wasn't like that at all. What really happened when one of them put forth an opinion at variance with my own was that I rolled my eyes and sighed (as much as to say, "I can't believe that my own flesh and blood could come up with such an idiotic idea"). *Then* I would assume the posture of accepting, sponsoring, and mentoring individual variances of opinion. I attempted to deny any such signal, only to be shouted down by a chorus of affirmations by other family members. "Dad," they said, "your opinions on everything are transparent. Don't you know that when you were bishop nobody ever watched the sacrament meeting speaker; everybody watched you to see how the speaker was doing."

Even more embarrassing was their further observation (they were on something of a roll at their dad's expense) that I walk ahead of everybody whenever we go out as a group—and sometimes even when I'm on a date with their mother. Ouch! What kind of a meta-message is that? So I'm trying to raise my consciousness on these matters and change my ways. But I figure that if *I* who give lectures and write books on this stuff can be so unaware of my own ungracious relational messages, others must find it challenging also. Certainly it is my observation as a therapist and as a people-watcher outside of therapy that I am not alone in this.

## The Law of the Harvest
## Principle 3: Protect from Predators

In the Savior's parable of the sower, some of the good seed was plucked up by fowls and consequently never survived to fulfill its promise. In this permissive and erotically super-saturated world we lose a lot of temple marriages to predators. Temple covenants are restrictive, oppressively so to some who observe all around them people of their own social class and standing enjoying the pleasures of the flesh with the approval of most of their associates. We live in a consumer-oriented culture, and many feel that the "Joneses" are having more fun than they themselves are. We have worked just as hard as they, yet we are being cheated of many of the gratifications and rewards that others demand as their right.

Others, who would never let themselves be tempted by such obvious Sodom and Gomorrah stuff, are yet led carefully away by ignoring the safety rules that ought to protect one's marital commitment. In their efforts to do good, to comfort those that mourn, to cheer up the broken hearted, they do not guard themselves from getting first emotionally and then physically involved with needy and appreciative people who happen not to be their spouses. I do not feel the need to belabor the point. If the promise of eternal marriage and exaltation is likened to a seed and a bird eats it, there won't be any rich celestial harvest, whatever the motivation of the bird.

## Conclusion

When it comes to celestial marriage it is not a matter solely of whether the marriage itself survives, but, as suggested by the title of this piece, whether the individual partners survive with their spiritual well-being intact. One of the hazards of making such lofty promises and indulging in such elevated hopes is that when it all turns sour, as it does in too many cases, the disappointment is as extravagant as the expectation had been. Sometimes Humpty-Dumpty can be put back together again, with or without the help of wise friends, sensitive priesthood leaders, or competent therapists. Sometimes it even happens that the loss of innocence is good for the relationship, in that each partner has learned through their painful experience the importance of principles they had too cavalierly overlooked.

Sometimes no resuscitation is possible. The wounding is too great, or one's partner has stubbornly turned away from and rejected the path that leads home. There is yet survival and even celestial promise for those who endure, faithful to the end. For some, a wiser, richer marriage with a worthy second partner. For some, a lonelier journey, lighted by the faith that every modern prophet has taught that our God will withhold no blessing from any of his children that they would willingly receive if the circumstances of their lives permitted it.

For the grateful majority of us, the marriage survives our mistakes, and serves, if we will permit it, as a continuing University of Advanced Gospel Application. The principles we learned in Primary. But the day-to-day applications—ah, there's the continuing challenge!

**Carlfred B. Broderick** *began publishing articles about marriage and the family more than forty years ago. To this point he has authored thirteen books and scores of articles and chapters on the subject. For almost a quarter of a century he has been the executive director of the Ph.D. program in marriage and family therapy at the University of Southern California. He and his wife, Kathleen, have eight children and a growing number of grandchildren. He is currently serving as a patriarch in the Cerritos Stake of the Church in Cerritos, California.*

# 3

# THE ISSUE IS
# A CHANGE OF HEART
## C. Richard Chidester

**M**y experience as a professional marriage and family counselor has confirmed for me personally the Lord's command to "say nothing but repentance unto this generation" (D&C 6:9). I have learned that for a marriage or a family to really improve, the people involved must experience a fundamental change of heart that comes only from true repentance—not from just an outward altering of behavior. Changes in behavior alone are cosmetic. Programmed actions are terrestrial at best. They lack the power to lift one to a celestial life.

But a change of heart can truly change people and ultimately the eternal quality of their marriage. It is a transformation in feeling and attitude, the result of repenting and yielding their hearts to God, to the Spirit (see Helaman 3:35). Samuel the Lamanite gave the formula: "Faith and repentance bringeth a change of heart" (Helaman 15:7).

### Finding Peace

I have been humbled and thrilled as I have seen clients turn to the Lord in the depths of their trials. As their hearts change, they find comfort, strength, and guidance—inspiration from a higher source. Some of them have spouses who are willing to repent and honestly improve. Together, they discover that as they exercise faith in Christ and yield to his Spirit their marriage relationship makes dramatic improvements.

Others have unrepentant spouses who are not yet willing to follow the same process. But even in these situations, as one spouse yields his or her own heart to the Lord and seeks divine comfort and guidance, bitterness and resentment are abandoned and the spouse is able to forgive. As hearts change, resentment is replaced with genuine compassion for the unrepentant companions; and they feel, for the first time, genuine peace.

## A Moment of Grace

I saw this process occur in a young man who came to see me. His wife had left him and gone home to her parents because of their marital difficulties. But instead of telling me about all the things *she* had done wrong, he spent an entire hour explaining to me what the Lord had taught him in the past few days about himself and what *he* had done to contribute to the reasons for her leaving.

He told me that for several days after she left he *was* filled with resentment and self-righteous pride and blamed her for most of their problems. Because of the hardness of his heart, he saw himself as the victim of an unreasonable wife who selfishly refused to give her heart to him or to their marriage. Hadn't he done his very best to cope with her unfair and hostile behavior? Little by little his resentment grew until, caught in a web of rationalization and self-justification, he completely distorted his outlook and was unable to see the truth about himself and his wife.

Then one day he was blessed with a moment of grace and insight. While praying, he began to listen to what the Spirit had to say to him. As he did so, he began to view his wife with compassion and realized that she had simply responded out of her own insecurity and in self-defense. He began to feel sorrowful, and he now missed her. His heart was softened and he was prompted to sincerely ask the Lord what he should do about his marriage. What he heard was very different from what he had expected.

## A Flood of Insight

The Spirit began to flood his mind with recollections of many things he had done to disrupt his relationship with his wife and to make things difficult for her: He had put his two jobs ahead of everything. He had made little effort to take time for her or to help her with her responsibilities. He had made light of her concerns as she tried to communicate her feelings to him about their marriage. He had put friends and athletics and selfish pursuits ahead of her. He had not led out in scripture study, home evening, family prayer, or husband/wife prayer as regularly as he should have. In short, he had neglected her needs and the needs of their marriage and had justified his actions by telling himself that he was pursuing her best interests in the long run.

After receiving this veritable flood of insight, he realized how selfish and neglectful he had been, and he felt deeply sorry. As the truth began to seep into his heart, he began to see a different woman than the one he had made his wife into. He began to see her as he had in days gone by. Now he realized that even though she had responded to him in the same way that he had treated her, he could have prevented the deterioration of their relationship by being more responsible himself. Seeing her as the problem had, itself, been the problem. It became obvious to him that the only person he had any direct control over was himself, and that changing himself was his best hope for changing the marriage.

This young man had truly humbled himself, desired to know the real truth, and asked in faith. And then he accepted responsibility for the things the Lord revealed to him. Trusting in the Lord and believing that the Lord would help him, he experienced a mighty change of heart. All of these realizations came to him without the help of a counselor—except the divine Counselor, the Holy Ghost.

I feel that my role, as I indicated earlier, is to "say nothing but repentance unto this generation"—and to help husbands and wives put themselves into a position to be able to receive this kind of divine help from the Spirit. I have witnessed this same pattern over and over again in the lives of those who truly humble themselves, seek the truth about themselves and their marriage, and experience a change of heart.

## The Natural Man

When we were born, we were innocent. However, as the Lord told Adam, "Inasmuch as thy children are conceived in sin, even so when they begin to grow up, sin conceiveth in their hearts" (Moses 6:55). After Adam and Eve had taught their children the gospel, Satan came among them and told them not to believe it. "And they believed it not, and they loved Satan more than God. And men began from that time forth to be carnal, sensual, and devilish." (Moses 5:13.)

When we refuse to follow the enticings of the Spirit or to live the gospel truths we have been taught, and we follow instead the enticings of Satan and the world, we experience our own personal fall and become a "natural man" and "an enemy to God" (see Mosiah 2:32–40; 3:19).

We are not somehow inherently defective or evil because of the fall of Adam. Our own sins are the culprit in our becoming "natural," or spiritually impure. Arthur Henry King wrote: "What is fundamentally wrong with human society and human beings is not psychological, it is not economic, it is not political, it is not anthropological, it is not cultural. It is more fundamental than that. It is sin." (*The Abundance of the Heart* [Salt Lake City: Bookcraft, 1986], p. 254.)

## The Effects of Sin on Relationships

As fallen mortals, we all struggle to one degree or another with sin. When people marry, they bring their own sins—and the consequences of those sins—into their marriage and family relationships. When we sin, our alternatives are (1) to acknowledge our wrongdoing and repent, or (2) to blame others or our circumstances. If we choose the second alternative, we are refusing to admit the truth and to repent. In doing so we violate our spiritual selves by deceiving ourselves and justifying our sin. Some rationalize by thinking to themselves: "I can't help it; it's the way I was raised." "Life hasn't been fair to me." "My emotions are too strong and I lose my temper." "My parents didn't love me."

The sin itself and the subsequent rationalizing cause us to feel guilty and to lose the Spirit. This self-deception creates defensiveness and anxiety, which in turn lead us to blame others for our misery, to harden our hearts, and to strike out at them. If the other person responds in a similar manner, a vicious cycle of mutual blaming and accusation is created. The inevitable result is alienation. Having impure hearts, we are unable to love others with a pure love.[1]

---

1. I am grateful to the Moral Studies group at Brigham Young University, and to C. Terry Warner in particular, for conceptualizing how sin is self-deception and how sin and self-deception undermine personal happiness and relationships.

## Cycles of Collusion

If a wife takes offense at her husband's provocations and strikes back at him she loses the Spirit also and becomes a party to the sin. When both husband and wife are caught up in the sin—blaming and accusing each other—they come into virtual collusion with each other, though that term usually signifies a deliberate conspiracy. It is as if they are cooperating in a mutual lie in which each person is trying to shift the blame and the responsibility to the other.

In this situation, both spouses can easily become engaged in an active crusade to defile the relationship, conducted under the pretense that each is only trying to cope with the difficulties the other spouse is creating for him or her. As a result, the relationship continues to deteriorate; it cannot be improved in an atmosphere of blaming, arguing, and self-deception.

When spouses are colluding with each other in this way they have their defenses up and treat each other with contempt. They are each absorbed in themselves and are out to protect themselves, and in effect each tries to manipulate the other in order to have his or her own needs met. They are on guard, each suspicious that the other will get the advantage. As a result they treat each other as objects to be controlled rather than as people with feelings and needs and ideas that long to be acknowledged.

In allowing themselves to become caught up in the sin, both husband and wife are resisting the enticing of the Spirit and betraying themselves—walking not in the light, but in darkness, and following the devil, "who is the father of contention" (3 Nephi 11:29). They tell themselves that the problem is the fault of the other person—forgetting that in order to have an argument, both spouses must be willing to cooperate. They ignore the fact that their spouse is only responding to them; that they are in on this together; and that to break the cycle of mutual recriminations, each must have a change of heart and give the spouse a different person to respond to.

I am constantly amazed at how effectively couples can argue with each other without hearing one thing. Because their defenses are so high, they are unable to listen on the feeling level. They are interested only in what they have to say or need to say in order to justify themselves.

Of course, by refusing to take or give offense in the first place, spouses can avoid this whole cycle of collusion.

## Force Is Not the Answer

In the natural world, force is used to bring about change. But it doesn't work in marriages and families.

I have seen husbands and wives and parents destroy their family relationships by using behavioral control techniques that threaten the identity, independence, and agency of others.

I have seen husbands and wives and children who have been the victims of forceful, controlling, and manipulative spouses or parents. They are broken in spirit, feel humiliated and intimidated, and have lost their confidence and vitality.

## Behavioral Techniques Are Not the Answer

Generally, rehabilitation techniques used by professionals focus on controlling and manipulating outward behavior. But it is the inner man and woman that must change.

I have seen clients who have been to marriage enrichment retreats, parenting classes, and communication seminars—and who are still without hope. Even with all the help the world could offer, they are still engaged in power struggles in their marriage and family relationships, and they wonder if family harmony is ever really possible. When they finally come to realize that the fundamental issue is a change of heart—not simply a change of behavior—they begin to feel hope.

We can engineer harmony temporarily by strict self-control and manipulative techniques—but it won't last. Without an honest change of heart, our feelings won't change. And unless the negative feelings in our hearts change, our behavior will not permanently change.

I am not suggesting that skill training is never helpful, or that it does not have a place in counseling. I'm saying that it is only a partial answer, because our skills will fail us if our hearts aren't right. Skills alone cannot override the power of accusing feelings and attitudes in our hearts. (I have learned this from communication experts who teach that communication skills are the answer, yet they cannot get along with their own spouses.)

## No Happiness Without Repentance

Since the root of personal problems and of broken relationships is sin, the cure is repentance. Indeed, through the grace of Jesus Christ it is possible for us to "put off," or to dispose of, the natural man.

Repentance is a *spiritual* solution. This is the reason why real peace cannot come through attending self-esteem workshops or by trying to find oneself through self-analysis, as the world teaches. Self-esteem workshops attempt to teach people how to feel good about themselves *without repenting*. But only a change of heart can truly change people—and their relationships. No wonder the Lord instructed the present dispensation to cry nothing but repentance!

If we are meek and lowly of heart, we will labor all our days trying to repent of our sins. Indeed, we will find happiness and peace to the extent that we liberate ourselves from sin's influence by submitting to our conscience and drawing on the power of the Atonement through repentance. As we do so, we become like children in the hands of the Lord: "submissive, meek, humble, patient, full of love" (Mosiah 3:19).

The Lord will help us repent if we ask him to soften our hearts and to give us the strength to confess our faults and to forgive. Because of the Fall, repentance is a full-time job. The greatest gift parents can give to their children is to repent, and the greatest gift husbands and wives can give to each other is to successively repent of their sins. As Elder Bruce R. McConkie pointed out, "Since all men repeatedly sin they must all gain successive remissions of their sins, otherwise none would eventually stand pure and spotless before the Lord and thus be worthy of a celestial inheritance" (*Doctrinal New Testament Commentary*, 3 vols. [Salt Lake City: Bookcraft, 1965–73], 1:179).

## Self-Honesty

The Lord said, "Ye shall know the truth, and the truth shall make you free" (John 8:32). It is only by living the truth, only through strict self-honesty, that we can become free—free from guilt, anxiety, and the bondage of sin.

However, before the truth can make us free it will first make us miserable as we recognize our personal weaknesses and sins. It is important to *want* the truth. Nephi explained that "the guilty taketh the truth to be hard, for it cutteth them to the very center" (1 Nephi 16:2), but "the righteous fear [the words of truth] not, for they love the truth and are not shaken" (2 Nephi 9:40). In other words, the unrepentant are "cut" by the truth and don't want to face it. But the repentant are pierced or deeply shaken by the truth, and it creates an attitude of obedience which motivates them to repent and improve. They want the truth so that they can rise above weaknesses and sin and improve their lives and relationships.

When we cease to strike out at each other and begin, instead, to respond to one another honestly as human beings with feelings and needs, we begin to have compassion. By dropping our defenses and allowing our spouse to touch our heart, we begin to feel love and concern. The change comes because we have begun to see honestly and to let the Spirit of the Lord touch us and soften and purify our hearts.

Elder F. Enzio Busche of the First Quorum of the Seventy said: "All learning leads to nothing unless it is centered on finding the roots of truth, which cannot be received without first becoming honest" (Truth Is the Issue," *Ensign*, November 1993, p. 25).

One of my favorite sayings is this one by Robert Louis Stevenson: "You cannot run away from weakness. You must sometime fight it out or perish. And if that be so, why not now and where you stand?" (*Richard Evans' Quote Book* [Salt Lake City: Publishers Press, 1971], p. 221.) As long as we are unwilling to face the truth about ourselves and do the things we know to be right, we will not be able to improve ourselves or our relationships. Conversely, if we are open to information about ourselves from others and from the Spirit, there is every hope for improvement.

One accusing, proud man I worked with was ready to divorce his wife. They came to me at the request of his bishop as a last effort to save their marriage. After watching the spouses blame each other for a while, I could see how self-righteous the husband really was and how accusing his wife was in return. I explained to them how self-deceived they both were. As I prayed in my heart, the Spirit descended in the room and I felt to confront him as directly as possible with his hypocritical behavior.

I asked: "When do you turn the other cheek? When do you forgive? When do you show your gratitude to her for the beautiful children she has borne and trained?" I continued asking questions such as these in an effort to help him see the disparity between his own life and the principles he was teaching in the Gospel Doctrine class.

He was shocked at first, and so was I for confronting him in this way. But I felt that it was not me but the Spirit that was communicating to him in this way. It humbled him, and through the promptings of the Spirit he saw himself clearly as the hypocrite he really was.

He reached over and took his wife in his arms. "I don't want to lose you or our wonderful children," he said. "I haven't treated you the way I should have. I have been critical and self-serving, and I need to apologize. Can you ever forgive me?"

She threw her arms around him and said essentially the same things.

I sat in grateful silence as they went on and on, confessing their sins to each other and begging forgiveness. It was truly wonderful to watch all of that repentance and healing taking place. They phoned their children that night and told them they were going to stay together and have a better marriage than they had ever known. They realized they had been living a lie, and in that moment of honesty and humility they experienced a change of heart that changed their lives forever.

## Taking Responsibility

For a person to have a change of heart in such circumstances, there must be a change in the way he perceives himself and his spouse. This change in perception comes as a spiritual transformation. It results from admitting the truth about oneself and one's spouse, both strengths and limitations. It means loving our spouse as he or she is—and forsaking the idea that any other person is responsible or blameworthy for anything we do.

Once spouses begin to take responsibility for their own behavior, they begin to feel freedom from the frustration and anxiety that come from seeing themselves as helpless and hopeless victims of forces outside of themselves. By living in greater harmony with what they know to be right, they begin to experience the peace and freedom of using their moral agency to love and repent and make changes for the better. They begin to realize that the problems they are having are not rooted in poor communication techniques, as the world teaches, but are the result of wrong attitudes and feelings in their own hearts, stemming from sin or from the false perceptions they are being influenced by.

## A True Change of Heart

In order to experience a genuine shift in behavior, then, there must be a true change of heart. A change of heart comes as we put off the natural man and begin to respond to the needs of others. King Benjamin taught that we can put off the natural man by yielding "to the enticings of the Holy Spirit" and becoming saints through the purifying influence of the atonement of Jesus Christ (see Mosiah 3:19). The key to becoming saints is to follow the enticings of the Spirit of Christ, which "is given to every man, that he may know good from evil" (Moroni 7:16).

The Savior said, "Out of the abundance of the heart the mouth speaketh" (Matthew 12:34). It is the feelings and attitudes in our hearts that come out in a crisis. When our hearts are right, when they are free from accusation and self-righteousness, we can spontaneously feel love and compassion and genuine concern for the welfare and needs of others. Such feelings stem from being in harmony with the Spirit, because the fruits of the Spirit are "love, joy, peace, longsuffering, gentleness, goodness, faith, meekness, temperance" (Galatians 5:22–23).

Consequently the change of heart comes as we hearken to the Spirit as it indicts and reproves us for our own unloving behavior and the misuse of our agency. It comes as we humble ourselves; confess our sins to ourselves, to those we have offended, to our priesthood leader when appropriate, and to the Lord. It comes as we seek forgiveness for our own irresponsible behavior and begin to take responsibility for our thoughts and actions. It comes as we begin to feel Christlike love, compassion, and forgiveness.

Honestly confessing our sins is the key to receiving forgiveness for them. By confessing them, we give them away to the Savior. He then pays the debt for them. But he cannot pay the debt unless we tell him, through our confession, how much we owe. If we confess only a portion of our sins, only partial payment can be made. We feel lighter after sincerely confessing our sins, because the Savior has transferred the weight of our guilt to himself. A simple "I'm sorry for the way I acted," or "I'm sorry for overreacting," is all that is sometimes required, and it opens the door for others to do the same.

A change of heart comes as a gift of the Spirit following our own honesty and repentance. Without this genuine change of heart, any outward change in behavior won't last.

## Family Harmony Through a Change of Heart

One man who came to see me complained that he was caught between his wife and his children whenever a power struggle developed. He always ended up feeling defeated, because no matter which side he joined he always lost.

When he was with his wife, the two of them made themselves into the victims of the children, and they saw the children as the problem. Of course, this alienated the children. When he was with the children, he joined their side as the victims of a self-righteous, controlling, unbending mother.

As a result, he had an accusing attitude toward both his wife and his children and felt that his job was to try to keep the lid on everybody. By moralizing and preaching to them about what responsible, gospel-oriented behavior was, he tried to get them to control themselves better.

I tried to help this man understand that neither his wife nor his children alone were to blame, that both sides were provoking each other into the very things they accused each other of, and that his own accusing attitude was a large part of the problem. His wife and children had been defending themselves against the perceived threats of the other, and he had been fueling the flames of contention by siding with one or the other and by self-righteously condemning them both.

Fortunately this man humbled himself, and his heart began to soften. He began to feel a new love for both his wife and his children. As he described it, he began falling in love with his family again.

As his heart changed, he began to see that the job of parents is not to try to take charge of their children and to force them into compliance—but to love and guide them. He realized that he had been treating his wife and children as objects to be controlled rather than as real people with feelings. Now he could see that his wife, with the best of intentions, had been responding from the incorrect perception that a parent's job is to ensure, through manipulation and control, that children do the right things—as her parents had done.

He apologized to his family for his own sinful and unloving behavior and asked for their forgiveness. He began to show love and respect for them by letting them resolve their own issues. He began to really empathize with each one by listening to feelings and responding with compassion. He ceased to see either side blamingly or indulgently, but simply communicated his expectation of responsible behavior in a low-key, matter-of-fact, respectful way.

His wife and the children were skeptical at first, since in the past they had not been able to trust him because of his sudden shifts from one side to the other. But as both he and his wife began to consistently apply the principles of self-honesty, repentance, forgiveness, and unreserved love for each other and the children, the relationships in the family began to change.

This husband and wife exercised faith by pleading with the Lord to bless them with a change of heart and to help them overcome their negative attitudes toward their children. Harmony began to replace dissension. It took time to overcome the old dysfunctional patterns that were so deeply rooted, but they did dissipate since there was no longer a need for them as a defense.

That family still has problems, as any family does, but they are solving them differently now. The parents realize that as they teach, love, and respect their children, and as they respect their agency, their children respond with more love, respect, and compliance. They realize that when their own feelings and attitudes toward their children are changed through their own repentance, the children's behavior can make a genuine and lasting shift. They realize that feelings in the heart are communicated through body language and verbal expressions, no matter how hard they may try to mask negative feelings by trying to be nice or by affecting feelings of love. By taking responsibility for themselves they are showing their children how to take responsibility for themselves.

Of course, a change of heart on the part of everyone is necessary for complete family harmony.

## Understanding Gospel Principles
## Helps to Bring a Change of Heart

In all of my counseling, whether the clients are members of the Church or not, I incorporate principles of the gospel because they are true principles. Observing gospel principles—such as self-honesty, humility, charity, repentance, and forgiveness—is the only way individuals, couples, and families will find happiness and harmony.

Elder Boyd K. Packer of the Quorum of the Twelve Apostles has noted, "The study of the doctrines of the gospel will improve behavior quicker than a study of behavior will improve behavior" ("Little Children," *Ensign*, November 1986, p. 17).

President Ezra Taft Benson said, "The Lord works from the inside out. The world works from the outside in. The world would take people out of the slums. Christ takes the slums out of people, and then they take themselves out of the slums. The world would mold men by changing their environment. Christ changes men, who then change their environment. The world would shape human behavior, but Christ can change human nature." ("Born of God," *Ensign*, November 1985, p. 6.)

The Sermon on the Mount in particular, and the scriptures in general, contain principles for relating to others in Christlike ways. The sermon focuses on the attitudes we need in order to live on a celestial level while living in a telestial world.

## Outward and Inner Behavior

The Jews of Christ's time were following the law of Moses, a terrestrial law, which focused on people's *outward* behavior (which is the focus of most worldly therapy). But Jesus came to lift people to the celestial level, which deals with their *inner* selves. He knew that when our attitudes and feelings are right, right behavior will follow.

I have found that most of us seem to have a difficult time in understanding and applying what the Lord teaches us in the scriptures. Paul said, speaking of detractors, "They zealously affect you, but not well" (Galatians 4:17). Likewise, I think we too are negatively affected by the worldly frames of reference that we assimilate from our culture, and these worldly doctrines are hindering our ability to comprehend the true meaning of Christ's teachings. It's as though we were reading them with a veil over our minds, because the principles aren't really penetrating our understanding or influencing our lives.

Therefore, some of us end up active in the Church but inactive in the gospel. Some of us become very successful in our Church callings and in our professional lives but fail in our own marriage and family relationships. And the true meanings of gospel principles remain a great secret, because we have been blinded by the teachings coming at us from worldly sources. We suffer untold misery as a result of not comprehending and applying the principles of the gospel in our relationships with our family.

Let me highlight a few of the Savior's teachings that can lift lives and bless relationships.

## Anger Is Sin

Throughout the Sermon on the Mount, the Lord contrasts the attitudes of the terrestrial law of Moses with celestial attitudes he wants us to incorporate into our natures. In Matthew 5:21–22 he teaches us that anger—as well as killing—is a sin. A telestial person may kill, and a terrestrial person may get angry. But the celestial attitude is to not even allow ourselves to become angry, because when we are blinded by this emotion we say and do things we would not normally do, things that are inconsistent with a celestial nature.

The world generally would scoff at such doctrine and write it off as unrealistic. However, if the Lord allowed anger on the part of his disciples, he would be justifying the horrible things people do in fits of rage.

A major goal of therapy, therefore, should be to help people realize that anger is a sin, in spite of what the world teaches, and that through the Lord's help we can control our emotions.

The worldly approach is that our emotions are caused by external forces and therefore they are automatic; there is not much we can do about them, they are natural. This erroneous thinking puts the responsibility for our feelings outside of ourselves, onto others, and justifies our conclusion that it is the circumstances we find ourselves in that justifies our anger.

However, the gospel teaches us that we are moral agents who are accountable for our thoughts, words, and actions (see Alma 12:14). We make the choice to perceive things as we do. Our choices lead to feelings, and our feelings lead to actions. By seeking to have pure hearts, by seeing others and ourselves honestly and compassionately and by accepting responsibility for our emotions, we can begin to avoid anger in our lives. And by repenting of our improper feelings and emotions we can be freed from negative, accusing emotions.

There are honest emotions and there are dishonest emotions. There is genuine sorrow for suffering and there is self-pity. One is pure, the other is not. If we are living under the influence of the Spirit our feelings will be pure and justified, whether they be righteous anger or sorrow or joy. In the Sermon on the Mount the Lord doesn't condemn righteous anger. But most of the human anger I see in others and experience myself is not righteous—it is the kind of

anger we work up when we are taking offense or are feeling victimized.

Of course, we cannot decide to control our emotions through self-
control or willpower alone. As fallen mortals we need the help of the
Lord, rather than the arm of flesh, to avoid anger.

## "Be Reconciled to Thy Brother"

In 3 Nephi 12:23–24 the Lord says that if we desire to come unto
him we must first be reconciled to our brother at whom we have been
angry. Then in Matthew 18:15 he says that if our brother trespasses
against us we must go to him and try to reconcile things. Apparently
it doesn't matter whether we are the one who did the offending or the
one who was offended. The responsibility for reconciliation is always
on us.

The celestial attitude, therefore, is to take responsibility—no
matter who started the conflict—and to do everything we can to resolve it. When we take and give offense and work up anger over differences, it is often wise to let emotions die down so that the truth
can seep in and we can see our own part in the problem. But then we
should seek a reconciliation as quickly as possible, for unresolved issues stay alive in our minds. The Lord says that after we have been
reconciled and then come unto him "with full purpose of heart, . . . I
will receive you" (3 Nephi 12:24).

It is not surprising that in marriages in which the husband and
wife are experiencing trouble one or the other oftentimes becomes
alienated from the Church. When there are unresolved differences, or
when we feel alienated from someone, we feel alienated from God.

I have learned from my own experience that I am not much
closer to God than I am to my wife or my children or my friends.
During one period of my life I was spending a great deal of time study-
ing the New Testament in preparation for teaching the life of Paul.
But even though I was in the scriptures all day I felt a lack of the
Spirit, and I was puzzled and uneasy about this.

One morning I read the verse in 3 Nephi about making reconciliation, and it came to me that I had been neglecting my wife and had
been insensitive to her needs. I needed to apologize. I picked up the
phone and told her I realized I had been caught up in myself and had

been neglectful of her needs. (She did not hesitate to agree with me.) As I apologized, I felt a spirit of peace that I had been lacking. I learned vividly that I could not be much closer to God than I was to my wife, and that she was one of the keys to my having the Spirit. That lesson has been reinforced over the years and has motivated me to try and stay close to her in order to have harmony in our relationship and the full blessings of the Lord.

## Turning the Other Cheek

Another Christlike attitude that the Savior taught us in the Sermon on the Mount is how to respond to provocation. A competitive, dog-eat-dog world teaches us to be ready to defend ourselves and stand up for our rights—to resist others and to strike back in self-defense. We see various forms of retaliation and vulgarity modeled for us in the cartoons children watch, in the steady stream of violence in movies and on television, and in the political and social arenas. It is little wonder we end up striking back in our family relationships.

But the Savior taught us not to resist evil, but to turn the other cheek (see Matthew 5:39). So often, we do not seem to understand the simple, clear meaning of Christ's words. We dismiss them as being impractical, convinced that non-resistance to evil won't work in our day, because people will walk on us and continue to take advantage of us if we don't strike back. It is sad that the very teaching that would revolutionize the whole world and that is at the heart of Christ's teachings is dismissed as being impractical, impossible for humans to live.

The law of non-retaliation is so critical, however, that the Lord reiterated it in section 98 of the Doctrine and Covenants. Here the Lord admonishes the Saints to repeatedly forgive their persecutors, whether the offending parties repent or not.

The Saints of Christ's day lived the principle of non-resistance and passed their lives in poverty and persecution, never returning evil for evil. Some Nephites lived the principle as well: "Some were lifted up in pride, and others were exceedingly humble; some did return railing for railing, while others would receive railing and persecution and all manner of afflictions, and would not turn and revile again, but were humble and penitent before God" (3 Nephi 6:13).

The Savior is the best example, and the last week of his life illustrates this principle. He refused to strike back, "because of his loving kindness and his long-suffering towards the children of men" (1 Nephi 19:9). And his example of perfect love is never better illustrated than in his forgiving and redeeming of the very soldiers who crucified him (see Luke 23:34).

If husbands and wives would refuse to strike back and would instead learn to solve their differences compassionately, there would be no arguments or enmity in relationships, and they could live in peace. And it is critical that parents do not allow their children to put each other down, not only because the contention will ruin the spirit in the home but also because the children will tend to do the same in their marriages later on.

Disagreement is healthy and normal, and openness is necessary because of differences; however, provoking and retaliating are nonproductive and destructive. We must learn to discuss differences at neutral times when hearts are right and emotions aren't high, so that we can resolve differences rationally. In sum, we must commit ourselves to non-resistance and then maintain right hearts through faith and the Spirit in order to keep that commitment.

One woman I worked with in therapy was caught in a power struggle with her ex-husband over child support, time with the children, and who should pay for what. She prayed earnestly for the Lord to show her the way to stop the enmity and constant bickering and competition between them and the children. The worldly advice she got was to be firm, to stand up to him, and to not back down or be a doormat.

When she finally humbled herself, turned to the Lord, and asked him what to do, the answers were just the opposite. He told her to withdraw from any opportunities to argue, to quit trying to force more child support from him because he was too irresponsible to earn more anyway, and to just be there for the children and help them as she could. When she followed that counsel, peace came into her heart and the bickering stopped. The children also backed down, and things began to go much more peacefully for everyone.

Although others might get a different answer in a similar situation, the main principle always applies: Trusting in the Lord and following his counsel and principles are the keys to peace.

## Replacing Evil with Good

Another principle in the Sermon on the Mount is the Lord's command to "love your enemies, bless them that curse you, do good to them that hate you, and pray for them which despitefully use you, and persecute you" (Matthew 5:44). In my experience, this commandment is also overlooked, or dismissed as impossible to live.

But it is one of the great keys to peace. As we follow it, all rancor and animosity are drained from our system. This commandment teaches us to have the kind of love the Lord has for his children, even when we do evil.

Our family has had experiences in which people have taken advantage of us and have brought real financial sacrifice and suffering into our lives. But these experiences have brought teaching moments in which we have been able to pray for these individuals, forgive them, go on with our lives, and find peace. The Lord promised he would not leave us comfortless—and he won't if we take his teachings at face value and follow them.

## Forgiving One Another

Another principle of emphasis from the Sermon on the Mount is the commandment to forgive (see Matthew 6:14–15). This is one of the most crucial and most difficult commandments for fallen mortals to live. C. S. Lewis wrote: "To forgive the incessant provocations of daily life—to keep on forgiving the bossy mother-in-law, the bullying husband, the nagging wife, the selfish daughter, the deceitful son—how can we do it? Only, I think, by remembering where we stand, by meaning our words when we say in our prayers each night 'Forgive us our trespasses as we forgive those that trespass against us.' We are offered forgiveness on no other terms. To refuse it is to refuse God's mercy for ourselves. There is no hint of exceptions and God means what he says." (*The Weight of Glory* [New York: Macmillan Publishing Company, 1980], p. 125.)

In essence, the scriptures teach that we must forgive or be damned! The Lord has said that failing to forgive someone is a more serious sin than the trespass that person has committed against us (see D&C 64:9). Forgiving others is absolutely essential for our own peace and salvation.

Many times I have seen people struggle to forgive horrible violations of trust, such as abuse or adultery. But many are able to do so because of their faith in the Atonement and their reliance on the Lord and his Spirit. Forgiveness and healing come as a gift through faith in Christ.

## Overcoming Pride

In the Sermon on the Mount, the Savior warned against the pride involved in beholding the mote in another's eye while overlooking the beam in our own (see Matthew 7:3–4).

President Ezra Taft Benson said that "pride is the great stumbling block to Zion" ("Beware of Pride," *Ensign*, May 1989, p. 7). Certainly pride is a great stumbling block to spiritual progress and to love and unity within marriage. As President Benson stated, pride is a sin that many are committing in ignorance. It seems to stem from all of the other categories of sin, which is a reason it is so deadly and may be considered the worst manifestation of sin.

There are two variations of pride. The first is worldly pride—haughtiness, arrogance, or self-conceit. It is the kind of pride the world thrusts upon us by teaching us to be the best, to be number one, to dress for success, and so forth. We have all learned to be proud; anyone who thinks he has not learned to be proud is very proud indeed!

The second kind of pride, spiritual pride, is far more deadly. Like cancer cells, spiritual pride destroys the good that surrounds it, ruining the possibility of inner peace and of loving, harmonious relationships.

Simply stated, spiritual pride is reliance on self as opposed to dependence on God. It is accepting ourselves as we are, without the need to put off the natural man and be born again.

President Benson noted that the central feature of pride is enmity—opposition toward God and our fellowmen. The spiritually proud man wants to do everything on his own, without relying on God or being told what to do by God or by anyone else. In such a state he hardens his heart against and resists the enticings of the Spirit. He seeks his own welfare, rather than being concerned for the welfare of others. He blames others and the circumstances for his emotional sufferings and for the problems he is confronted with in life. He cannot learn from his weaknesses or mistakes, because he is blinded to the truth as he seeks to justify himself in all things and to shift the responsibility for his problems or marriage difficulties onto his spouse or family.

While one is blinded by pride, it is impossible to repent or to make improvements in the marriage, because the proud man does nothing wrong in his own eyes. He cannot receive help from God, "for none is acceptable before God, save the meek and lowly in heart" (Moroni 7:44). Being meek and lowly in heart is the opposite of being proud. These virtues open the door to the companionship of the Lord and to greater unity and love in marriage.

The only thing that can break down the wall of pride in some people, or get their attention, is a significant emotional event—such as being served with divorce papers, being ordered out of the house, or having a spouse move out. Even shocking experiences such as these won't necessarily soften a heart if a person is too proud and unrepentant to take an honest look at himself and to be willing to negotiate some changes.

The antidote to pride is humility, which is an acknowledged recognition of our dependence upon a higher power. Alma advised us to "acknowledge [our] unworthiness before God at all times" (Alma 39:14)—to never forget we are unworthy and always need the Lord's help. President Benson said that we can choose to be humble by "esteeming [others] as ourselves . . . , receiving counsel and chastisement . . . , forgiving those who have offended us . . . , rendering selfless service . . . , going on missions . . . , getting to the temple more frequently . . . , *confessing and forsaking our sins and being born of God* . . . , [and] submitting our will to His, and putting Him first in our lives." ("Beware of Pride," p. 7, emphasis added.) The essence of humility is putting God first in our lives, following his example, and trying to do what he would have us do.

## Learning—and Unlearning

As we begin to recognize how sin has corrupted our lives and our happiness, we realize that we not only need to *start* doing certain things but also to *stop* doing certain things. It is not just what we need to *learn*, but also what we need to *unlearn*.

C. S. Lewis said: "Repentance is no fun at all. It is something much harder than merely eating humble pie. It means *unlearning* all the self-conceit and self-will that we have been training ourselves into for thousands of years. It means killing part of yourself, undergoing a kind of death. In fact, it needs a good man to repent. And here comes the catch. Only a bad person needs to repent: only a good person can repent perfectly. The worse you are the more you need it and the less you can do it. The only person who could do it perfectly would be a perfect person—and he would not need it." (*Mere Christianity*, [New York: Macmillan, 1952], p. 59.)

## A Change Can Come Quickly

One man I worked with in therapy saw in *one session* how he had been provoking his wife and how, with contrived emotions, he had been holding her and the circumstances responsible for actions of his own choosing. He could see that she was doing the same and that many of their interactions were rooted in manipulation and self-deception. And he decided to forsake the idea that she was responsible for anything he did.

Having recognized the truth for what it was, he felt a new love filling his heart. He went home that night and started treating his wife as he did when they were first married. She responded immediately with love and forgiveness. They felt love and joy and peace return in one evening, and were amazed at how quickly things changed when their hearts had changed. The husband learned that his change of heart opened the door for hers.

## "Can Ye Feel So Now?"

Whether the changes come quickly or more gradually, the challenge is to maintain a right heart. As Alma addressed the Saints, he asked: "If ye have experienced a change of heart . . . I would ask, can ye feel so now?" (Alma 5:26.) The key word is *now*. We must seek to maintain a right heart in our relationships in the same way we maintain it with God—by keeping ourselves blameless (see Alma 5:27) through first principles and ordinances—faith in the Lord and each other, repentance, keeping our covenants, seeking the Spirit, and enduring in righteousness to the end.

## Becoming as a Little Child

The solution to marriage and family problems, then, is to become more Christlike and to seek a change of heart. The Lord gave us the key: "Repent, . . . and become as a little child" (3 Nephi 11:38). Little children are the best teachers of persistence, forgiveness, and unconditional love. Little children trust, want to please, and like to imitate their parents because they love them. (Imitation is the highest form of worship, which is why the Savior commanded us to imitate him [see 3 Nephi 27:27].) Children care nothing for wealth. They know nothing of social aspirations or ambition.

It is the *heart* of a child that Jesus loves, and the broken heart is a childlike heart filled with charity. Joseph Smith taught us much about the kind of charity we need in our marriages and families when he said: "If you do not accuse each other, God will not accuse you. If you have no accuser you will enter heaven, and if you will follow the revelations and instructions which God gives you through me, I will take you into heaven as my back load. If you will not accuse me, I will not accuse you. If you will throw a cloak of charity over my sins, I will over yours—for charity covereth a multitude of sins." (*Teachings of the Prophet Joseph Smith*, sel. Joseph Fielding Smith [Salt Lake City: Deseret Book Co., 1938], p. 193.)

If we try to maintain a remission of our sins we will be filled with love and won't take offense at the sins of others. We will be brokenhearted when we see others hurting themselves by taking offense or by their own wrongdoing. We won't see others as hurting us but as hurting themselves. We won't worry about nursing our own wounds, but will feel charity. Charity is the greatest power for good in the whole world, and without it we will be found wanting at the last day. To love people and to provide an atmosphere free from accusation is one of the greatest gifts we can give them.

Charity, inspiration, guidance, knowledge of weaknesses and sins, forgiveness, and the gifts of the Spirit are rooted in fervent prayer and in faith in the Lord. It becomes evident why Mormon said that if we have faith in Christ we will have hope in Christ—that through him and his atonement we can be purified. If our hope is in Christ and not in the arm of flesh, we will have charity. Then, through Christ, we will "become holy, without spot." (See Moroni 7:39–41; Moroni 10:33.)

**C. Richard Chidester** *teaches at the institute of religion at the University of Utah and is also a practicing marriage and family therapist. He received his B.A. degree from the University of Utah; his M.A. degree in guidance and counseling and his Ph.D. in marriage and family therapy from Brigham Young University. He lives in Bountiful, Utah, and is married to Kathryn Midgley. They are the parents of eight children.*

# 4

# THE CREATION, THE FALL, AND THE ATONEMENT: THE GREAT AND ETERNAL PLAN FOR FAMILY RELATIONSHIPS

*Daniel K Judd*

Several years ago I received a phone call from a member of my ward stating that he and his wife were going to go through with the divorce they had been contemplating. As their bishop, I had been working with them but hadn't been successful in helping them. As with most troubled couples, they each continued to see their problems as being the fault of the other. Even though I had already spent many hours with them, I asked if I could see them before they carried out their decision. While I felt somewhat helpless and didn't know what I was going to say, I felt that I should try once again to assist them.

Between their phone call and the time I was to meet with them, I was preparing to teach a class, when I re-read the following words by President Ezra Taft Benson: "We need to use the everlasting word to awaken those in deep sleep so they will awake 'unto God' [see Alma 5:7]. I am deeply concerned about what we are doing to teach the Saints at all levels the gospel of Jesus Christ as completely and authoritatively as do the Book of Mormon and the Doctrine and Covenants. By this I mean teaching the 'great plan of the Eternal God,' to use the words of Amulek (Alma 34:9). Are we using the messages and the method of teaching found in the Book of Mormon and other scriptures of the Restoration to teach this great plan of the Eternal God?" ("The Book of Mormon and the Doctrine and Covenants," *Ensign*, May 1987, p. 84.)

In his remarks President Benson describes the "great plan of the Eternal God" as being founded on the doctrines of the Creation, the Fall, and the Atonement. He also asks us to declare and make application of these doctrines in our teaching and in our day-to-day lives. That day, as I was discussing these ideas with my students, I quietly realized that while I had been teaching the "great plan of the Eternal God" as a teacher, I hadn't been doing the same as a bishop. I had been giving the distressed couple competent counsel, but I had not been teaching and counseling them in the manner the Lord would have me. As I thought about what I had learned, I no longer felt the helplessness I had earlier but began to feel a growing eagerness to meet with the couple and once again try to help.

During the weeks that followed, this couple and I were blessed with understanding and guidance relative to their family problems as we viewed their situation in light of the Creation, the Fall, and the Atonement. We discussed how their dating, courtship, and early days of marriage had been (in a metaphorical sense) like the Creation, and then how their sins, adversity, and opposition had brought about their fall as individuals and as a couple. We then spoke of the beauty and power of the Atonement and of how reconciliation between them was possible as they reconciled themselves with their God.

This couple represents literally hundreds of thousands of others who labor and at times are heavy laden, but they can have hope, for there is a plan, even "the great plan of the Eternal God."

## The Creation

In the books of Genesis, Moses, and Abraham, we read the different scriptural accounts of the creation of the world (see Genesis 1–2, Moses 2–3, Abraham 4–5). At first glance, one may wonder how the doctrine of creation, introduced thousands of years ago, can in any way relate to the solving of our present problems, but it is really quite fundamental. One of the most basic reasons for the detailed manner in which the Creation is outlined is to teach the divine origin and potential of man. In Moses we read: "And I, God, created man in mine own image, in the image of mine Only Begotten created I him; male and female created I them" (Moses 2:27). This verse follows a detailed account of how the various forms of animal and plant life were created "after their [own] kind" (see Moses 2:11–12, 21, 24–25). One of the truths which can be understood from this sequence of verses is that Adam and Eve were not the evolutionary products of lesser life forms. Neither were they mystically created *ex nihilo* (that is, out of nothing), as many would have us believe. (See 1909 First Presidency statement "The Origin of Man" in James R. Clark, comp., *Messages of the First Presidency*, 6 vols. [Salt Lake City: Bookcraft, 1965–75], 4:200–206.) This knowledge of our divine origin illuminates what our true heritage and potential are. We are not merely a higher order of animal, with the accompanying animalistic appetites, drives, and patterns of behavior. We are sons and daughters of God in the process of developing his same "character, perfections, and attributes" (*Lectures on Faith* 3:4).

A 1909 First Presidency message states: "Man is the child of God, formed in the divine image and endowed with divine attributes, and even as the infant son of an earthly father and mother is capable in due time of becoming a man, so the undeveloped offspring of celestial parentage is capable, by experience through ages and aeons, of evolving into a God" (*Messages of the First Presidency* 4:206).

As we come to understand the character of God, we can come to comprehend who we really are. The Prophet Joseph Smith taught, "If men do not comprehend the character of God, they do not comprehend themselves" (*Teachings of the Prophet Joseph Smith*, sel. Joseph Fielding Smith [Salt Lake City: Deseret Book Co., 1938], p. 343).

God is our Father and wants us to understand that we can become like him. As God is, man may become. This is the fundamental message of the Creation.

### Conscience

It is through our conscience that we first come to perceive the promptings of our Father in Heaven as well as begin to understand what we are. Elder Boyd K. Packer observed the following concerning our conscience:

*Conscience* is a most interesting word. It is made up of the prefix *con,* meaning "with," and the word *science,* meaning "to know." The *Oxford English Dictionary* says it comes from the Latin *conscientia,* meaning "knowledge [knowing] within oneself." The first definition listed there is "inward knowledge, consciousness, inmost thought, mind." The second one is "consciousness of right and wrong," or in just two words, "moral sense."

Our conscience might be described as a memory, a residual awareness of who we really are, of our true identity. It is perhaps the best example of the fact that we can become aware of truths because we *feel* them rather than by knowing them because we perceive them through the physical senses. (" 'The Law and the Light,' " in *The Book of Mormon: Jacob Through Words of Mormon, To Learn with Joy,* ed. Monte S. Nyman and Charles D. Tate, Jr. [Provo: Religious Studies Center, Brigham Young University, 1990], pp. 3–4.)

The prophet Mormon stated the following concerning the Light of Christ, another term for conscience:

> For behold, the Spirit of Christ is given to every man, that he may know good from evil; wherefore, I show unto you the way to judge; for every thing which inviteth to do good, and to persuade to believe in Christ, is sent forth by the power and gift of Christ; wherefore ye may know with a perfect knowledge it is of God.
>
> But whatsoever thing persuadeth men to do evil, and believe not in Christ, and deny him, and serve not God, then ye may know with a perfect knowledge it is of the devil; for after this manner doth the devil work, for he persuadeth no man to do good, no, not one; neither do his angels; neither do they who subject themselves unto him. (Moroni 7:16–17.)

Our conscience, or the Light of Christ, can be experienced in different ways. If we are living truthfully, we will experience our conscience as a gentle invitation to do good. We may have even reached a point of selflessness where we aren't even aware that we are being prompted or acting upon the prompting. We are living spontaneously, without self-regard (see 3 Nephi 9:20).

If we are not living truthfully, we will experience our conscience as something demanding and irritating, as an uncomfortable reminder of what we have to do. Living truthfully and following our conscience leads us to peace and greater understanding, while not being true to who we really are is always the beginning of greater problems to follow. Note the following example of a "prompting of conscience" from my colleague C. Terry Warner:

> Marty was lying in bed, wrapped in the comfort of a deep sleep. He was a young, ambitious businessman concerned about climbing the career ladder and preoccupied most of the time with corporate assignments. As he slept, the four-month-old baby began to cry in the nursery just off the master bedroom. Marty roused, lifted his head, and looked at the clock: 2:30. His wife, Carolyn, wasn't stirring. Marty told his story: "At that moment I had a fleeting feeling, a feeling that if I got up quickly I might be able to see what was wrong before my wife woke up. I don't think it was even a thought because it went too fast for me to say it out in my mind. It was a feeling that this was something I really ought to do. But I didn't do it." (*Bonds of Anguish, Bonds of Love* [unpublished manuscript, 1990], chap. 2, p. 2.)

Why didn't Marty follow his prompting of conscience to awake, arise, and care for his child? Was it maybe that his spirit was willing but his flesh was weak? We will come back to Marty's story later, but first let's examine the question from a doctrinal perspective. Why aren't we always true to what we know is right?

## The Fall

Most of the Christian world teaches that we (mankind) inherited an evil, sinful nature from Adam and Eve because of their partaking of the forbidden fruit in the Garden of Eden (see LaMar Garrard, "The Fall of Man," in *Principles of the Gospel in Practice* [Salt Lake City: Randall Book Co., 1985], pp. 39–70). Consequently, according to this view, our evil desires and actions are indirect results of this "original sin." Because of such teachings, many Christians are led to view Adam and Eve with disdain, thinking that if our first parents had not partaken of the forbidden fruit, we would all be living in a state of peace and prosperity in the Garden of Eden. They teach that thus we would not be plagued by our sinful, carnal nature. These ideas, which permeate the great majority of Christianity, are simply false. As we will discuss later, the idea of mankind's carnal nature, when taught in this manner, can become a rationalization for sin.

## The Restoration View of the Fall

Our Heavenly Father, being all-knowing, understood that for us to become like him we would have to attain that exalted condition in the same manner he did. We would need to come to an earth and experience growth through opposition. (See Joseph Smith, *Teachings*, pp. 345–47.) The Book of Mormon prophet Lehi taught his sons this truth in the following words: "And to bring about his eternal purposes in the end of man, after he had created our first parents, and the beasts of the field and the fowls of the air, and in fine, all things which are created, it must needs be that there was an opposition; even the forbidden fruit in opposition to the tree of life; the one being sweet and the other bitter" (2 Nephi 2:15).

In order to experience righteousness and joy, there must be the possibility of sin and misery. The very purpose behind the Lord's placing the tree of knowledge of good and evil and the tree of life in the same garden was that Adam might exercise his moral agency: "Wherefore, the Lord God gave unto man that he should act for himself. Wherefore, man could not act for himself save it should be that he was enticed by the one or the other." (2 Nephi 2:16.)

While some espouse the notion that we would be in a state of happiness if Adam and Eve had not partaken of the fruit, the prophet Lehi teaches us the truth of the matter:

> If Adam had not transgressed he would not have fallen, but he would have remained in the garden of Eden. . . .
>
> And they [Adam and Eve] would have had no children; wherefore they would have remained in a state of innocence, having no joy, for they knew no misery; doing no good, for they knew no sin.
>
> But behold, all things have been done in the wisdom of him who knoweth all things.
>
> Adam fell that men might be; and men are, that they might have joy. (2 Nephi 2:22–25.)

Just as many Christians bemoan the fall of Adam and Eve, many of us lament the fact that we have to experience the bitter in order to comprehend the sweet. The couple I spoke of at the first of this paper resented the fact that their marriage wasn't in the same state of "creation" as it had been during their early days of courtship and marriage. The reality of children, finances, Church assignments, sickness, and job-related problems had replaced the relative innocence and simplicity they had once shared. They—like most of us, most of the time—preferred the ease of a Garden-of-Eden-like existence in which all the grass is green, the water is clear, and the skies are blue. They didn't understand the doctrine that for there to be true joy, there "must needs be . . . an opposition in all things" (2 Nephi 2:11). When many of us experience opposition we respond with feelings of resentment toward our spouses, families, jobs, or other life circumstances. Some of us falsely believe that our problems are caused by our circumstances and we attempt to solve them by changing our environment. We falsely believe that a divorce, job change, or other modification in our circumstances will bring the happiness we seek. Scriptures that describe the Judgment also seem to suggest the fallacy of pinning our hopes for happiness on outward, environmental factors, for regardless of circumstance, it appears, "he that is happy shall be happy still; and he that is unhappy shall be unhappy still" (Mormon 9:14). Eventually most of us come to the realization that even though our spouse, job, or other circumstances may change, our problems remain the same. The changes that need to come about are not in our circumstance but in our hearts.

Note the following words from President Ezra Taft Benson: "The Lord works from the inside out. The world works from the outside in. The world would take people out of the slums. Christ takes the slums out of people, and then they take themselves out of the slums. The world would mold men by changing their environment. Christ changes men, who then change their environment. The world would shape human behavior, but Christ can change human nature." ("Born of God," *Ensign*, November 1985, p. 6.)

The scriptures clearly teach that the possibility of personal sin and misery must have existed for Adam and Eve and must exist for each of us if we ever hope to experience righteousness and joy. One cannot have the latter without the former.

The fall of Adam and Eve introduced spiritual and physical death into the world—spiritual death in the sense that Adam and Eve were no longer in the presence of God, and physical death in that their immortal bodies became mortal, subject to death. However, through the atonement of Jesus Christ all mankind has been redeemed from the fall of Adam and Eve. We are not "born in sin," as many would have us believe, but are born "innocent before God." In section 93 of the

Doctrine and Covenants we read: "Every spirit of man was innocent in the beginning; and God having redeemed man from the fall, men became again, in their infant state, innocent before God" (D&C 93:38).

From the age of accountability, we pass beyond innocence and begin to be accountable for our own fall, which follows as a consequence of our own disobedience and our adopting the false traditions of our fathers. Continuing in section 93, we read the following: "And that wicked one cometh and taketh away light and truth, through disobedience, from the children of men, and because of the tradition of their fathers" (D&C 93:39).

It is important to emphasize that while the influence of our fathers may have been for good or for evil, there comes a time in each of our lives when we are accountable and responsible for our own righteousness or wickedness. Samuel the Lamanite taught this doctrine in the following words: "And now remember, remember, my brethren, that whosoever perisheth, perisheth unto himself; and whosoever doeth iniquity, doeth it unto himself; for behold, ye are free; ye are permitted to act for yourselves; for behold, God hath given unto you a knowledge and he hath made you free. He hath given unto you that ye might know good from evil, and he hath given unto you that ye might choose life or death." (Helaman 14:30–31.)

I have had the privilege of working with many individuals who have been physically and emotionally abused. Many of these individuals have literally suffered "the iniquity of [their] fathers" (Numbers 14:18). Those who have successfully worked through the implications of this kind of abuse have eventually come to the same conclusion as that stated by the Savior in the Gospel of Mark: "There is nothing from without . . . that . . . can defile him: but the things which come out of him, those are they that defile the man" (Mark 7:15). In other words, even though we may have been sinned against, it is not what others have done to us that defiles us; it is our own actions that lead to happiness or despair (see 2 Nephi 2:26). Note the following example of this truth in the words of one of my former students, Laura:

> As a child I was abused by my older brother. At the time I knew what my brother did was wrong, yet I still loved him. As I grew older, however, I learned to hate him. As I came face to face with the everyday problems of life, I didn't accept the responsibility for my own mistakes

and faults. I looked for an excuse—a way out. I looked for someone or something else to blame. I began having problems with my physical health, but when I began to get well I refused to accept it. I didn't want to return to the everyday problems that would be waiting for me. That was when the hate for my brother really grew. In my mind, all of my problems were his fault. I realize now, it was then that it became my sin. My hate, my anger was what hurt me—it made me sick. The hate for my own brother had grown so strong and fierce that it left him behind. I hated myself, my family, my friends, this earth and its creator. I think that when you hate everyone the void is so powerful that if you don't find love, if you don't give love, you die. That's where the gospel came in. That was when I finally realized there was something more to life than my bitterness. Being part of the Church had never really been important to me. It became worthless, because I didn't do my part. So I began for the first time to work, to really live the gospel. I found that in return Heavenly Father began to give more to me than anything I could ever give him. My happiness and peace became his gift to me. With each day of my life as I give all that I can give, I can't even comprehend the blessings he gives me. (Personal correspondence with the author.)

This young woman came to understand that it was her hate and anger and not her brother's sin (as heinous as it was) that was consuming her life. It is also true that it is our own sins and not Adam's transgression that bring about many of the problems we experience in life. The following verses clarify this doctrine by teaching that Adam and Eve's children acquired their own carnal nature as a consequence of their own sins and not their parents' transgression: "And Adam and Eve blessed the name of God, and they made all things known unto their sons and their daughters. And Satan came among them, saying: I am also a son of God; and he commanded them, saying: Believe it not; and they believed it not, and they loved Satan more than God. And men began from that time forth to be carnal, sensual, and devilish." (Moses 5:13; see also D&C 20:20 and Articles of Faith 1:2.)

Just as most of Christianity places the blame for our fallen condition on our first parents (Adam and Eve), many people see their problems as being caused by someone or something else. Also, many social scientists and practitioners place the blame for a person's existing problems on his "dysfunctional family"—namely his mother and father. Freud taught that our personalities are formed at an early age in direct response to "early childhood experiences," particularly the influence of our parents. Freud and his followers maintain that later in life, our tendencies to think, feel, and behave as we do are determined by these early factors. From this principle follows the notion that we are not responsible for being the way that we are; our personalities are the psychic product of the way in which our parents raised us. The best that we can expect is insight into this cause-and-effect process and how we can learn to cope with it.

Even though there are many semantical and practical differences between the different psychological theories and therapies, many share the common theme that our personalities are determined by forces beyond our agency. These theories embody the idea that we are either the victim or the beneficiary of our environment, whether that environment be physical, emotional, mental, or biochemical.

Many of us may believe we would be in a state of peace and prosperity if our parents hadn't been alcoholic, abusive, emotionally distant or enmeshed. Influenced by these ideas, many of us have grown up with the idea that our problems are the result of our environment. From this hopeless perspective, our problems are always someone else's or something else's fault. We deny individual responsibility and accountability. A key point here is that if we blame our circumstances for our present problems we also give up any hope for real peace, for circumstances (especially if they exist in the past) are out of our control. This isn't to say that the fall of Adam and Eve, the sins of our parents, or our circumstances in general don't influence us—they do, and they are oftentimes difficult to bear; but they haven't made us evil, nor do they need to ruin our lives.

Our own fall and the fall of both sets of parents (that is, Adam and Eve and our immediate parents) have significant meaning to each of us as to the very purpose of our earthly existence. Mortality and its accompanying challenges, including our own weaknesses (see Ether 12:27), provide an opportunity for wholeness (holiness) that we couldn't experience in any other way.

I have always been moved by the scriptural account of our ancestor Joseph (Jacob's son) making himself known to his brothers, who had previously sold him as a slave:

> And Joseph said unto his brethren, I am Joseph; doth my father yet live? And his brethren could not answer him; for they were troubled at his presence.
> And Joseph said unto his brethren, Come near to me, I pray you.

And they came near. And he said, I am Joseph your brother, whom ye sold into Egypt.

Now therefore be not grieved, nor angry with yourselves, that ye sold me hither: for God did send me before you to preserve life. (Genesis 45:3–5.)

Further on in the record, we read what happens after Jacob dies:

And when Joseph's brethren saw that their father was dead, they said, Joseph will peradventure hate us, and will certainly requite us all the evil which we did unto him.

And they sent a messenger unto Joseph, saying, Thy father did command before he died, saying,

So shall ye say unto Joseph, Forgive, I pray thee now, the trespass of thy brethren, and their sin; for they did unto thee evil: and now, we pray thee, forgive the trespass of the servants of the God of thy father. And Joseph wept when they spake unto him.

And his brethren also went and fell down before his face; and they said, Behold, we be thy servants.

And Joseph said unto them, Fear not; for am I in the place of God?

*But as for you, ye thought evil against me; but God meant it unto good, to bring to pass, as it is this day, to save much people alive.*

Now therefore fear ye not: I will nourish you, and your little ones. And he comforted them, and spake kindly unto them. (Genesis 50: 15–21, emphasis added; see also D&C 100:15.)

The scriptures not only are replete with counsel for those who have suffered at the hands of oppressors, but also give warning and counsel to those who are the oppressors: "Ye have come unto great condemnation; for ye have done these things which ye ought not to have done. . . . Ye have broken the hearts of your tender wives, and lost the confidence of your children, because of your bad examples before them; and the sobbings of their hearts ascend up to God against you." (Jacob 2:34–35.) But to those who will repent and seek righteousness come these motivating words of Isaiah: "Though your sins be as scarlet, they shall be as white as snow; though they be red like crimson, they shall be as wool. If ye be willing and obedient . . ." (Isaiah 1:18–19.)

President Spencer W. Kimball stated:

Is there not wisdom in giving us trials that we might rise above them, responsibilities that we might achieve, work to harden our muscles, sorrows to try our souls? Are we not exposed to temptations to test our strength, sickness that we might learn patience, death that we might be immortalized and glorified? . . .

Should all prayers be immediately answered according to our selfish desires and our limited understanding, then there would be little or no suffering, sorrow, disappointment, or even death, and if these were not, there would also be no joy, success, resurrection, nor eternal life and godhood. (*Faith Precedes the Miracle* [Salt Lake City: Deseret Book Co., 1972], p. 97.)

While a terrible proportion of our suffering is brought upon us by no fault of our own, the scriptures and our prophets have taught that the most persistent cause of our suffering is our own personal violation of the commandments of God. Note the words of President Kimball:

There are many causes for human suffering—including war, disease, and poverty—and the suffering that proceeds from each of these is very real, but I would not be true to my trust if I did not say that the most persistent cause of human suffering, that suffering which causes the deepest pain, is sin—the violation of the commandments given to us by God. . . . If any of us wish to have more precise prescriptions for ourselves in terms of what we can do to have more abundant lives, all we usually need to do is to consult our conscience. (*The Teachings of Spencer W. Kimball*, ed. Edward L. Kimball [Salt Lake City: Bookcraft, 1982], p. 155.)

Sin, such a simple doctrine—but the doctrine of sin has nearly been lost from our culture. We seem to have replaced the word *sin* with words like *mistake* and *error*, which lessen the degree of responsibility we have to take for the act. In the book of James we read the following definition of sin: "Therefore to him that knoweth to do good, and doeth it not, to him it is sin" (James 4:17). To some, committing a sin means committing some grave act like murder or adultery. While these sins are indeed most serious and bring grave consequences, there are other sins which are more subtle and, in time, just as destructive. Remember the story of Marty mentioned earlier? Let's continue with what Marty had to say as to why he didn't follow his "prompting of conscience":

I didn't get up to see what was wrong with the baby. But I couldn't go back to sleep either. It bugged me that Carolyn wasn't waking up. I kept thinking it was her job to take care of the baby. She has her work and I have mine, and mine's hard. It starts very early in the morning. I was exhausted, and she can sleep in. On top of all that, I never really know how to handle the baby anyway.

I wondered if Carolyn was lying there waiting for me to get up. Why did I have to feel guilty and lose my sleep, when the only thing I wanted was to be able to get to work fresh enough to do a good job? What's so selfish about that? Besides, she's the one who wanted to have the kid in the first place. (As quoted in Warner, *Bonds of Anguish, Bonds of Love,* chap. 2, p. 2.)

In order to go against our conscience and continue to feel good about ourselves, we have to deceive ourselves into actually believing and living our own lie. We are not just pretending; we can reach a point where we actually eclipse ourselves from the truth and believe what we are doing or not doing is justifiable. John the Beloved taught, "If we say that we have no sin, we deceive ourselves, and the truth is not in us" (1 John 1:8).

While it may seem extreme to label what Marty didn't do as a "sin," it was. To paraphrase the writing of James, Marty knew to do good and did it not; therefore to him it was sin (see James 4:17). Even though Marty's excuses were logical and provided him with sufficient reasons not to get up, they were immoral, as they allowed him to not live truthfully.

### Hypocrisy (Self-Righteousness)

Not all sin is as simple to see as Marty's. Note the following example of Phillip:

I was riding home on the train from work this one night, and I read a magazine article about being a loving parent. It inspired me. I made a resolution. After an orderly dinner, with no squabbling and no stern looks from me, I would gather our three little children around the fireplace and read them a story. I had gone too many years preoccupied with my work without tucking them in and kissing them and telling them I loved them.

On our front step I gathered up the paper and went through the door determined to be cheerful and kind. But dinner wasn't on the table. Marsha wasn't even getting it ready. She had her housecoat on (there was egg and mucus and whatever on it), the lunch dishes were still on the table, the breakfast dishes were still in the sink, and the kids had strewn things all over. I should have known better than to expect she'd have things under control.

For a moment I felt I ought to help her out; I felt she must be in need of me. But then I just got bitter, thinking how many times she had done this to me. And here on the night when I wanted things to be right, she did it again.

I felt like letting out a bellow. How could I ever be the kind of father I'm supposed to be when there was disorder everywhere? It wasn't fair, and most important, it wasn't right, either.

But I didn't let out a bellow. I never do. I did what I always do. I hung up my coat (so there would be at least one thing put away in the house) and went to work cleaning up the mess. First, I put the children in the tub and got them properly cleaned. Then I did the dishes and put away clothes and vacuumed everywhere.

Marsha said, "Please, stop, will you?" I'm sure she felt humiliated to have someone else get the mess cleaned up when she couldn't bring herself to do it. People who don't take their responsibilities in hand are going to feel humiliated by people who do. That's a problem they create for themselves.

But I didn't say anything back. I know a lot of husbands who would've given her "what for," and a lot more who wouldn't have helped her at all. But I wasn't going to stoop to her level. The house had to get cleaned up, and so I just kept cleaning it. And I tried not to have an angry expression or anything, even though it was hard. I'd like to think I'm above that childish sort of thing.

It took till after midnight. When we went to bed, she was still upset. After all these years I know her well enough to say that if I had worked all night long, she still wouldn't have appreciated it. I didn't know she was going to be like that when I married her. (As quoted in Warner, *Bonds of Anguish, Bonds of Love*, chap. 4, pp. 1–2.)

Phillip was "doing" all the right things. If Phillip had been in Marty's situation, he would have risen and taken care of the crying baby. But as is evident from reading the story, Phillip's problems are not behavioral. Let's read the Savior's words regarding individuals whose attitudes were similar to Phillip's: "Woe unto you, scribes and Pharisees, hypocrites! for ye are like unto whited sepulchres, which indeed appear beautiful outward, but are within full of dead men's bones, and of all uncleanness. Even so ye also outwardly appear righteous unto men, but within ye are full of hypocrisy and iniquity." (Matthew 23:27–28.)

Some advisors would have Phillip give up the notion of "control" and express or "vent" his anger. While there is much controversy in the world (and sometimes among Church members) regarding the control or expression of anger, I have found the scriptures enlightening on the subject. With respect to anger, note the following comparison between the Bible and the Book of Mormon. From the King James Version (KJV) of the New Testament we read these words from Jesus' Sermon on the Mount:

> Ye have heard that it was said by them of old time, Thou shalt not kill; and whosoever shall kill shall be in danger of the judgment:
> But I say unto you, *That whosoever is angry with his brother without a cause shall be in danger of the judgment:* and whosoever shall say to his brother, Raca, shall be in danger of the council: but whosoever shall say, Thou fool, shall be in danger of hell fire. (Matthew 5:21–22, emphasis added.)

The passage from a similar sermon given by Jesus in the Book of Mormon reads this way:

> Ye have heard that it hath been said by them of old time, and it is also written before you, that thou shalt not kill, and whosoever shall kill shall be in danger of the judgment of God;
> But I say unto you, *that whosoever is angry with his brother shall be in danger of his judgment.* And whosoever shall say to his brother, Raca, shall be in danger of the council; and whosoever shall say, Thou fool, shall be in danger of hell fire. (3 Nephi 12:21–22, emphasis added.)

Likewise, Joseph Smith's translation (JST) of the passage in Matthew does not contain the phrase "without a cause" (see JST, Matthew 5:23–24).

Note the following comparison between the KJV and the JST with respect to Paul's teachings on anger:

> Be ye angry, and sin not: let not the sun go down upon your wrath (KJV, Ephesians 4:26).

> Can ye be angry, and not sin? let not the sun go down upon your wrath (JST, Ephesians 4:26).

Lastly, note the selflessness of the Savior's anger:

And he entered again into the synagogue; and there was a man there which had a withered hand.

And they watched him, whether he would heal him on the sabbath day; that they might accuse him.

And he saith unto the man which had the withered hand, Stand forth.

And he saith unto them, Is it lawful to do good on the sabbath days, or to do evil? to save life, or to kill? But they held their peace.

*And when he had looked round about on them with anger, being grieved for the hardness of their hearts,* he saith unto the man, Stretch forth thine hand. And he stretched it out: and his hand was restored whole as the other. (Mark 3:1–5, emphasis added.)

The Savior's anger is an expression of selfless justice, as His every act centers on "doing all things for the welfare and happiness of his people" (Helaman 12:2). The natural man's anger (including my own) is an expression of his natural, normal, but ungodlike selfishness.

### Looking Beyond the Mark (Perfectionism)

Another problem many of us participate in is commonly called perfectionism, but a possible scriptural term would be "looking beyond the mark" (Jacob 4:14). Here's an example taken from the Church's family relations manual:

Esther was trying to be the perfect wife and mother. Every morning she woke up announcing to herself: "This is the day I will be perfect. The house will be organized, I will not yell at my children, and I will finish everything important I have planned." Every night she went to bed discouraged, because she had failed to accomplish her goal. She became irritable with everyone, including herself, and she began to wonder what she was doing wrong.

One night Esther knelt in prayer and asked for guidance. Afterward, while lying awake, a startling thought came to her. She realized that in focusing on her own perfection, she was focusing on herself and failing to love others, particularly her husband and children. She was being not loving, therefore not Christlike, but essentially selfish. She was trying to be sweet to her children, not freely, out of love for them, but because she saw it as a necessary part of *her* "perfection." Furthermore, she was trying to get a feeling of righteousness by forcing her husband and children to meet her ideal of perfection. When her children got in the way of her "perfect" routine, she blamed them for making her feel "imperfect," and she became irritated with them and treated them in a most unloving way. Likewise, if her husband did not meet her idea of perfection when he came home from work, she judged him as failing and was critical of him as a way of reinforcing her sense of her own righteousness.

Esther remembered the Savior's commandment to be perfect *as he is perfect* (see 3 Nephi 12:48). She realized that this perfection includes loving as he loved (see John 13:34), and she realized she had been pursuing the wrong goal. (*Teach Them Correct Principles: A Study in Family Relations* [Salt Lake City: The Church of Jesus Christ of Latter-day Saints, 1992], p. 7, italics in original.)

As was the case with Esther, most of us who have some challenges with perfectionism are not committed to selflessly serving others but to serving ourselves by showing the world how competent we are. We are constantly on the run, doing a lot of things for a lot of people and usually becoming physically ill in the process. Like Martha of New Testament times, perfectionists are "careful[1] and troubled about many things" (Luke 10:41). Martha's being "cumbered about much serving" (Luke 10:40) was a form of self-justification for not choosing "that good part" (Luke 10:42), as did her sister, Mary. A perfectionist's flurry of activity is usually some sort of "virtuous" excuse for not being true to who he or she really is.

### Evil for Evil

We are social beings. Our lives have always been and always will be lived in relationships with others. In the Doctrine and Covenants we read that the "same sociality which exists among us here will exist among us there [celestial sphere]" (D&C 130:2). It is in our relationships with others that we have the greatest potential for beauty or pain. Speaking of the love between a man and a woman, Elder Boyd K. Packer observed: "No experience can be more beautiful, no power more compelling, more exquisite. Or, if misused, no suffering is more excruciating than that connected with love." (*Eternal Love*, Brigham Young University Speeches of the Year [Provo, 3 November 1963],

---

1. The word *careful* (KJV) is one translation of the Greek word *merimnao*, which means "to be anxious about" (see *Strong's Concordance*, p. 3309).

p. 9.) While Elder Packer was referring to romantic relationships, I believe that all relationships have potential for great joy or misery. Just as love requires some kind of relationship, so does misery. Note the following example of David and Diane:

David and Diane had been married for two years. Their relationship had regressed, and criticism filled their conversations together. Neither seemed to be able to find pleasure or happiness in their marriage. They felt their burdens were increased because they were both working long hours and trying to complete their schooling. Their expectations about their marriage were not even remotely being fulfilled. David felt Diane was not spiritual enough and was failing in her duty to support his priesthood decisions. Diane felt her contribution to the family equaled his and that he was constantly judging her unfairly. After a hurtful night of arguing, Diane moved back to her parents' home, convinced that she had made a terrible choice of a husband, an irreversible mistake.

For three weeks they did not see or hear from each other. At first David thought Diane would come back, but she had become reimmersed in the love of her former home and was enjoying the familiarity and security. Meanwhile, David kept reliving in his mind all the wrong things Diane had done and how justified his actions were. Each night he prayed to the Lord to help Diane to change, to become a better person, more like the person he thought he married.

One night, while writing in his journal, he reviewed some of the entries of the preceding months. He became acutely aware of how much criticism of Diane filled those pages. He suddenly realized that his belittling, criticism, and lack of concern for her welfare was a direct contradiction to the spirituality he professed. No wonder she could not support his so-called priesthood decisions. He knelt in prayer, this time with a broken heart and a contrite spirit, and prayed for forgiveness. He prayed, not that the Lord would change Diane, but that the Lord would change him and help him to become the husband Diane thought she had married. This contrition, when humbly offered to Diane, rekindled her willingness to try again. His sincere efforts softened her heart and brought about a new admiration and regard for him. (*Teach Them Correct Principles*, pp. 101–2.)

In the Epistle to the Romans, the Apostle Paul counseled that we should "recompense to no man evil for evil. Provide things honest in the sight of all men." (Romans 12:17.) However, when others provoke us, the "natural" (see Mosiah 3:19) thing to do is to live the lesser law and exchange "life for life, eye for eye, tooth for tooth, hand for hand, foot for foot, burning for burning, wound for wound, stripe for stripe" (Exodus 21:23–25), or, in Paul's words, "evil for evil" (Romans 12:17).

As sad as it may seem, sometimes we even rejoice in another's iniquities, as that person's faults serve as justification for our own. The fact that the other person is treating us badly allows us to maintain our accusing attitudes towards that individual and not love him or her as we should.

When I work with couples in conflict, I often hear this phrase, "See . . . see . . . you're doing it again!" In other words, "Aha, you've just given me the evidence I need for the accusing attitudes I have toward you." Personally I have never worked with a couple where both parties weren't responsible for the problems. If it were possible to assess responsibility, let's say that one partner was 99 percent responsible. Whatever it was that the person who was 1 percent responsible was doing would serve as justification for the 99-percenter to continue what he or she was doing! This may have been what the Savior was referring to when he taught us concerning the mote and the beam:

> Judge not, that ye be not judged.
> For with what judgment ye judge, ye shall be judged: and with what measure ye mete, it shall be measured to you again.
> And why beholdest thou the mote that is in thy brother's eye, but considerest not the beam that is in thine own eye?
> Or how wilt thou say to thy brother, Let me pull out the mote out of thine eye; and, behold, a beam is in thine own eye?
> Thou hypocrite, first cast out the beam out of thine own eye; and then shalt thou see clearly to cast out the mote out of thy brother's eye. (Matthew 7:1–5.)

It has been my experience that many forms of negative emotions that we may experience—such as anger, low self-esteem, depression, boredom, anxiety, and so on—are actually assertions or judgments we make against others in order to justify our own sins. We are not caused to think, feel, or act in the ways we do by the actions of others. While many people are threatened by this doctrine, it is actually a very hopeful, liberating truth. If indeed our fallen state (negative emotions, thoughts, and actions) is something we are responsible for creating or doing, then it is also true that we don't have to create it. As Lehi taught, people are free "to act for themselves and not to be acted upon" (2 Nephi 2:26). On the contrary, if our problems are the effect of a prior cause initiated by someone or something else, there is nothing we can really do about it but wait for our circumstances to change. What a hopeless perspective!

While the fall of Adam and Eve may appear to be a curse, it was in reality a great blessing. The fall provided Adam and Eve and all mankind the opposition necessary to grow and progress. Note the following words of Adam and Eve:

> And in that day Adam blessed God and was filled, and began to prophesy concerning all the families of the earth, saying: Blessed be the name of God, for because of my transgression my eyes are opened, and in this life I shall have joy, and again in the flesh I shall see God.
>
> And Eve, his wife, heard all these things and was glad, saying: Were it not for our transgression we never should have had seed, and never should have known good and evil, and the joy of our redemption, and the eternal life which God giveth unto all the obedient. (Moses 5:10–11.)

As each of us struggles with the problems of life, it is important to remember that there is a great purpose in opposition and adversity. From the writings of President Ezra Taft Benson we read: "It is in the depths where men and women learn the lessons which help them gain strength—not at the pinnacle of success. The hour of man's success is his greatest danger. It sometimes takes reverses to make us appreciate our blessings and to develop us into strong, courageous characters. We can meet every reverse that can possibly come with the help of the Lord." (*The Teachings of Ezra Taft Benson* [Salt Lake City: Bookcraft, 1988], p. 465.)

## The Atonement

While there is much that we can do on our own to achieve peace in this world and eternal life in the next, all of us, in one sense or another, remain in a fallen state and are under the bondage of our own sins. The Apostle Paul taught, "For all have sinned, and come short of the glory of God" (Romans 3:23). No matter what our personal possessions of power, prominence, prestige, intellect, wealth, or righteousness, we cannot save ourselves from our own sins. Neither can we be saved "in [our] sins" (see Alma 11:37). Each one of us is in vital need of the merits, mercy, and grace of Jesus Christ: "Wherefore, how great the importance to make these things known unto the inhabitants of the earth, that they may know that there is no flesh that can dwell in the presence of God, save it be through the merits, and mercy, and grace of the Holy Messiah" (2 Nephi 2:8).

Through our own sins, each of us gradually distorts his or her agency and becomes "carnal, sensual, and devilish" (Alma 42:10) and is "bound down by the chains of hell" (Alma 13:30). We become the "natural man" and an "enemy to God" (Mosiah 3:19) spoken of by an angel to King Benjamin. As President Spencer W. Kimball explained, "the 'natural man' is the 'earthy man' who has allowed rude animal passions to overshadow his spiritual inclinations" ("Ocean Currents and Family Influences," Ensign, November 1974, p. 112). While most negative feelings such as anger, depression, rebelliousness, and so on are certainly "natural," they are not godly and need to be given up. While one can learn to control these natural feelings, he or she can only be free of them through Christ. The scriptures teach us that this freedom is possible only through faith, repentance, and following the promptings of the Holy Spirit. In Alma we read:

> And now, my brethren, I wish from the inmost part of my heart, yea, with great anxiety even unto pain, that ye would hearken unto my words, and cast off your sins, and not procrastinate the day of your repentance;
>
> But that ye would humble yourselves before the Lord, and call on his holy name, and watch and pray continually, that ye may not be tempted above that which ye can bear, and thus be led by the Holy Spirit, becoming humble, meek, submissive, patient, full of love and all long-suffering;
>
> Having faith on the Lord; having a hope that ye shall receive eternal life; having the love of God always in your hearts, that ye may be lifted up at the last day and enter into his rest.
>
> And may the Lord grant unto you repentance, that ye may not bring down his wrath upon you, that ye may not be bound down by the chains of hell, that ye may not suffer the second death. (Alma 13:27–30.)

Without the atonement of Christ there is no true peace: "For it is expedient that an atonement should be made; for according to the great plan of the Eternal God there must be an atonement made, or else all mankind must unavoidably perish; yea, all are hardened; yea, all are fallen and are lost, and must perish except it be through the atonement which it is expedient should be made" (Alma 34:9).

It is my belief and experience that the majority of the psychological/emotional problems we face can be alleviated by understanding and living the gospel of Jesus Christ. Indeed there are problems which are not the result of our own sins nor the sins of our parents, but these are the exception. Note the following exchange between the Savior and his disciples: "And as Jesus passed by, he saw a man which was blind from his birth. And his disciples asked him, saying, Master, who did sin, this man, or his parents, that he was born blind? Jesus answered, Neither hath this man sinned, nor his parents: but that the works of God should be made manifest in him." (John 9:1–3.) The disciples understood the rule; the Savior taught them the exception.

The majority of our problems result from sin; God allows other problems (adversity) to occur to bring to pass his purposes (see Ether 12:6, 27; Job 1:22, 2:9–10). Inasmuch as the Atonement is infinite, it also has application to our afflictions. Elder Neal A. Maxwell has written: "Since not all human sorrow and pain is connected to sin, the full intensiveness of the Atonement involved bearing our pains, infirmities, and sicknesses, as well as our sins" (*"Not My Will, But Thine"* [Salt Lake City: Bookcraft, 1988], p. 51).

An important question we need to ask ourselves when facing social and emotional problems is, "Do I understand the gospel and am I living in harmony with all of God's laws?" President Ezra Taft Benson teaches us this truth in the following:

> In the Book of Mormon we read that "despair cometh because of iniquity." (Moroni 10:22.) . . . Sin pulls a man down into despondency and despair. While a man may take some temporary pleasure in sin, the end result is unhappiness. "Wickedness never was happiness." (Alma 41:10.) Sin creates disharmony with God and is depressing to the spirit. Therefore, a man would do well to examine himself to see that he is in harmony with all of God's laws. Every law kept brings a particular blessing. Every law broken brings a particular blight. Those who are heavy-laden with despair should come unto the Lord, for his yoke is easy and his burden is light. (See Matthew 11:28–30.) ("Do Not Despair," *Ensign*, October 1986, p. 2.)

While many of the problems we face in life have nothing to do with the choices we make, it is my opinion that many of us are too quick to blame our problems on another or upon circumstances which we deem "beyond our control." We feel that if the other person would change, or our circumstances would change, our problems would be solved. Also, it is possible to blame ourselves in a way that gives us an excuse for sin. We think and feel things like, "I'm such a terrible person, how can I possibly do whatever it is that is being asked of me?" Sometimes feelings of guilt can be the evidence we provide so we can continue to sin!

## Conclusion

The scriptures are filled with examples of great men and women who found the answers they were seeking by petitioning God and living by his word in spite of the magnitude of the challenges they were facing (see Isaiah 31–37, 2 Kings 5:1–14, Joseph Smith—History 1, D&C 121:1–10).

The Savior taught that "the key of knowledge [is] the fulness of the scriptures" (JST, Luke 11:53). The restoration of the fulness of the scriptures through the Prophet Joseph Smith provides the means by which we can learn to understand ourselves, the world around us, and the heavens beyond. Many will argue the point that the gospel truths are "too simplistic" to address the complex problems of our day. I have observed that it is not the gospel which is too simplistic; it is our understanding and obedience that are lacking. Nephi taught us this truth in the following words: "[The Lord] sent fiery flying serpents among them [the ancient Israelites]; and after they were bitten he prepared a way that they might be healed; and the labor which they had to perform was to look; and because of the simpleness of the way, or the easiness of it, there were many who perished" (1 Nephi 17:41).

While the scriptures do not necessarily promise us temporal prosperity, prestige, or freedom from the problems of the world, they do contain promises of peace in the midst of adversity if we live the principles taught therein. The Savior taught: "Peace I leave with you, my peace I give unto you: not as the world giveth, give I unto you. Let not your heart be troubled, neither let it be afraid." (John 14:27.)

We are children of a Heavenly Father who loves us. He has given us a plan, even "the great plan of the Eternal God," that we may have joy in this life and eternal life in the world to come.

Therefore, cheer up your hearts, and remember that ye are free to act for yourselves—to choose the way of everlasting death or the way of eternal life.

Wherefore, my beloved brethren, reconcile yourselves to the will of God, and not to the will of the devil and the flesh; and remember, after ye are reconciled unto God, that it is only in and through the grace of God that ye are saved.

Wherefore, may God raise you from death by the power of the resurrection, and also from everlasting death by the power of the atonement, that ye may be received into the eternal kingdom of God, that ye may praise him through grace divine. Amen. (2 Nephi 10:23–25.)

*Daniel K Judd was born and reared in Kanab, Utah. After completing a mission in San Diego, California, he earned a bachelor's degree in zoology and chemistry from Southern Utah University. He also holds an M.S. in family science and a Ph.D. in counseling psychology from Brigham Young University. In addition to having been a seminary and institute instructor in Arizona, Utah, and in Michigan, he was also a professor of family science at Rick's College in Rexburg, Idaho. He has served as a bishop and is now president of the Young Men in his home ward. He is presently an assistant professor of Ancient Scripture at BYU, where he also conducts research studying the relationship of religion and mental health. He and his wife, Kaye Seegmiller, are the parents of four children and live in Orem, Utah.*

# 5

# THE KEYS OF MARITAL SUCCESS— PART 1

## Douglas E. Brinley

*I*n a letter to Ann Landers, a lady from Louisiana offered her husband, free of charge, to anyone willing to take him off her hands! Follow-up letters from readers brought responses like this one:

> Dear Ann Landers: The woman from Louisiana who offered her husband to anyone who would take him described his virtues: a good family man, church-going, in excellent physical condition, who doesn't drink, smoke or gamble. Then she listed his flaws: mean, selfish, critical, deceitful, miserly, demanding, rude, vain, inflexible, unforgiving and, she added, "He sucks the joy out of life on a daily basis." She has stayed with him 40 years.

Then the writer continued:

> Anyone who wants that man's twin brother can find him in Cleveland. I married him. As an added incentive, he plays the piano. No notice necessary. I can have him packed and ready immediately. One caveat: no deposit and no return. —Also Fed Up

Ann's response:

> Dear Fed: I think you're stuck with your husband, dearie. I have at least 12,000 letters on my desk from readers who would like to unload their spouses. Read on:

She then proceeded to quote from her mail:

> "Louisiana" has a good many soul sisters. My husband had every fault she mentioned plus a few more. He died last June, and God forgive me, I sang to myself all the way home from the cemetery.

Another one:

> Back in the mid-'70s when so many men were dumping their wives, I kept praying someone would run off with my husband. I tried dressing him up and sending him to places where lonely women gathered. An hour later he'd be back. Too many women settle for a warm body without realizing that with it comes his laundry, the dishes and a lifetime of boredom.

And another one:

> I'll go "Louisiana" one better. She offered to give her husband away. I will pay $1,000 to any woman who will take mine.

I hope your spouse was not one of those twelve thousand who wrote in, or would have written had he or she known about the opportunity! Can you imagine twelve thousand individuals sitting down to write Ann Landers on just this one topic? It makes you wonder how many thought about it but didn't take the time to write, or how many didn't have a stamp handy!

Why is marriage such a difficult relationship for so many, when it ought to be the most enjoyable thing we do? Certainly our culture is filled with messages of love, romance, and marriage. Consider all of the love songs and movies built around romantic themes.

Then we have so many modern conveniences that should help free up time for us to be together with our spouses. The days of pioneering and physical hardship, which included time spent clearing land and farming unproductive soil by oxen or primitive implements, are over. Many of the deadly diseases that took so many children of our ancestors have been conquered. Most likely all of your children will be able to live to adulthood. Gone too are the days of washing clothes in the river, drinking tainted water, hooking up the horses to ride into town. Burning, looting, persecution, and other threats to health and longevity are minimal in our modern era. Wrinkle-free fabrics nearly eliminate ironing, while microwaves and dishwashers decrease time spent in the kitchen. A thermostat calls heating or cooling equipment into action. No more chopping wood or living in sweat houses. Men no longer must leave wives and children to serve on missions or in the military while the family ekes out an existence. We have phones to keep in touch with each other even when we are separated. We can cross the country in a day by plane and be home the same evening! We have such comfortable lives compared to our forebears.[1] If our families are a priority with us, we can spend more time with our companions and children; yet we seem to suffer more marital instability than ever.

## Deterrents to Strong Marriages

All right, so what is wreaking havoc in our modern relationships to the tune of 40 to 50 percent of married people giving up or bailing out of marriage? If you were to compose a list of marital problems that you think contribute to the breakup of marriages, what items would you put down?

### Money and Money Management

No doubt money is a major factor in most unhappy relationships. But why? What is there about money that makes it an emotional element in marriage? Is it the amount of money? Do we not know poor people with great marriages (perhaps you are one of them!)? On the other hand, many financially sound couples find their marriages floundering—movie stars immediately come to mind. Well, there are several factors concerning money and money management that impinge on marital happiness:

1. One factor has to do with what money means to you. Family scientists have concluded that we use money the same way we use other resources such as time or talents. If a person is tightfisted with money, the thinking is, there is a strong probability that he or she is a tightwad in sharing emotions and feelings. For many of us, spending money is like hemorrhaging, or giving away vital pieces of our bodies; we simply struggle to part with it.

---

1. There are, of course, some downsides. Children are out of the home more as teens. They are more mobile, have more access to media, and are exposed to more peer influences than ever before.

2. Individuals with low self-esteem may try to compensate for their feelings of inadequacy by buying expensive gadgets—cars, homes, electronic equipment, and so on, in order to show others they are successful. You have to admit that it feels good to spend money. It does have a therapeutic effect. If you have money to spend, there is some satisfaction in having nice things. However, this behavior usually leads to financial debt and increases the chances for marital arguments, for as consumers, our wants are unlimited. Money, it is thought by many, represents the "good life"—power, prestige, and status.

3. Money becomes a tool to manipulate or control others. A spouse may use money to dominate or control other family members; after all, the financial manager controls the purse strings, which often forces others to come on bended knee for a mere pittance. The keeper of the treasury may claim that family members are poor money managers, when his control of such matters is really a veiled way to control others. Sometimes parents, for example, can't understand why their children do not "love them" when they have given those same children so many "things," including cash, which to the parents represents "love."

Arguments over money are generally a function of personality weaknesses, a lack of self-discipline, or ignorance of money management principles—all of which can be corrected or overcome with persistent effort.

### Sex

Sex is another important element of marital happiness and stability. President Spencer W. Kimball explained its importance this way: "If you study the divorces, . . . you will find there are one, two, three, four reasons. Generally sex is the first. They did not get along sexually. They may not say that in the court. They may not even tell that to their attorneys, but that is the reason." He went on to say:

> Husband and wife . . . are authorized, in fact they are commanded, to have proper sex when they are properly married for time and eternity. That does not mean that we need to go to great extremes. That does not mean that a woman is the servant of her husband. It does not mean that any man has a right to demand sex anytime that he might want it. He should be reasonable and understanding and it should be a general program between the two, so they understand and everybody is happy about it. (*The Teachings of Spencer W. Kimball*, ed. Edward L. Kimball [Salt Lake City: Bookcraft, 1982], p. 312.)

Most couples experiencing conflict in their relationships who go to counselors or ecclesiastical leaders for help do not initiate discussions about sexual incompatibility in such visits. But upon inquiry of how these couples' present conflicts impact their intimate relationships, President Kimball's comments come into focus. Let me explain.

As Latter-day Saints we know that, in addition to having the purpose of bringing children into the world under the protection of the family umbrella, sexual relations are an essential form of therapy to a married couple. The complexities of marriage and adult life—bearing and rearing children, earning a living, budgeting, traveling freeways, dealing with supervisors and bosses and fellow employees, and other tests—all take their toll on us personally. The Lord has provided that each married couple can periodically, in their own private, intimate world, renew their commitments and feelings for each other through an experience together in which they share their emotions and enjoy a physical stimulation that renews their vision and common goals.

Through sexual relations, in other words, a husband has the opportunity to send this message to his wife: "Honey, I love being married to you. I appreciate all that you do for me and our family. Thank you for being my companion." It is a chance for a wife to convey: "I love you, sweetheart, and I'm grateful for all that you do for me and the children." Thus marital intimacy was commanded by Deity, in part, to be a renewal for married couples, a chance to check in with each other, to express mutual love and appreciation. A couple who can cooperate physically and emotionally usually have a good basis for resolving most of the external challenges to their unity.

Unfortunately we live in a society that desecrates the true purposes of intimacy. Merchandisers, it seems, can't pitch their automobiles or soda pop without half-naked bodies. Even when you are watching something fairly decent on television, they want to show you clips of upcoming programs, hoping to entice you to view their steamy scenes. In a related vein, Elder Neal A. Maxwell has pointed out that some of today's talk shows "feature not real conversation but exhibitionism and verbal voyeurism among virtual strangers" (" 'Behold, the Enemy Is Combined' [D&C 38:12]," *Ensign*, May 1993, p. 77). We are bombarded with sexual messages that tend to keep this subject of sex uppermost in our minds.

For marrieds, sexual relations is a natural expression of the positive feelings and regard that already exist between them. Problems develop in a marriage when a couple allows irritations to disrupt this relationship, which then influences their feelings for each other in negative ways. What spouse feels like sharing physical, emotional, and spiritual gifts with a companion who is unappreciative of the spouse's gift of self? Every counselor has heard the "wife's refrain": "The only time my husband ever tells me he loves me is when we are being intimate." Or, "He doesn't really love me, he simply enjoys getting his pleasure at my expense."

Or, as one wife told me, "My husband comes home from work about 5:00 P.M., miserable and complaining about the day until about 9:30 P.M. Then he suddenly turns into this sweetheart for about an hour and a half until we make love. Then before I know it, he is upset again about something—when I thought we just reaffirmed our love for each other! That is, if he doesn't fall asleep first." The message— "I love you as long as you service my needs"—is not a message wives appreciate. What President Kimball was saying is that when we cannot enjoy each other's presence physically and emotionally, the foundation for resolving other marital issues becomes flawed. We look for blemishes in our spouses to justify our actions, and we become disenchanted with marriage. Sexual intimacy, it turns out, is a fairly reliable barometer of the quality of the marriage, for if a couple can come together in this private, intimate time and express mutual love feelings and devotion, their marriage is sufficiently strong to withstand inevitable shocks and jarrings.

Argument and contention have a direct bearing on the quality and frequency of intimate contacts between spouses. Quite often I learn that even young marrieds who are having disagreements will go months without sexual relations when marital tension exists. (I recall one couple who had gone thirteen years without sexual relations, and they were not in their sixties or seventies yet, either! When I run into such couples, I always ask: "Do you two happen to reside in the same state, city, neighborhood, house, and sleep in the same bed?" They claim they do. "Don't you ever run into each other in the night!") Such couples seem determined to avoid each other regardless of the damage that is caused to their relationship. Unfortunately pride and selfishness can destroy feelings when we are not sufficiently humble to repent and seek forgiveness. The side effects of such behavior are often immorality and sexual transgressions.

### In-laws

Many would list troubles with in-laws as a significant marital problem. Our hope, when we marry, is that all in-laws will jump off the matrimonial ship at the time of launching, but most of us, at some time in our lives, will experience a conflict with in-laws. (I have observed that *before* marriage, engaged persons often don't show off their entire families. They only trot out some of the impressive ones to make the prospective spouse think he or she is marrying into good stock!) Though mother-in-law jokes are common, fathers-in-law can be controlling and manipulative too.

### Children

Is it possible that children can ruin an otherwise great marriage? I know many Latter-day Saints who get along well—except when it comes to rearing their children. Rearing children and disciplining them are not topics two head-over-heels lovers usually discuss before marriage. Most of us naively assume at that point in time that if we can figure out how to have them, we will know what to do with them once we get them! Experienced parents will agree that the most difficult task in life, and a frequent challenge to marital harmony, is bringing up the next generation. Husbands often think wives are too lenient in their child-rearing practices, while wives may feel their husbands leave too much for them, the mothers, to do. Wives sometimes feel that husbands either ignore problems or deal with them brusquely, while husbands often think they are excused from helping with the children.

Because Latter-day Saints generally have large families, we increase the possibilities for married couples to disagree over child-rearing practices. Too, in this modern day, many fathers are gone from home on business excursions, and their absences may create some guilt in their minds concerning the amount of fathering they are doing. They may bring home trinkets, gadgets, and surprises for the kids, perhaps to compensate for their lack of parenting time. If a husband comes home from a trip passing out candy bars to the kids, for example, without knowing that his wife has grounded them for misbehaving, an interesting discussion usually ensues. She becomes upset because he is rewarding the kids at the very time she is trying to discipline them. He argues that he was just thinking of his kids, as any good dad should, and soon the two are off on a trivial debate on the merits of peanuts and chocolate for children. Parenting as partners is a major challenge in our nation as well as among Church members.

Men are typically raised to see their marital role like this: "Look, honey, this is the way I've got it figured out. Your job is to have the kids—I think it says that in Genesis somewhere if you need a reference. My job is to earn the bread. I'll do the best I can to see that we eat regularly, and I'll ask the Lord to bless you in *your assignment!* Now, if you *should* have any trouble with the kids, don't hesitate to call me. You've got my work number on the fridge—so buzz me and I'll see if I can get someone over to help you out! Maybe your mother could come down for a week or so." Wives often become frustrated with a husband's lack of help with the children. Wives believe that because it takes two people to bring children into this world, it requires two to raise these children to adulthood—and that includes the father.

## Power Struggles

I'm not sure that many of us men in the Church have ever figured out this patriarchal-order business. It is interesting to watch men run their little kingdoms. There seems to be a continuum: On the left side is the man I call Brother Milquetoast—a man who functions as his wife gives him permission. It may be that he detests, and therefore avoids, confrontation with others, so he passively yields to others. There is no question who runs the family business. Mom is the boss and it is obvious to everyone. When I see that arrangement I am reminded of a statement by Elder Orson Hyde: "I will here venture the assertion, that no man can be exalted to a celestial glory in the kingdom of God whose wife rules over him; and as the man is not without the woman, nor the woman without the man in the Lord, it follows as a matter of course, that the woman who rules over her husband, thereby deprives herself of a celestial glory" (in *Journal of Discourses* 4:258).[2]

---

2. In this connection, President Spencer W. Kimball, referring to the term *rule* in Genesis 3:16, said, "But I like the word *preside*," which gives a much better connotation to this term (see *The Teachings of Spencer W. Kimball*, ed. Edward L. Kimball [Salt Lake City: Bookcraft, 1982], 316).

On the other end of the continuum are men who think that if their wives do not agree with their every opinion, or the children fail to salute as they go by, the whole bunch are not honoring his priesthood! Unfortunately there are some of those characters running around loose. Actually a husband and father's task is much like that of the bishop or stake president. The bishop counsels with his counselors and comes to a joint decision. Can you imagine a situation like the following? A bishop asks his first counselor: "What do you think we ought to do in this case?" He listens to the counselor's response and then says, "Thanks." He then asks the second counselor: "What do you think we ought to do in this case?" He listens and then responds: "Sorry, men, but we are going to do it my way!"—without regard to their counsel. Such a situation is unlikely to endear him to his counselors.

The husband presides; that is God-ordained. The wife is the first counselor and the children are members of the family (or patriarchal) quorum. Most of the time we will do well if we run our homes similar to a Church council, considering the views of everyone. But Dad has the responsibility to see that councils are held, and that presidency meetings are held! Like the bishop, the husband-father counsels with his counselor and the quorum members until they come to a consensus on the best course of action. President Kimball put it best when he said: "When we speak of marriage as a partnership, let us speak of marriage as a *full* partnership. We do not want our LDS women to be *silent* partners or *limited* partners in that eternal assignment!" (*The Teachings of Spencer W. Kimball*, p. 315.)

## Solutions

Enough about problems: Let's look at some typical solutions. Most people think that there are three main solutions to marital problems:

1. *Increased communication.* Because we do not live on farms anymore, and family members go in many directions, it is thought that modern couples simply do not spend enough time talking with each other to succeed in marriage.

2. *Increased communication skills.* Most of us, it is generally believed, are not sufficiently skilled to know what to say, when to say it, or how to say it in a manner in which it will not cause anger on the part of the spouse or family members.

3. *Increased listening skills.* Most of us, it is commonly held, are not very good listeners. We are impatient when others talk and are anxious to have the other party finish so that we can get in our two bits.

If we could improve in these three areas, the thinking goes, we could probably solve 90 percent or more of marriage and family problems. Despite the fact that this sounds good (it is the approach of pop psychology), these three points are not solutions proposed by the Lord, the prophets, or the scriptures.

Let me explain. Most of the training of counselors revolves around helping people communicate more effectively by learning about the need for two-way communication, and the need for all parties to be better listeners, to really hear what a spouse or child is saying. Though this approach has some value, a key element is missing. I learned this principle when a prophet of the Lord declared, "Every divorce is the result of selfishness on the part of one or the other or both parties to a marriage contract. Someone is thinking of self-comforts, conveniences, freedoms, luxuries, or ease." ("Marriage and Divorce," in *1976 Devotional Speeches of the Year* [Provo: Brigham Young University Press, 1977], p. 148.)

Every divorce, when you think about it, is a fairly high percentage! This statement grabbed my attention because I had never heard the word *selfishness* during my academic training. But here was a prophet of the Lord saying it was *the* primary factor in the breakup of marriages. My first reaction to the statement was: "I wonder what books President Kimball is reading. We Ph.D.'s know that the real problem revolves around poor communication and listening skills."

Having taught a class in the Church Educational System for many years entitled "The Teachings of the Living Prophets," however, I was trained in the principle that when a prophet speaks, we are hearing the truth and we need to listen. I remembered that the Lord usually has a different answer or approach to most human problems than we do. But I did not quite understand the application of the principle.

So, the next time I visited with a couple I was determined to look past the communication problems and think in terms of how selfishness could be destroying their relationship. It is not easy to spot without being sensitized to it, for one of the most obvious things about troubled couples when you meet them for the first time is their poor communication patterns. They struggle so. If the wife gets out two sentences, the husband feels compelled to interrupt and get in his licks. If he talks first, she can't let him say too much without jumping into the fray. If the helping person is not careful, it is easy to think that the couple's only or main problem is one of communication. Having been forewarned, however, by a prophet, when I visited with troubled couples I looked past their obvious communication difficulties to identify the principle. I noticed that when I talked to the wife, and she with me, and *neither one of us was mad at the other*, she was very clear about her concerns and what she would like to see changed. The same held true with her husband. Because *he and I were not mad at each other, we did not interrupt each other* and he effectively articulated his worries and concerns as to what he would like to see changed in his marriage.

So, here is the first principle I would like to stress: When we are mad or upset with someone, we do not use the same communication skills we do when we are dating, attending public functions (ward dinners or stake conference), trying to impress a client, seeking employment through an interview, or talking to prospective in-laws. On those occasions we all seem to be mannerly, fun-loving, and relaxed, attempting to put our "best foot forward." When our self-interest is at stake, we seem to be quite adequate. In other words, we do possess the skills. However, when we are angry, we do not use the same communication and relationship skills that we do when we are in a good mood!

It is easy for those who are not angry or emotionally involved in a couple's differences to suggest to a couple that what they need to do is to communicate more, for to those who are not angry, that is the normal way people resolve their problems. How else can change occur, we argue, if couples don't talk? But consider your own experience: Are there certain people in your circle of acquaintances with whom you find that the more you talk to them, the more frustrated you become? Telling people to increase the amount of communication between them when they are angry with each other is not a peacemaking technique. In fact, it usually makes things worse.

I recall two political candidates arguing with each other on television before a general election. Neither could agree with anything his opponent said, obviously, or he would lose face. They reminded me of a married couple! To tell two politicians to "talk more" or "communicate more" to resolve their differences is simply to compound the problem. To tell married people who are in a combat mode that what they need to do is talk more to each other concerning their problems is to simply increase the tension. They are already talking too much! Something else must happen first before they can talk calmly and resolve their differences.

I am convinced that all of us have sufficient skills to succeed in marriage. Consider this point: If you are presently married—I mean if you have, in days past, faked someone into marrying you, if you have actually convinced someone to join your marital act—then you have proof positive that you are already adequate in your communication skills! Believe me, it is not easy to talk someone into marriage. (Now, you may have become a little strange since you married, but at one time, at least in those romantic, heady days of courtship, you were quite skillful in communicating—sufficiently so, at least, to attract a spouse!)

Well, you ask, if communication is not the primary solution, what must be its antecedent? The answer can be understood in connection with what might be termed a "heart problem." The best example is found in the Book of Mormon. Consider this experience of the Nephites: "And it came to pass in the thirty and sixth year, the people were all converted unto the Lord, upon all the face of the land, both Nephites and Lamanites, and there were no contentions and disputations among them, and every man did deal justly one with another" (4 Nephi 1:2).

You recall that the Lord appeared to the Nephites following his resurrection in Jerusalem. Their conversion seemed to affect the way they treated each other. The record continues: "And now, behold, it came to pass that the people of Nephi did wax strong, and did multiply exceedingly fast, and became an exceedingly fair and delightsome people. And they were married, and given in marriage, and were blessed according to the multitude of the promises which the Lord had made unto them." (4 Nephi 1:10–11.)

Then a little further on we read of a key element of the Nephites' happiness: "And it came to pass that there was no contention in the land, because of the love of God which did dwell in the hearts of the people" (4 Nephi 1:15).

The solution to marriage and family problems is to have the love of God in our hearts! Consider how this condition would have influenced the way these Nephites treated each other. I think that the love of God they possessed was generated by their personal experience of the Savior's appearance, their physical contact with him (see 3 Nephi 11:14–15), and the realization that here was a resurrected being standing before them, a person no longer subject to death, yet very much as they were. They could see that he was a male and they could understand that if they were faithful to the gospel, they too would be resurrected as a male (or female), and thus marriage and family relations could be eternal if two married people were faithful to the message the Savior taught. This knowledge would be an important force in their living without contention, because of their knowledge and understanding of who they were and of their potential. The record then describes the behavior that resulted from this change of heart, this understanding of the plan of salvation:

> And there were no envyings, nor strifes, nor tumults, nor whoredoms, nor lyings, nor murders, nor any manner of lasciviousness; and surely there could not be a happier people among all the people who had been created by the hand of God.
>
> There were no robbers, nor murderers, neither were there Lamanites, nor any manner of -ites; but they were in one, the children of Christ, and heirs to the kingdom of God.
>
> And how blessed were they! For the Lord did bless them in all their doings; yea, even they were blessed and prospered until an hundred and ten years had passed away; and the first generation from Christ had passed away, and there was no contention in all the land. (4 Nephi 1:16–18.)

The Lord's solution to our marital problems seems to be this: If we can build the "love of God" into our hearts, there will be no contention or arguing between married partners or between family members. Such contention would be too petty, too inconsequential, given our eternal possibilities. Such a perspective or vision would allow us to establish Zion in our homes, wards, and stakes and to extend righteousness into the entire community.

When the love of God abounds in our hearts, communication skills are natural and simple, for Christlike individuals do not purposely offend others, and because no offense was intended, none is taken. Don't misunderstand; all of us can improve in our communication and listening skills, but unless our hearts are right, we will not make any lasting improvements. What we say and how we say things must be genuine, and must issue from a righteous heart and proper motives. Under these conditions, no one would take offense at what we say, because people would recognize that our hearts are free from any desire to hurt, manipulate, smother, offend, or dominate.

Perhaps it could be said this way: If you simply help people with communication skills, without reference to the need for a change of heart, all you have done is make them more clever fighters, for their improved techniques allow them to zing each other even more effectively than before! But when hearts are right, men and women become teachable, they want to improve, to do better. Then charity replaces justice. Have you noticed that when mistakes occur, a genuine, humble apology heals a wounded heart? With the love of God in our hearts we are not too proud to seek forgiveness and repair damages we have caused. Christlike people forgive easily—so no grudge is held, there is no retaining of grievances. The need to go over and over trivial events is unnecessary, for from a pure heart come honest, genuine feelings, with no intent to hurt or embarrass the other.

Our goal, then, is to develop this love of God in our hearts so that we may become even as the Nephites were for almost two centuries, with "no contention in all the land" (4 Nephi 1:18). How we develop this profound love of God is the subject of part 2.

# 6

# THE KEYS OF MARITAL SUCCESS— PART 2

## Douglas E. Brinley

*I* suggested in the previous chapter that the key to success in marriage is to establish in our hearts the love of God. The precedent was set by the Nephites following the ministry of Christ as recorded in 4 Nephi. Our challenge may be more difficult than theirs, for we must develop this love in a day when we do not see and converse with the Savior as they did at the temple in Bountiful, though we have had resurrected beings minister in these latter days.[1]

### The Temple, Our Model: Worthiness, Perspective, Covenants, and Practice

The model in our day, one that can bring the love of God into our hearts, is to be found in temples, the Lord's modern counterpart to his visit to the Nephites. The first criterion for this educational and empowering process is to be worthy to enter the temple, which the Lord defines as a "house of prayer, a house of fasting, a house of faith, a house of learning, a house of glory, a house of order, a house of God" (D&C 88:119). We must be clean (or become clean through sincere

---

1. Resurrected beings that have appeared in this final dispensation include Moroni, Peter, James, John the Baptist, Moses, Elias, and Elijah.

repentance) before entering that holy place. The promise is: "And inasmuch as my people . . . do not suffer any unclean thing to come into [the temple], that it be not defiled, my glory shall rest upon it; yea, and my presence shall be there, for I will come into it, and all the pure in heart that shall come into it shall see God" (D&C 97:15–16). A temple recommend indicates our worthiness. Within sacred precincts of the temple we receive divine instruction as to what we must comprehend, what we can do, and how we must live if we are to establish a Zion people and individually and as couples prepare for eternal life.

Second, in the temple we are instructed in what I call perspective—the "big picture." It is important for our understanding that we know something of our divine origin and destiny, that we know God has power to redeem worlds and therefore individuals and couples. He is not a laboratory technician experimenting with us as his guinea pigs. We are his children, his offspring. He has created many worlds—too numerous for man to number, in fact (see Moses 1:33, 35)—to bring his children, if they will, to his exalted state.

In the temple we are involved in a great educational and empowering curriculum designed to qualify us for "immortality and eternal life" (Moses 1:39). The Holy Ghost, a member of the Godhead and our gift at baptism, supervises our spiritual growth and development if we hearken to his counsel. In that holy house our faith is increased in both our Father's plan and the mission of the Son, for through their gifts we may qualify for immortality and eternal life through the resurrection. Christ is, therefore, the central figure in this plan, for without him we could not obtain a celestial body and return to the presence of our Father, because of our sinful and fallen condition and the choices we make. As we come to understand the great plan of redemption and our place in it, our eternal perspective is enhanced. We are free to covenant with our Father to live in harmony with his plan—comprised of doctrines and ordinances—called the gospel of Jesus Christ, so that we may inherit all that he has if we are obedient to those laws and ordinances upon which exaltation is conditioned (see D&C 130:20–21). From such perspective and covenants comes power to live on a higher plane than the surrounding telestial environment.

The doctrines of the gospel provide us with an eternal perspective so that we can exercise our agency in light of our eternal potential. Elder Boyd K. Packer explained the process: "The study of the doctrines of the gospel will improve behavior quicker than a study of behavior will improve behavior. . . . That is why we stress so forcefully the study of the doctrines of the gospel." ("Little Children," *Ensign*, November 1986, p. 17.) Elder Neal A. Maxwell taught the value of the plan of salvation and its impact on our behavior:

> One of the great blessings flowing from amplifying, latter-day revelations is the crucial, doctrinal framework known as the marvelous plan of salvation, the plan of happiness, or the plan of mercy. . . .
> So vital is this framework that if one stays or strays outside it, he risks . . . misery. In fact, most human misery represents ignorance of or noncompliance with the plan. A cessation of such mortal suffering will not come without compliance to it. ("The Great Plan of the Eternal God," *Ensign*, May 1884, p. 21.)

This helps to explain why the Lord's prophets counsel us to study the scriptures on a daily basis so that we might keep uppermost in our minds the basic doctrines of the plan of salvation and thus ensure that our hearts will be filled with the love of God. Logically, behavior coincides with our understanding of doctrine and then our committing ourselves to use our agency to comply with God's requirements. It is my intent here to show that coming to understand doctrine helps us focus on the plan of salvation and its centerpiece, Jesus Christ, so that we too can develop the same level of the love of God that inspired righteousness in the Nephites during their golden era. Then, like those of the first century, we too can experience "no contentions and disputations among [us], and every man [will] deal justly one with another" (4 Nephi 1:2). In our day we call such a society a Zion people, a people who are seeking exaltation.

## Doctrines That Help Us to Be Better Married Partners

Following are five doctrines that can have a powerful influence on our behavior, in particular on the way we treat our spouses and children: (1) the premortal life and our purpose in coming to the earth, (2) eternal marriage, (3) the three degrees of glory, (4) the damnation of Lucifer, and (5) the identity of our mortal children and the purpose of parenthood for us.

## The Premortal Life and the Purpose of Mortality

The doctrine of the premortal life teaches us that we are the literal offspring of heavenly parents, parents who have attained a resurrected state of immortality. We lived in their presence as male and female children before our mortal birth. President Brigham Young explained:

> You are well acquainted with God our Heavenly Father, or the great Elohim. You are all well acquainted with him, for there is not a soul of you but what has lived in his house and dwelt with him year after year. . . .
>
> There is not a person here to-day but what is a son or a daughter of that Being. In the spirit world their spirits were first begotten and brought forth, and they lived there with their parents for ages before they came here. (*Discourses of Brigham Young*, sel. John A. Widtsoe [Salt Lake City: Deseret Book Co., 1941], p. 50.)

Spirit bodies are similar in appearance to our mortal bodies (see Ether 3:16–17; D&C 77:2). However, as premortal spirits, we were incapable of reproducing; consequently marriage was not an option for us at that time. A primary purpose in coming to this "second estate," in fact, was for us to obtain a body of element—flesh and blood—which would endow us with powers and privileges unavailable to us in that premortal sphere, marriage and procreation being two of the most obvious. The earth was created so that we could have this wonderful experience, and it is in these functions and powers that we most approximate the work of the Gods. The Lord declared in a modern revelation: "I say unto you, that whoso forbiddeth to marry is not ordained of God, for marriage is ordained of God unto man. Wherefore, . . . they twain shall be one flesh, and all this that the earth might answer the end of its creation; and that it might be filled with the measure of man, according to his creation before the world was made." (D&C 49:15–17.)

This earth, then, is the residence where our spirit bodies are united with bodies of element in an environment where we can be tested outside of God's presence to see if we will be obedient to those laws and principles that will prepare us to live the kind of life that he lives. That plan calls for us to be born as infants and grow to be adult men and women, to the same stature as our spirit bodies. As adults we may then marry and be given the authority to exercise our powers of creation to prepare bodies for other children of our Father. In this way we "may bear the souls of men; for herein is the work of my Father continued, that he may be glorified" (D&C 132:63). This is the first time in our long existence as males and females that we are privileged to participate in these functional roles.

How long did we wait for this opportunity to marry and become parents? Even a conservative estimate suggests that we waited a substantial period as "single adults" for the privilege of coming to this earth.

In that premortal realm the only family relationships we experienced were those we had as sons and daughters of God and as brothers and sisters to one another. We were never in a marriage relationship with the ability to create children, for our bodies were incapable of such functions in the premortal sphere. In comparison to this lengthy premortal period of singleness, in this life we are married for only a brief period—fifty to seventy years at most. Yet the staggering reality is that the quality of our marriage and family relations in this life greatly influences whether the privilege to continue marriage will be extended to us into eternity. Here we may avail ourselves of the opportunity and privilege to form an eternal partnership.

Should not this perspective influence us to be our very best selves in order to be eligible for such an eternal opportunity? Should it not create in us a love of God, a love that would motivate us to attain that same station the Father enjoys, to be obedient to the laws that the God of heaven has set forth because he is the one who has implemented the plan to return us to his presence?

### Eternal Marriage

A major doctrine that affects our behavior is that of eternal marriage itself. From modern scripture we learn that "the spirit and the body are the soul of man. And the resurrection from the dead is the redemption of the soul." (D&C 88:15–16.) The soul, then, consists of two separate "bodies" which come from two different sets of parents— one set being mortal, the other immortal. Our flesh-and-blood bodies were created by parents who transmitted to us the effects of the Fall. Neither our physical bodies nor those of our children will escape death and dissolution. But the parents of our spirit bodies are immor-

tal and resurrected, and therefore our spirits are not subject to death.[2]
Sexual relations, conception, and birth are important elements in the
creation of a soul, for these processes join these two bodies in an
earthly probation. The accompanying chart (see page 88) illustrates
the origin of our physical and spirit bodies, the effect of death, the
meaning of the resurrection, and our ultimate state as eternal companions and immortal parents capable of producing spirit children
even as we were organized in the distant premortal past.

At death the mortal body and the eternal spirit separate, and
while our physical remains are consigned to the earth, our spirit bodies inhabit the spirit world.[3] Once resurrected there will be no further
separation of body and spirit, for a resurrected person cannot die (see
Alma 11:45). Concerning a group of spirits awaiting the resurrection,
President Joseph F. Smith perceived in vision that "their sleeping dust
was to be restored unto its perfect frame, bone to his bone, and the
sinews and the flesh upon them, the spirit and the body to be united
never again to be divided, that they might receive a fulness of joy"
(D&C 138:17).

The Savior's atonement made possible our resurrection. This resurrection enables our eternal spirit bodies to be restored to their former physical bodies (the materials of which are now refined and purified as male and female beings no longer subject to death. Such
exalted beings have bodies capable of generating spirit children.[4] Our
association as husbands and wives in that sphere will be "coupled

---

2. We speak of spirit bodies, but these are, nevertheless, bodies of matter. "There
is no such thing as immaterial matter. All spirit is matter, but it is more fine or pure,
and can only be discerned by purer eyes; we cannot see it [in our finite, mortal state];
but when our bodies are purified [resurrected] we shall see that it is all matter." (D&C
131:7–8.)

3. The spirit world is apparently here on this earth. "The earth and other planets
of a like sphere have their inward or spiritual spheres as well as their outward, or temporal. The one is peopled by temporal tabernacles and the other by spirits. A veil is
drawn between the one sphere and the other whereby all the objects in the spiritual
sphere are rendered invisible to those in the temporal." (Parley P. Pratt, *Key to the
Science of Theology* [Salt Lake City: Deseret Book Co., 1978], p. 80.)

4. In mortal life we create bodies subject to death and dissolution. However, in
the resurrection, since we will no longer be subject to death, we will have the power
to organize bodies that cannot die—an endowment greater than that given us in
mortal life.

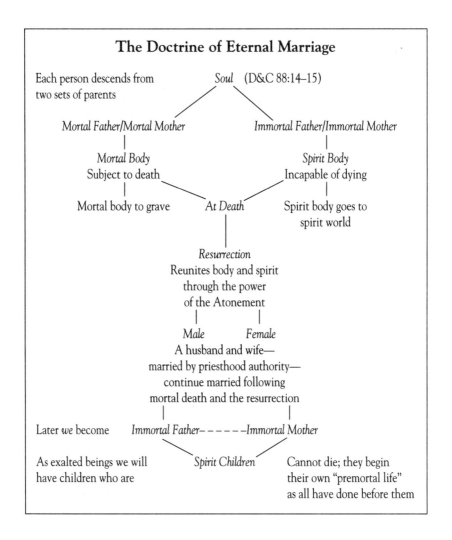

## The Doctrine of Eternal Marriage

Each person descends from                    *Soul*   (D&C 88:14–15)
two sets of parents

              *Mortal Father/Mortal Mother*              *Immortal Father/Immortal Mother*
                            |                                              |
                      *Mortal Body*                              *Spirit Body*
                    Subject to death                          Incapable of dying
                            |                                              |
           Mortal body to grave        *At Death*        Spirit body goes to
                                              |                       spirit world

                                    *Resurrection*
                              Reunites body and spirit
                                  through the power
                                  of the Atonement
                                    |        |
                               *Male*    *Female*
                              A husband and wife—
                         married by priesthood authority—
                            continue married following
                          mortal death and the resurrection
                                    |                        |
Later *we* become      *Immortal Father*– – – – –*Immortal Mother*

As exalted beings we will        *Spirit Children*        Cannot die; they begin
have children who are                                     their own "premortal life"
                                                          as all have done before them

with eternal glory, which glory we do not now enjoy" (D&C 130:2). Priesthood keys restored through Elijah to Joseph Smith allow the sealing of husband and wife for time and eternity (D&C 110:13–16).

When a couple are married by priesthood authority (the authority of an eternal being), are faithful to their covenants, and develop the attributes of Christ in their natures, they are entitled to come forth in the resurrection clothed with immortality and eternal lives—meaning that they will have the capacity to have spirit children. "Then shall they be gods, because they have no end; therefore shall they be from everlasting to everlasting, because they continue" (D&C 132:20). In a 30 June 1916 statement, the First Presidency explained this principle of "eternal lives":

> So far as the stages of eternal progression and attainment have been made known through divine revelation, we are to understand that only resurrected and glorified beings can become parents of spirit offspring. Only such exalted souls have reached maturity in the appointed course of eternal life; and the spirits born to them in the eternal worlds will pass in due sequence through the several stages or estates by which the glorified parents have attained exaltation. (In *Messages of the First Presidency*, comp. James R. Clark, 6 vols. [Salt Lake City: Bookcraft, 1965–75], 5:34.)

## Degrees of Glory

The Doctrine and Covenants indicates that only those couples who attain the highest degree of glory will enjoy the blessings of exaltation, which would include those of eternal marriage and eternal increase: "In the celestial glory there are three heavens or degrees; and in order to obtain the highest, a man must enter into this order of the priesthood [meaning the new and everlasting covenant of marriage]; and if he does not, he cannot obtain it. He may enter into the other, but that is the end of his kingdom; he cannot have an increase." (D&C 131:1–4.)

Elder Melvin J. Ballard explained:

> What do we mean by endless or eternal increase? We mean that through the righteousness and faithfulness of men and women who keep the commandments of God they will come forth with celestial bodies, fitted and prepared to enter into their great, high and eternal glory in the celestial kingdom of God; and unto them, through their preparation, there will come spirit children. I don't think that is very difficult to comprehend. The nature of the offspring is determined by the nature of the substance that flows in the veins of the being. When blood flows in the veins of the being the offspring will be what blood produces, which is tangible flesh and bone; but when that which flows in the veins is spirit matter, a substance which is more refined and pure and glorious than blood, the offspring of such beings will be spirit children. (*Melvin J. Ballard: Crusader for Righteousness* [Salt Lake City: Bookcraft, 1966], p. 211.)

In a temple marriage, couples enter into the same covenant as that of Abraham, wherein he was promised innumerable seed (see Abraham 2:9–11; Genesis 13:16; 22:17). Elder Bruce R. McConkie wrote: "Those portions of [the Abrahamic covenant] which pertain to personal exaltation and eternal increase are renewed with each member of the house of Israel who enters the order of celestial marriage" (Mormon Doctrine, 2d ed. [Salt Lake City: Bookcraft, 1966], p. 13). Powers and blessings associated with this covenant were restored by Elias, who appeared to Joseph Smith and Oliver Cowdery in the Kirtland Temple on 3 April 1836. He restored the dispensation of the gospel of Abraham, "saying that in us and our seed all generations after us should be blessed" (D&C 110:12). In the resurrection, where death is no longer possible, an exalted couple's seed shall, in the eternities, be as innumerable as the "sand upon the seashore" (D&C 132:30).

This conception should help us to see that the person we select as our eternal partner should be treated as if we are going to live together forever. Who would want to live with someone who is ornery, rude, insensitive, vulgar, or abusive? Can you see the need for that never to happen, or if there are any mistakes, to repent?

### The Damnation and Curse of Lucifer

Limitations were placed upon Lucifer for his rebellion in the premortal world. His damnation consists, in part, of never having the privilege to marry or become a father. "The adversary is jealous toward all who have the power to beget life," said Elder Boyd K. Packer. "He cannot beget life; he is impotent." ("Our Moral Environment," Ensign, May 1992, p. 66.) He is destined to be single forever, and he aggressively seeks to make all men and women as he is. He does not want any who kept their first estate and who presently enjoy the powers and blessings associated with marriage and the family to retain those powers and blessings beyond this life. He knows that we can lose these powers and blessings after this life if, having had the opportunity, we fail to build a marriage worthy of exaltation. Elder Orson Pratt spoke of the blessings of the righteous and the penalty for those who are unworthy of exaltation:

> God . . . has ordained that the highest order and class of beings that should exist in the eternal worlds should exist in the capacity of husbands and wives, and that they alone should have the privilege of propa-

gating their species. . . . Now it is wise, no doubt, in the Great Creator to thus limit this great and heavenly principle to those who have arrived or come to the highest state of exaltation, . . . to dwell in His presence, that they by this means shall be prepared to bring up their spirit offspring in all pure and holy principles in the eternal worlds, in order that they may be made happy. Consequently, He does not entrust this privilege of multiplying spirits with the terrestrial or telestial, or the lower order of beings there, nor with angels. But why not? Because they have not proved themselves worthy of this great privilege. (In *Journal of Discourses* 13:186.)

Individuals who suffer the "deaths" spoken of in Doctrine and Covenants 132:25 are those who can no more propagate their species. On another occasion Elder Pratt explained Satan's loss and the promises to the righteous:

Could wicked and malicious beings, who have eradicated every feeling of love from their bosoms, be permitted to propagate their species, the offspring would partake of all the evil, wicked, and malicious nature of their parents. . . . It is for this reason that God will not permit the fallen angels to multiply: it is for this reason that God has ordained marriages for the righteous only [in eternity]: it is for this reason that God will put a final stop to the multiplication of the wicked after this life: it is for this reason that none but those who have kept the celestial law will be permitted to multiply after the resurrection. ("Celestial Marriage," *The Seer*, October 1853, p. 157.)

What a wonderful privilege to obtain a physical body, learn to discipline these bodies, and become valiant sons and daughters in our marriage and parenting stewardships! Satan will go to any lengths to destroy the plan of God, and he tries to do it by destroying families. He has no power over us as long as we keep our covenants. Who would want to be like Satan—denied the opportunity to be with a member of the opposite sex as companions forever?

### Rearing the Children of God

Another powerful doctrine that influences our behavior has to do with children. When we speak of "our children," we actually mean the spirit children of our heavenly parents, who place great trust in us when they assign to us their offspring to rear in their behalf.

If couples were to decide not to have more children (and in our society today, many are making that decision), the Father's plan would come to an abrupt halt. We are honored to assist God in his great work to bring his posterity to their mortal probation. We thereby help them to fulfill their eternal destiny, the same as our parents have done for us.

Could there be a greater trust given to two people than to have the children of Heavenly Father assigned to them with the responsibility to nurture them and bring them to maturity in preparation for their own exaltation? Certainly our heavenly parents have a great interest in how we rear their children in their behalf in this probationary state. An understanding of this doctrine would surely prevent any physical, verbal, and mental abuse of these choice spirits.

## Doctrine Leads Us to Develop Christlike Attributes

The doctrines discussed above are basic principles which can influence our perspective and our practice of Christlike behavior, particularly in our family life. These doctrines remind us of the purpose of life, how marriage and children fit into the eternal scheme. We know that to succeed in this endeavor, our model must be Christ, for he taught us the qualities we need to succeed in family relations. He made the Father's plan operational through his atonement, and he came to teach us character traits that we need if we are to join a society of celestial people where couples love each other and parenthood is a part of godhood. As we learn and apply gospel doctrines as well as make and honor gospel covenants, it is more likely that we will develop the necessary character traits. The Doctrine and Covenants identifies a number of these traits:

- *Charity* (D&C 4:5–6; 6:19; 12:8; 42:31, 45; 52:40; 59:6; 108:7)
- *Faithfulness* (D&C 5:22; 9:13; 10:69; 50:5)
- *Gentleness* (D&C 121:41)
- *Gratitude* (D&C 59:7, 15)
- *Honesty* (D&C 8:1; 124:15)
- *Hopefulness* (D&C 18:19)
- *Humility* (D&C 1:28; 12:8; 20:37; 29:2; 54:3; 104:79; 112:10)
- *Joyfulness* (D&C 19:39)
- *Meekness* (D&C 19:23; 25:5, 14; 32:1; 38:41)

- *Mercy* (D&C 64:9)
- *Modesty* (D&C 42:40)
- *Patience* (D&C 4:6; 6:19; 24:8; 31:9; 63:66; 67:13; 98:23–24; 107:30; 121:41)
- *Peaceableness* (D&C 98:16)
- *Prayerfulness* (D&C 6:11, 14–15; 9:8; 10:5; 19:38; 30:6; 31:12; 46:7)
- *Purity* (D&C 100:16)
- *Seeking for Wisdom* (D&C 16:7)
- *Temperance* (D&C 4:6; 6:19; 12:8; 107:30)
- *Virtue* (D&C 38:24; 46:33)

How could a marriage fail if each spouse possessed these qualities in his or her character? Such attributes would make us more attractive, lovable, and competent marriage partners. On the other hand, if we emulate Satan's traits (temper, anger, contention, arrogance), we become unlovable and repulsive; consequently, our relationships suffer. Our goal is to be emotional, spiritual, mental, and physical reflections of the Savior. If we follow his example and counsel, our marriages will be strong and our children will adopt our values. Understanding the Atonement and resurrection brings an appreciation for Christ, because by overcoming physical and spiritual death he made it possible for marriage and family life to be eternal. The resurrection restores our bodies to our spirits as well as our relationships sealed by his priesthood power. We do not lose in the resurrection the deep and poignant feelings of heart and soul that are so important to our happiness in this state of our existence.

When Elder Parley P. Pratt was taught this doctrine, he marveled:

It was at this time [the winter of 1839–40] that I received from him [Joseph Smith] the first idea of eternal family organization, and the eternal union of the sexes in those inexpressibly endearing relationships which none but the highly intellectual, the refined and pure in heart, know how to prize, and which are at the very foundation of everything worthy to be called happiness. . . .

It was from him that I learned that the wife of my bosom might be secured to me for time and all eternity; and that the refined sympathies and affections which endeared us to each other emanated from the foundation of divine eternal love. It was from him that I learned that we might cultivate these affections, and grow and increase in the same to all eternity. . . .

I had loved before, but I knew not why. But now I loved—with a pureness—an intensity of elevated, exalted feeling, which would lift my soul from the transitory things of this grovelling sphere and expand it as the ocean. (*Autobiography of Parley P. Pratt*, ed. Parley P. Pratt, Jr., Classics in Mormon Literature [Salt Lake City: Deseret Book Co., 1985], pp. 259, 260.)

A person armed with this understanding of the potential of marriage would do his or her utmost to be eligible for an eternal spouse and the privilege to continue as a parent.

## Application

Knowing the importance of marriage in this life as a preparation for eternity and considering the waiting period we have passed through in our anticipation to come to the earth; understanding that Christ's atonement and resurrection restores physical bodies and marriage and family relationships; knowing that at the Judgment some men and women will be assigned to kingdoms where no marriage or family life exists; seeing Lucifer's damnation as no possibility for marriage or parenthood (which explains his relentless effort to prevent us from having these blessings beyond mortality); and realizing that our children are on loan to us by eternal parents who ask us to rear them in their behalf—understanding all these things provides us with powerful reasons and incentives to be our best as companions and parents.

Ponder this for a few minutes. Practically speaking, how could a person who understands these doctrines abuse a spouse or child? How could a person with this eternal perspective of family life, one who has covenanted with the Author of the plan, use anger and temper to control or manipulate or intimidate those he or she has promised to safeguard with his or her life? Why would one want to use Satan's techniques to achieve some selfish end? Would a person who violated this position of trust as a spouse or parent ever, in all eternity, be allowed to function in those roles again especially when, as a resurrected being, he or she would never be able to die? It is not reasonable that God would allow a being with that temperament to remain in a marriage or continue in a parenting role in the eternal realm. A degree of glory with no marriage or children would best satisfy justice in such cases. Further opportunities to parent would no doubt be closed.

These concepts should humble us, soften our hearts. When you think about it, we know so little about marriage or parenting from our brief experience in these roles during the few short years we are married on this planet. Why do you suppose we consider ourselves experts on marriage matters or parenting practices when our time in these roles has been so brief? Marriage is a commitment to do the best we can, to work together with a kindred spirit to succeed in this first-time venture. We must be good students of marriage and family life, willing to learn from each other and children, sensitive to their perceptions, needs, feelings, and responses, which may vary from our own. Of course parents must be firm, insist on obedience to common-sense rules, for they are responsible for the direction and destiny of the family. They have been down the road a little farther. But even then, our teaching must be charitable and kind toward those we are helping along the path. If we choose to be angry (because of our own spiritual immaturity), and offend others, when we regain our senses (perspective), surely we would seek forgiveness from those we offended. Would we not be anxious to restore our relationships to their former state through apology and repentance? Would we not strive to make things right with the most important people in our lives? How relieved we should be to know that an atonement has been made that allows us to change and seek forgiveness not only from God but also from those who are kin forever. When we offend others, we offend God. Anger's penalty is a withdrawal of the Spirit, and that departure should serve as a reminder to repent and repair any damage if we expect to regain the Spirit's companionship.

Too, a Christlike attitude causes us, when others thoughtlessly err against us, to quickly forgive, for we realize how shallow it is to take offense at others when none was intended and when we know we have made similar errors. The Golden Rule applies. How easily we should be able to forgive little children, who are innocent! In fact, the more a man or a woman comes to understand and live the plan of salvation, the less inclined he or she will be to take offense at the words or actions of any family member.

Well, it sounds simple, doesn't it? But why shouldn't this be the outcome? Perhaps we fail to follow this model because we do not review these doctrines on a regular basis. Perhaps that is one of God's reasons for the Sabbath—a time to reflect on our origin and destiny as well as on our spiritual condition, to count our blessings, to check our testimonies, to renew our perspective, to rethink our covenants. Or, perhaps we have not been back to the temple for a refresher, or we have not drunk deeply from the scriptural well. Without these sources to renew vision, we lose the ideal of marriage, and the carnal side of our natures tends to prevail. At such times we are more like the "natural man"; we model Lucifer more than Christ, and darkness prevails. When we lose our temper, or say hurtful things, or make cruel statements that devastate, such behavior must cease and it is time to get our hearts right before God. No wonder the gospel is repentance-oriented. We have short memories. Perhaps that is why the Lord has us renew our covenants weekly with him. It is a time to remind us of our dependence on a higher source. Otherwise we lose the Spirit of the Lord, turn inward, and become insensitive to the needs and feelings of others, our family thus suffering from our pride and arrogance.

Too often we fail to repent because we justify and defend our behavior by blaming others for our failures. An arrogant attitude, one mirroring personal pride and selfishness, prevents us from a humbling of our hearts and usually results in a refusal to change.

With gospel doctrine guiding our minds and hearts, we do not allow anger or negative feelings to generate in the first place. We *are* free agents. We *can* choose how we respond to events. We *can* act civilized and charitable in our homes. We surely had that ability to choose how we would respond when we were dating. When a date missed a golf or tennis ball, we laughed; when a family member misses the ball, we are sarcastic and critical. We have the ability to change our attitudes quickly. Have you ever been angry with another family member, only to have a friend call you and suddenly your voice and demeanor are different? Have you noticed that many times we are more civilized with strangers, who have no eternal connections to us, than we are with those of our own household, whom we have invited to join us eternally? Have you noticed that when our self-interest is at stake, we can exhibit adequate communication and listening skills? On those occasions we do exercise self-control, which is evidence that we can determine our actions.

It was this ability to choose responses that made the Savior perfect. Though he was "in all points tempted like as we are" (Hebrews 4:15), he did not respond unrighteously or in ways that hurt honest souls. The exception (for example, the oft-cited case of his driving the money changers from the temple, in anger), came in response to the hypocrisy of his enemies. He confronted them and they *chose* to take offense rather than repent. His understanding of doctrine and his role as the Son of God gave him a perspective and love for his Father and his brothers and sisters that made it possible for him not to sin against people. That was the case with the Nephites after the Savior's departure, as was alluded to in the previous chapter. Modern prophets have emphasized selfishness and pride as common reasons we take offense, delay repentance, or remain unforgiving—traits that were never a part of Christ's nature. Our sins are often a result of our carelessness in losing our perspective and becoming entangled in worldliness. Sometimes we act as if we enjoy being offended, so that we have an excuse to retaliate! Or we hold grudges to justify our attitudes, which really represent a "littleness of soul" (see D&C 117:11). It seems that at times we prefer being cantankerous to being forgiving and charitable. When we behave that way, we emulate Satan more than Christ.

The Lord said in a modern revelation: "Ye ought to forgive one another; for he that forgiveth not his brother his trespasses standeth condemned before the Lord; *for there remaineth in him the greater sin.* I, the Lord, will forgive whom I will forgive, but of you it is required to forgive all men. And ye ought to say in your hearts—let God judge between me and thee, and reward thee according to thy deeds." (D&C 64:9–11, emphasis added.) How could disciples who were oriented to gospel principles do otherwise? No wonder repentance is at the heart of the gospel and is connected to the Atonement so that we might repent and be forgiving.

## Covenants Give Us Power

Covenants give us power to live in a fallen world and yet live higher principles. To illustrate: I traveled on one occasion to Las Vegas for a speaking assignment. After the meeting, on the way back to the motel, I noticed there were some interesting establishments in that city!—most of which were out of harmony with gospel principles. Do you think that my wife, at home in Provo, was concerned about my being alone in a city with tempting circumstances all about me, late at night? Why not? Because my wife knew, and I certainly knew, that the two of us had been before our Heavenly Father in a sacred setting and that in a special way we promised each other that we would not do anything that would jeopardize our eternal relationship. On the other hand, while I was alone in that great desert city and my wife was far away, do you think I worried about her succumbing to sinful practices? Seeking other companionship while I was away? Of course not! And why was I not worried about her? Because I knew that she knew, as did I, that we had made covenants that we would not do anything to destroy our eternal goals. What a wonderful and sacred privilege it is to be married, and covenants add strength to avoid the sins of this generation.

## Personal Application

When we talk of marriage and family, we touch on the things of eternity, for we are eternal beings. We touch on the true source of happiness, on the fountain of life, on the most profound feelings and emotions. God established that neither man nor woman should be alone. Through marriage we may develop that companionship and intimate relationship that are sacred and the genuine source of our happiness.

I admit that the longer I am married to my wife, the more I love her and cherish our association. The more we share our feelings and experiences, the stronger my love and appreciation for her grow. The more intertwined our lives become through our unique personalities, children, goals, intimacy, even our finances, and as we learn to meet each other's needs and deal with mortal limits—mainly aging factors—the more I have come to know what love is all about.

Imagine a different plan of salvation, one in which we came to earth, gained our bodies, married and bore children, spent our mortal years in marriage and parenting, and then, after all the cherished experiences and emotional affiliations gained through those associations, we were allowed to die and lose our family connections and ties in the grave. If that were the end result of this mortal experience, I would want nothing to do with so-called religion. What a tragic ending that would be! If the atonement of Jesus Christ did not have the power to restore to me a resurrected body and my family associations (knowing that we must be worthy), I could not worship the God who presented it. Such a theology would cause us to live in constant fear that we might lose our lives and cut our family associations short. The death of a loved one would be disastrous. Every honest soul would ask himself, under such assumptions, "Why would God perpetrate such a hoax? Why would a being who knows all things and who has all power implement such a useless and wasteful plan?" Surely one would be compelled to ask, "What is the purpose of it all? Why marry? Why bear and rear children?" As a song of our day says, "If love never lasts forever, tell me, what's forever for?"

I want my association with my wife to last forever, and I feel the same about my association with my children. I find myself deeply involved in their lives, wanting to know how to help and assist them, without interfering, of course. Each child is important to me and contributes to my happiness. It is my work (and perhaps my glory) to contribute to their eternal life in any way that I can. From my own limited experience with my little family, I know, in some small degree at least, how my Heavenly Father must feel about each of his offspring. And these feelings should cause any husband or wife, mother or father, to want to please God and to guard against satanic efforts that would destroy the family.

## Summary

Elder George Q. Cannon summarized the potential of this noble adventure of marriage and family:

> We believe that when a man and woman are united as husband and wife, and they love each other, their hearts and feelings are one, that that love is as enduring as eternity itself, and that when death overtakes them it will neither extinguish nor cool that love, but that it will brighten and kindle it to a purer flame, and that it will endure through eternity; and that if we have offspring they will be with us and our mutual associations will be one of the chief joys of the heaven to which we are hastening. . . . God has restored the everlasting priesthood, by which ties can be formed, consecrated and consummated, which shall be as enduring as we ourselves are enduring, that is, as our spiritual nature; and husbands and wives will be united together, and they and their children will dwell and associate together eternally, and this, as I have said, will constitute one of the chief joys of heaven; and we look forward to it with delightful anticipations. (In *Journal of Discourses* 14:320–21.)

This principle of the eternal nature of the family is one of the great and joyous truths revealed in the present dispensation. That is the reason for modern temples. The Lord told Joseph Smith: "And verily I say unto you, let this house be built unto my name, that I may reveal mine ordinances therein unto my people; for I deign to reveal unto my church things which have been kept hid from before the foundation of the world, things that pertain to the dispensation of the fulness of times" (D&C 124:40–41). Marriage and family life were meant to be eternal, for we ourselves are eternal.

Adam and Eve made mortality possible, and it was Jesus Christ who made it possible for marriage to never end. No wonder we "shouted for joy" in the premortal life at the prospect of earth life (Job 38:7). This is our opportunity to marry, to plumb the depths of another soul in an emotional outpouring and sharing of feelings and passion while participating in the miracle of conception and birth. What a profound experience for a husband to watch his wife bring forth one of their offspring—to bring into mortality another being, a kindred spirit, with similar desires to accept this mortal stewardship to fashion his or her own eternal family unit. Marriage connects our past eternity of singleness to a never-ending future of marriage and family life!

This is our destiny: to come to know in this life what love really means so that we may look forward to its blessing our lives forever. Truly we may have the "love of God" in our hearts because of what we know.

***Douglas E. Brinley*** *earned bachelor's and master's degrees in economics from Utah State University and a Ph.D. in family studies from Brigham Young University. He served as the director of several LDS institutes of religion. He is presently an associate professor on the Religious Education faculty at BYU. He served as mission president in Dallas, Texas. He and his wife, Geri, are the parents of six children and a foster daughter.*

# 7

# WELL, WHAT DO YOU EXPECT?

## Charles B. Beckert

*I*t was about three in the afternoon when Maria walked into my office. The intake information sheet indicated that she was concerned about her fourteen-year-old son because he was finding it difficult to make it to school more than one or two days a week. I was not prepared for what I saw. Maria was in some pain, grimacing as she gently seated herself in the side chair. Her left eye was black, she had scrapes and bruises on her cheeks, her lip was split, she limped, and her right arm was in a half cast! I asked if she felt okay. She said she was fine, and then she proceeded to request advice and counsel concerning her consistently truant son. I was, of course, curious about the origin of her physical problems, but since she did not bring them up, I didn't feel right about prying.

We talked about her son, his dad, other family members, and possible motives for the boy's reluctance to attend school. We had a nice conversation, and I felt that the ideas and suggestions concerning her son were helpful to her and that she saw a direction she could go.

We ended our conversation, and she was about to leave the office when my curiosity got the better of me and I inquired as to how she sustained her cuts and bruises. I was certain she would relate a story of an automobile, bicycle, or some other accident. But she did not. She matter-of-factly stated that her condition was the direct result of a beating she had received from her husband. But to my amazement, neither her voice nor her face showed any anger, frustration, or contempt. I pursued the topic and asked if the two of them were still living together. She said, "Certainly. Why shouldn't we be?" At this point I realized I was in deeper than I wanted to be. After all, I was the one who initiated this conversation. She did not seem concerned at all. She rather flatly stated something like: "He is a good man. He earns a good living and provides well for me and the children. He means well, and he only hits me when he is drunk, and it occurs no more often than once or twice a year." I was dumbfounded. Here was a woman who had been beaten by her husband, something she endured once or twice a year, and she was not even angry with him. Most women I know would have either clobbered him or at least left him. There would be no way they would have remained in that relationship. But Maria seemed satisfied with her marriage.

Now, why would she tolerate her husband's behavior? Why would some women stay and others run in a similar situation? I think the answer resides in the *expectations* of each individual. I realize that sounds simple, but based on my counseling and personal experiences, I believe it to be true. And it is these expectations that I would like to discuss in this chapter: Where do they originate? How are they maintained? Are they realistic or unrealistic? Can they be altered and/or adjusted, and if so, how? This chapter will also address how expectations can be clarified and why that is important; the role they play in marital satisfaction; and how they can be used to encourage a more positive marriage relationship.

## The Critical Factor

The following statement is one I encourage (require) my students and clients to commit to memory. To me, it is at the very heart of marital problems:

> *A major cause of marital dissatisfaction is the unwillingness and/or inability of one partner in a marriage relationship to behave in the manner expected by the spouse.*

It may sound simplistic, but in my experience it is generally true. The reason Maria was not unhappy in her marriage was that she did not expect her husband to behave other than the way he did. It was as if she expected occasional abuse from him. Not all examples of expectations are as dramatic as hers, of course.

One evening my wife and I were visiting an older couple. In the process of our conversation, the husband asked his wife of more than sixty years for a drink of apple cider. She dutifully brought him a glass, about one-quarter filled with cider. He looked at her, then at the glass, then back at her and said, "Do you call this a drink of cider?" His response was saturated with sarcasm. Her response was equally interesting. "I never know what you want or expect. Sometimes you want only a sip or two, and other times you want a full glass. Often you leave more in the glass than you drink. You can get your own next time!" In this case expectations were unknown, undeclared, and apparently unfulfilled. Result: two sarcastic people. Yet they seem to really love each other.

## Why Do People Hurt Each Other?

Over the years I have spent literally thousands of hours working with married couples who have been experiencing some form of pain. Generally I can remain objective to their impaired relationships, not carrying their burdens beyond the office. But as I get older I seem to feel their pain more and more. I feel sorry for so many of them because marriage for me has been so joyful and happy. I find myself wanting them to have fun with each other as my wife and I do and to get along on a daily basis. In some cases they do not have that many more years of marriage left. But they do not get along or enjoy their lives together. Even though they may say they love each other, there is some motivation on the part of each one to hurt his or her spouse.

Brenda and Tom had been married less than a year. In the few months since their wedding, they had had several minor and even a few major eruptions. After a blowup, they would look at each other and actually shed tears over what they had done. As I talked with them, they seemed puzzled as to why each would knowingly do things he or she knew would be destructive to the partner and the marriage. They talked much about feeling frustrated on those occasions, but at the time they did not (could not) comprehend what they were doing to each other. It was not until later, as they would look back on their altercations, that they recognized that their troubles stemmed from unfulfilled expectations. In other words, they did not get what they wanted or expected from each other. In the latest fiasco Brenda had expected Tom to pick her up from school at 4:15 P.M. Tom had planned to be there on time but found when he started to work on his truck that it took more time than he expected. Consequently he arrived at the university nearly thirty minutes late. Brenda was furious. How could he be so inconsiderate? Why had he not called when he knew he would be late? To her it seemed like common sense, completely rational, something that any husband who loved his wife would naturally do.

Tom, on the other hand, was almost beside himself. He wondered who this girl was that he had married. He thought she should realize you can't always plan things to the minute. He expected Brenda to understand his tardiness and not yell at him about it. He knew he was late, but to him it was not a major issue. He thought she could figure it out for herself. He was hurt because Brenda was so inflexible regarding a schedule he was unable to meet. From this point on their discussion turned nasty, and both said things to each other in anger and frustration, things which were very devastating. And yet, they loved one another.

Here is a flowchart suggesting how this negative interaction comes about.

1. A major cause of marital dissatisfaction is the unwillingness and/or inabilty of one partner to behave so as to meet one or more expectations of the spouse.
2. An expectation remains unfulfilled when an individual is unwilling or unable to fulfill it (or might be ignorant of its existence).
3. Frustration develops from an unfulfilled expectation.
4. Anger, pain, disappointment, discouragement, or indifference are the result of unresolved frustration.
5. The desire and motivation (conscious or unconscious) to retaliate or strike back often find their roots in anger, pain, disappointment, discouragement, or indifference.
6. People strike back at each other, causing hurt and pain.

One night I received a telephone call from a young couple who had been married just over four months. The husband placed the call, and from his shaky voice it was obvious he was in great emotional pain. He said he and his wife had just had a major fight and needed help immediately. I went to their apartment. They were seated opposite one another, he on a couch and she on the kitchen chair. Both were very frustrated and upset over what had just happened. They had been fighting, physically. She had rushed him, trying to wrestle with him. He turned to free himself from her grasp and accidently elbowed her in the mouth. A couple of teeth had been chipped. They both felt terrible about it, but they had not made up, either. They just glared at each other, as if they could not believe such a thing as this was actually happening to them in their marriage.

Again it turned out to be a matter of unfilled expectations. She wanted to talk through a problem which had surfaced at dinner. He wanted to retreat for a while and consider what he was feeling and thinking so he would not say or do the wrong thing. She interpreted his retreat to be a withdrawal and knew they would never solve the difficulty if they kept silent. He knew if he talked about it right then, things could really get out of hand. She expected him to talk with her. He expected her to give him time and space to work things out first in his own mind. The harder she pushed for talking, the more he withdrew, and the more he withdrew, the harder she pushed him to resolve the issue. Finally, as it often does, frustration turned to anger. And in an emotional state most of us do things for which we are later sorry.

After about thirty minutes of my explaining what I thought had happened, their faces softened. Tears were visible in all four eyes. They moved together, held hands, and looked deeply into each other's eyes. The desire to hurt was gone, and kindness and gentleness had again entered the relationship. No doubt they would live in harmony and peace until they discovered other expectations which were not being fulfilled in the marriage.

## Personal Luggage

Sometimes I marvel at how wonderful most marriages are. What a challenge it is to bring two strangers together to set up house, to live so intimately together, and to come to know each other on such a personal basis!

We all bring what I call "luggage" into marriage. I believe we begin packing this personal luggage in childhood. It consists of what we think, our fears and phobias, prejudices, attitudes, habits, beliefs, temper, dreams, goals, commitments, and so on. To us they represent our valuables, our "expectations" as to what we expect to receive (and give) in marriage. Obviously in our premarital state we do not know exactly what is going to occur in marriage. We do not even really know if we will ever marry. And yet, there are certain things packed away in our personal luggage relative to marriage that will turn out to be very important to us once we begin living with someone else in a trust relationship. Certainly there are things packed into our trunks of which we are not yet even conscious. Some expectations are so natural to us we just take them for granted. And we assume that everyone else feels the same way we do about them, especially our spouse.

## What Are Your Expectations?

It is often surprising to many couples, once they marry, to discover how different some of their basic expectations are. I have used the following list of expectations several times in presentations, and almost without exception husbands and wives are a little surprised when they learn how their spouses feel about certain issues and what each partner actually expects of the other in marriage.

You and your spouse try the following survey, indicating whether you agree or disagree with each statement. I would suggest that you each complete the entire list separately according to how you genuinely feel about each topic and that then the two of you compare your choices. It can be a learning device—an eye-opener on the one hand and a way to solidify your compatibility on the other. Here is the list:

1. If there is a difference of opinion regarding where to live, the husband should decide.
2. Husbands and wives should share housework equally.
3. A wife should be as well informed as the husband concerning the family's financial status and business affairs.
4. Wives should combine career and motherhood.
5. A husband should leave the care of the children entirely up to the wife when they are babies.
6. It is more important for the wife to be a good cook and housekeeper than to be an attractive, interesting companion.
7. Unless there are unusual circumstances, each spouse should agree to participate in physical intimacies when the other is interested.

8. Keeping the yard, making repairs, and doing outside chores should be the responsibility of whoever wishes and has the time to do them.
9. The husband and the wife should have equal privileges in such things as going out at night.
10. The husband and the wife should have equal voices in decisions affecting the family as a whole.
11. After marriage a woman should forget an education and become primarily a homemaker.
12. It is more important that a husband be congenial and loving than that he earn a good living.
13. Husbands should spend most of their energies in getting ahead and becoming a success.
14. Being married should cause little or no change in either the husband's or the wife's social or recreational activities.
15. The wife should fit her life to her husband's more than the husband should fit his life to hers.
16. Husbands and wives should feel equally responsible for the children.
17. Traditional views on which jobs men and women should do around the house should be completely ignored and interests and abilities should determine who does what.
18. As children grow up, the boys should become more the responsibility of the father and the girls the responsibility of the mother.
19. Each spouse should know where the other spouse is and what he or she is doing in his or her spare time.
20. Neither spouse should purchase anything over ten dollars without consulting the other.
21. The husband should be willing to give up some things which are important to him to help his wife's personal growth.
22. The wife's opinion should carry as much weight as the husband's in money matters.
23. Money earned by the wife should be considered her money.
24. Both husband and wife should be expected to drop what he or she is doing to listen to the other's problems.
25. Education and career training are less important for the wife than for the husband.

How did you do? Did you experience any surprises? Are your expectations as compatible as you thought they were, or even more so? Have you learned that there are many things that the two of you can and need to talk about? Whatever the results, I hope you learned something about your own and your partner's expectations. Now you know what I am talking about in this chapter.

One of my favorite thought questions in working with couples is: "What has surprised you most in your marriage?" The responses are as varied as the people you meet. I remember one young man answering, "The amount of toilet paper a woman uses." He was raised in a family with four brothers and no sisters. A young woman answered this question with: "I never thought I would have to ask my husband to take care of me when I was sick. I thought he would know what I needed him to do." Of course, before marriage she did not know that she had this particular expectation.

Once married, we often surprise ourselves when we identify our own expectations, and no doubt some of the expectations of our spouses are a shock to us as we learn about them. During the dating stage neither partner thinks they are of sufficient import to check them out.

Cindy had always wanted a happy marriage. Her desire was to be a good wife and a terrific mother to her children. She did not expect to work outside the home when the children came, because she wanted to spend all her time with them. She and George had not talked much about this before marriage, I guess because George was going to school at the time they met and Cindy was working full-time at a local bank. Unknown to Cindy was the notion that George had that she would continue to work to support him through school. George wanted children, of course, but expected they would find an appropriate day-care center for their children while Cindy worked. Cindy was approaching her sixth month when the two of them discovered their incompatible expectations. They really had a tough time working through it, but because the event was closing in on them, there was not much either of them could do about their situation. Their solution was for Cindy to work part-time, spending most of the day with the newborn, and for George to take fewer credit hours, which enabled him to add a few more hours to his job. Things worked out, but both admitted it would have been easier had they discussed this issue at an earlier time in their relationship. Had they understood how strongly each one felt about this issue, they might have planned things differently.

My wife and I had the opportunity to attend a lecture by a marriage and family therapist friend. His topic was "Negotiating Scripts." He explained how each of us comes into marriage with his or her own "script" as to how things are supposed to happen in each area of marriage. (His "scripts" were the same as what I call "expectations," only perhaps a little more formal.) He had us write down our scripts in two areas he suggested. My wife wrote her script and I wrote mine, and then we compared notes. Maybe we have been married so long we already have a "joint script." For us it was not a problem. Our scripts were very similar, certainly compatible. Some of the younger married couples, however, did not have such an easy time. It was a real struggle for a number of them. One couple in particular had problems when they were comparing their personal scripts on "how to act around in-laws." The diversity of their scripts almost resulted in a battle royal, so different and contradictory were they from each other. Their mutual conclusion seemed to be that neither would spend longer than twenty-four hours in the home of an in-law at one time period. I felt certain they both would mellow in time, but it was evident that there was a need to "negotiate scripts" in the days ahead.

As I have spoken on this topic over the years, one thing I have enjoyed is providing seminar or workshop participants with an opportunity to confront one another on some "silly" (yet sometimes serious) differing expectations to illustrate that we all have expectations, even on simple matters. Here are eight of them, presented in a question-and-answer format, for you and your spouse to review and do together. These items relate to common situations that can stir controversy in any household. Until these common expectations are understood and accepted, irritation often results, which may then lead to contention.

## Expectations in Marriage: A Test

1. *Who should control the thermostat in the home?*
   A. The wife
   B. The husband
   C. They should take turns
   D. They should live in separate houses

2. *What should be done with the soiled clothing at night?*
   A. Put in a hamper or hung up
   B. Piled in a certain place
   C. Dropped wherever convenient and taken care of in the morning
3. *How should the toothpaste tube be squeezed?*
   A. Only from the bottom
   B. Anywhere from the middle of the tube down
   C. Anywhere on the tube
4. *How should a sick spouse be treated?*
   A. Fussed over
   B. Generally left alone, checked on from time to time
   C. Basically left alone
5. *How should the toilet paper be placed on the dispenser?*
   A. So the paper comes "up and over"
   B. So the paper goes "down and under" (Story: One man said one time in a large gathering that he did not care how the paper rolled when he walked into the bathroom, but it would be "down and under" when he left—regardless of whose bathroom it was!)
6. *How should the toilet seat be left after being used?*
   A. Both seat and cover up
   B. Seat down, cover up
   C. Seat and cover down
7. *How should personal feelings be handled?*
   A. Express them and get things out on the table
   B. Keep them in, don't say too much, and allow time to heal
   C. Keep them in until ready to explode and then explode
8. *Who should initiate physical intimacy in marriage?*
   A. The husband
   B. The wife
   C. Both should (Story: Another man in a session responded in a rather loud manner: "I really don't care who initiates it, as long as somebody does!")

A couple can have a lot of fun discovering each other's expectations. But discovery is not enough. If the differing expectations are significant to one or both partners, some form of change or adjustment must occur if the couple are to avoid conflict and contention.

## Discovering Expectations

The number of ways a couple might uncover or discover their expectations other than in a crisis is limited only by the level of creativity of the individuals involved. I would like to suggest a few methods that could be helpful to you.

### *"I See Me . . . I See You . . . I See Us . . ."*

Although this first exercise requires time and effort, it has proven to be very helpful to most couples. First, the two of you identify an area of marriage which could potentially produce different and perhaps incompatible expectations. These areas might include the following: "yard work," "housekeeping," "home repairs," "earning a living," "managing finances," "initiating physical intimacy," "organizing family recreation," "maintaining relationships with relatives and/or friends," "caring for the children," "disciplining children," "religious activities in the home," "maintaining effective communication," "planning for and preparing family meals," "sharing personal thoughts and feelings," and so on. You could add as many additional topics or areas as you like.

This exercise involves writing three short, basic paragraphs that would describe the following three items:

1. How you *see yourself* functioning in this particular area of marriage
2. How you *see your partner* functioning in the same area
3. How you would like to *see the two of you* working together on this topic or area of marriage

Each partner writes these three paragraphs and then the two of you compare what you have written. If the expectations match, fine. If they do not, some discussion, adjustment, and negotiating must take place.

Here is an example from one husband who wrote about yard work around the home.

> *I see me* having the primary responsibility for the yard work. It will be my task to mow the lawn, spade the garden, rake the leaves, care for the garden, etc.

*I see you* being willing to help with the yard work when you have opportunity and time. I also see you helping whenever you wish. I see you taking care of the flower bed on the east of the house as per your request.

*I see us* discussing the needs of the yard together, planning what we would like to grow, and especially working together in the vegetable garden. I also see us both enjoying the fruits of our labors at harvest time.

The wife then responds to this topic with her three paragraphs. Then the two come together, listen to each other, and as a couple create a "mutual agreement" or a "joint script" relative to the yard work at home.

This exercise can be powerful and helpful in clarifying expectations. It is also very useful for engaged couples as they attempt to enter their marriage as prepared as possible.

### *"I Would Like . . ."*

A second exercise provides further practice on clarifying expectations. This strategy requires both partners to work together on the experience.

First, a couple chooses an area of marriage to discuss. It could be any of those listed above or one specific to your marriage. Both spouses should be willing to consider this area of marriage jointly.

Once the subject has been selected, one partner starts. Here is an example: A wife wants to talk about the spiritual atmosphere (actually the lack of it) in the home. She has had the expectation that the television set would be turned off on Sunday and that they, as a couple, would spend time together studying, talking, listening to music, visiting relatives, and so on—"appropriate Sunday activities." Her husband is a God-fearing man, but he also loves the Dallas Cowboys, the Atlanta Braves, and the Utah Jazz. He has expected that he would attend church but then would be free to enjoy his sports on the tube. The couple has spent some very unhappy hours arguing about this situation. The husband is very willing to come in for counseling to see if they can resolve this issue. To him it is "not that big a deal."

Step two requires that one partner, generally the one who raises the concern in the first place, expresses what it is he or she expects, or "would like," to happen in the marriage. In our example, the wife starts the conversation.

"I would like to enjoy our Sundays without the interruption of the television set and sports programs."

The third step might comically be labeled the "fast-food-drive-through-order routine." Let me explain. When you drive through the take-out lane of a fast-food restaurant, the individual inside the restaurant asks, "May I take your order?" You respond by verbally stating the order. Now comes the helpful routine. Having heard your order, and perhaps having made some kind of note of it or having punched prelabeled buttons on the cash register, the individual repeats the order back to you, in detail, to make sure your order has been accurately understood and received. In our example, the husband repeats, in his own words, what he understands his wife's wishes to be.

"If I understand what you are saying, you would like to have me not watch TV on Sunday, but rather spend the day with you and our family doing religious things."

Back at the drive-through station, after the order-taker has repeated back to you your order, you indicate whether or not the order was taken correctly. This is step four of our exercise. The wife responds back to her husband, "Yes, that is what I would like, but it doesn't mean we can't do some fun things together. I just think television ruins the spiritual atmosphere in our home most of the time. Besides, I thought that one of the reasons why we purchased our video recorder last year was so we could tape those programs that you really want to see at another time."

Now that the expectation or desire has been declared and understood, two questions remain. They are directed at the husband. (After the first time or two that this exercise is used, no one has to ask, they come up automatically.)

Question one is, "Is this something you can do?" In other words, is it within your power not to watch TV sports on Sunday? Here a simple yes or no is all that is needed for a response. If the answer is yes, the second question is, "Will you do it?" The response to this question may not be quite as simple. The husband could say, "Of course I will. I would do anything for you and our marriage." Or he might say, "Yes and no. I am willing to do it most of the time, but I do not want to commit to *never* watching a sports program on Sunday." He is obviously thinking about the Super Bowl or the baseball World Series.

If his answer is yes, the dialogue is over and the two of them can live happily ever after—at least relative to this particular issue. If the answer is other than yes, some negotiation will need to take place. Perhaps a counteroffer, or an adjustment in the expectation, allowing Sunday TV on special occasions.

This simple technique could be beneficial for literally hundreds of situations found in marriages. It does require time, mutual trust, an understanding heart, and a willingness to compromise and allow others to have their choices honored. In my experience, this strategy has worked best when a couple takes turns bringing up issues. One major key to remember is that the process must be a *discussion to understand rather than an argument to win.* Both hearts must be open. (Variations of the initial question could be used; for example, "I would feel better about things if you would _____.")

It is important at this point to understand that if a partner indicates that he or she "can't" do what is expected, this may not be just an excuse. There really are some things we cannot do even though a partner may truly want us to do them.

Sometime ago a wife indicated that she would like her husband to be with her when she was not feeling well. She did not like being alone and really did have a personal fear of dying when no one was around. Her expectation was that her husband would always be there when illness struck. The husband promptly responded that this was one thing he could not do. It was not that he did not want to. It was that he could not take the time from school and/or his job. Most employers do not take kindly to workers who do not show up to the job on a regular basis!

There are also some good reasons why a partner may choose to say "I won't" even if he or she "could" do something. A case comes to mind in which a husband indulged himself in massive amounts of hard-core pornography. His appetite had been whetted and he wanted his wife to act out some of the seamy scenes he had viewed on video. When asked if she "could" do this, the wife said yes, she could. But when asked if she "would" do these things, her answer was a resounding "No!"

## What If Our Expectations Don't Match?

What if your expectations and your spouse's don't match? This is a good question, because in my experience they quite often don't.

Once in a while couples are blessed with compatible scripts, but most often the scripts need to be negotiated and written together.

Remember that one of my initial statements suggested that the level of marital happiness can be traced to the difference between how one partner interprets a spouse's actions and what expectations existed in the first place. What we need is a strategy to decrease differences. There are basically three alternatives to assist us in accomplishing this task.

1. The "expecting" spouse may choose to adjust his or her expectation. (Note: I use the word *adjust* rather than *lower* because too many people tend to resist "lowering" anything. They think it is a sign of weakness or wrongness.)

When my wife and I were first married I had a great dream about the two of us spending countless hours on the tennis courts. Not that I was any good, but it seemed like a nice "couple sport." Her physical condition would not allow her to participate in the sport. It truly was something she "could not" do. I had to adjust my expectations. I did not want to play tennis alone and I did not really want to spend that amount of time with someone else. Eventually we solved our dilemma by our both picking up the game of golf. This has turned out to be one of the greatest decisions we have made. We both can do it. We both want to do it. And we both really enjoy spending this time together.

2. A second option is for the "target spouse" to do whatever it takes to improve his or her behavior. If a wife expects her husband to spend more quality time at home with the family and her expectation is not unrealistic, he would do well to adjust his schedule, maybe giving up something here or there in order to accommodate her desires.

3. A third alternative might be a combination of the first two. The expectation could be adjusted *and* a particular behavior improved. This would also decrease the distance between the partners' expectations.

I would like to suggest a fourth option. It could be labeled "compensation." In this instance the specific expectation would not be met, but the "unhappy" spouse would be provided something which could make up for the loss. I remember a man who loved deer hunting. He admitted the tremendous cost per pound of meat when he did get one (and the even higher cost if he didn't). But to him, it was worth the effort. His wife did not want to be alone for the week of the deer hunt and she felt rejected. She saw it not only as a waste of family funds but also as a lonely time for her. She had no desire to join him on the hunt, nor did the husband really want her there; it was too primitive. So they worked out a compromise. The wife could have the same amount of money the husband spent for the hunt. This enabled her to fly home to spend the week with her family or do whatever else she might choose. This agreement was acceptable without any qualifications by both spouses.

Thus, when marital expectations do not match, you can (1) adjust the expectation, (2) adjust the behavior, or (3) make adjustments in both expectations and behavior. And if these do not work, you can provide an acceptable compensation that will meet the needs of both partners.

## Summary

It really makes little difference what you call them—expectations, scripts, luggage, or something else. The phenomenon is real. This statement is true:

*A major cause of marital dissatisfaction is the unwillingness and/or inability of one partner in a marriage relationship to behave in the manner expected by the spouse.*

If we want to enhance our marriage relationships, we would do well to become aware of our own and our partners' expectations, understand them, and accept them as they are or work out the necessary adjustments. Humility (being open) and unselfishness are two essential keys for success in these matters.

Whether or not you enjoyed this chapter depends upon how closely the ideas presented came to matching your expectations. You see? You cannot get away from them!

**Charles B. Beckert** *has been married to Olga Madsen for over thirty-four years, and they are the parents of four sons and numerous grandchildren. He holds a Ph.D. in marriage and family therapy from Brigham Young University, and has a private counseling practice in Ogden, Utah. He has been a bishop twice, is a published author, and has recorded several tapes on marriage and family topics.*

# 8

# READY OR NOT—
# HERE WE ARE

*David T. Seamons*

Tom and Julie had been married almost two years. They discussed with me how they met and courted, and it sounded pretty close to the Cinderella-Handsome Prince story. Yet here they were, only a short time after marriage, reporting that the "spark" had gone out of their relationship. Apparently the same shoe that fit so well on the night of the ball didn't feel as comfortable in the daylight of marriage. In fact, now they found it difficult to even go to the ball at all! Their likes and dislikes seemingly had changed. Prior to marriage, time with each other had been something they greatly anticipated. Now it was something to avoid. Tom's conclusion: "I guess we have fallen out of love." He sounded as if he had caught a germ or virus for which there was no cure; as if he could not "fall back in love" again.

Julie jumped in after a minute or two: "Is our relationship beyond repair? Is there any hope? I hate to file for divorce. I thought marriage was going to be so wonderful, but it is not what I expected."

The story of Tom and Julie, unfortunately, is not so unusual. It appears to be almost acceptable and commonplace for couples to use the initial disappointments that can arise in marriage as an excuse to justify the need for divorce. The discovery that a spouse is not perfect—which seemed so improbable in those heady days of courtship—seems to throw so many into a state of confusion.

Each of us brings into marriage certain expectations and assumptions about how our marriage will unfold over time. We expect this new relationship will fulfill our personal needs for intimacy and close-ness. It seems easy for many to make this jump: "We enjoy dating, don't we? Imagine what marriage will be like, when we can actually live together as a married couple, sharing everything, where we can fully function as sexual beings and not have to say good-night at the doorstep." We can easily envision such wonderful days ahead of us as our dreams become our realities.

It is true that we discuss many different things while dating; topics such as how many children we should have and what they will look like, our educational goals, wedding and honeymoon plans, how we can finance our marriage, where to live, how we will furnish our apartment, what it will be like to attend a regular ward. These are normal concerns that couples anticipate as they look forward to mar-riage. At that point in time, however, expectations are not very de-tailed in their minds, while others of which they are not even con-scious yet may turn out to be more significant in the long run.

So many of our expectations regarding what we think is "right" or "wrong" behavior, or "normal" to us, do not surface until our lives be-come more complicated by earning a living; a variety of homemaking tasks; car insurance, loans, and maintenance; debt; intimacy; preg-nancy; colicky babies; how we reconcile after a spat; and myriad other potential trouble spots. Marital satisfaction—how well marriage satis-fies our personal goals—is influenced in important ways by how well our known and yet-to-be-discovered expectations mesh as married partners.

Where do we acquire all of these expectations about marital scripts or roles, anyway? From childhood on we observe different people in our lives and how they relate with each other. We see our parents, brothers and sisters, relatives, neighbors, and friends interact, and we unconsciously absorb from them ideas about proper and appropriate behavior—role expectations. These are assumptions we have about what kind of behavior is typical or normal for a number of marital roles such as housekeeping, sexual intimacy, parenting, in-laws, reli-gious practices, wage-earning, and so forth. In addition, powerful ex-amples of relationships are presented on television, movies, and videos, and in books and magazines.

Of course, some of these relationships fare well while others are unhealthy, but it is never made clear to us as young people what makes the difference. We acquire and store large amounts of data gathered from years of observing and absorbing ideas, but we do not know until we marry how we will apply that information which is stored on our personal "chip." Yet when that special young man or young woman comes along, we suddenly begin to pull from this reservoir of observations, ideas, beliefs, and expectations on how we and our soon-to-be spouse ought to function in these marital roles.

During the dating years we seek a mate who has the characteristics we think we want in our spouse—traits that will complement ours and enrich the relationship. While we do talk about a number of topics while dating, the process of defining and talking through mutual expectations and goals before marriage is often handled very superficially for at least two reasons: (1) If this is our first marriage, we are not familiar with the details of these marriage roles for either us or our new companion; our ideas are not clearly formulated; and (2) Hormones and emotions often become the focus and driving force of this new relationship, ofttimes compromising our judgment. Many buy into the myth that sexual intimacy will compensate for any character deficiencies we brushed by in dating. Many believe that marital intimacy will resolve any concerns that showed up in our premarital searching. Then, when we marry, we find differences that we did not anticipate. Said President Spencer W. Kimball:

> One comes to realize very soon after marriage that the spouse has weaknesses not previously revealed or discovered. The virtues that were constantly magnified during courtship now grow relatively smaller, and the weaknesses that seemed so small and insignificant during courtship now grow to sizeable proportions. The hour has come for understanding hearts, for self-appraisal, and for good common sense, reasoning, and planning. The habits of years now show themselves; the spouse may be stingy or prodigal, lazy or industrious, devout or irreligious, kind and cooperative or petulant and cross, demanding or giving, egotistical or self-effacing. The in-law problem comes closer into focus and the relationships of the spouses to them is again magnified. (*Marriage and Divorce* [Salt Lake City: Deseret Book Co., 1976], p. 13.)

Heavenly Father's instructions to us are to marry and become parents (see D&C 49:15–17; Moses 3:18, 24). We are forbidden, however, to marry one from our own family, thus virtually ensuring that we will marry someone from a family where ideas and practices were carried out in ways different from our own. Also, we marry someone of the other gender, one socialized to see and feel and interpret things differently than we do. What I am saying is that built into marriage is the probability that the two people, coming together from different perspectives and backgrounds, will find a number of "role discrepancies"— differences in what each had supposed would happen in the marriage relationship.

It is in marriage that we find out just how Christlike we are, what all of those meetings, youth conferences, testimony meetings, and missions made of us as singles in preparation for marriage. The gospel teaches us a style of living designed to assist us in developing personal strengths that allow us to handle with charity a number of differences that arise in marriage. In order to be successful in this new enterprise we must incorporate the Savior's characteristics and attributes into our own natures. I can think of no relationship which requires more patience, gentleness, compassion, understanding, selflessness, forgiveness, and repentance than the role of a spouse and/or parent.

## Expectation Assessment

In order to answer the questions Tom and Julie proposed concerning the future of their relationship, we began identifying specifically what each one's self and spouse expectations were, and what responsibilities they believed should be shared. Worksheet number 1 was given to them to begin this process. Both filled out the worksheet separately, and then they came together to compare their responses. This helped to identify and clarify their beliefs and expectations on who should accept responsibility for various areas of the marriage.

Immediately their similarities and differences became obvious and specific, where they could be addressed as a team. Tom was surprised to learn, for example, that Julie expected her husband to oversee car maintenance and repairs, whereas he had been raised in a family where each driver took care of the maintenance of his own car. Julie now learned that Tom expected his wife to personally be in charge of cleaning the house *and* overseeing the upkeep of the yard too. This was certainly different than what she had expected. Both agreed that child discipline and money management should be a joint effort.

These expectations gave them a lot to discuss. I reminded them both that differences did not mean that their marriage was in jeopardy, and I helped them to understand that marriage is a profound

# Worksheet No. 1
## Responsibility in Marriage

Instructions: List in the space below what responsibilities you think you, your spouse, and both of you expect in your marriage.

| Husband | Both | Wife |
|---|---|---|
| I think the husband should accept responsibility for the following areas: | We should both be willing to accept responsibility for the following: | I think the wife should accept responsibility for the following areas: |
| | | |

Adapted from John Narcisco, Ph.D.

commitment in which each of us has much to learn from his or her companion. It turns out that as marriage partners both are students and teachers of one another. Teaching requires charity and patience, for one spouse may not see what the other sees; and this works both ways. Teaching and learning are therefore best accomplished in an atmosphere of trust and love, without negative emotion or criticism, so that each can understand and appreciate each other's way of seeing reality. From our family backgrounds we bring a number of solutions to typical problems, but we also will fashion solutions that will be uniquely ours. Tom and Julie came to realize that changing or redefining individual expectations for a variety of marriage roles is an ongoing process for every couple. Expectations are basic building blocks for all marriages.

Once the basic responsibilities of Tom and Julie were clarified through discussion and a measure of agreement was reached, then came the question of *how* each would like to have expectations carried out. Worksheet number 2 is designed to help with that process. Nine major areas around which most marital relationships revolve are listed. Individually Tom and Julie filled out this form. Each stated in specific terms what he or she would like to have happen in each of these nine categories if it were up to him or her, and what the corresponding spouse's behavior would be in each area. This exercise required some extensive soul-searching for the two of them. They, like most of us, operated on what might be called core beliefs which often go unexpressed. We think, or at least hope, that the person we marry will have the same core beliefs as we do.

As to these core beliefs, it turned out there was a classic difference between Tom and Julie. For example, Tom's idea of leisure activities was watching football and basketball games. He learned that while Julie enjoyed athletic events, she wanted to attend cultural activities too, such as plays, the ballet, and symphony concerts. This process of sharing wishes and expectations shook them in a positive way. They thought they knew each other pretty well before they married, and in many respects they did, but they did not know specifics with regard to what each other really wanted and expected to happen in marriage.

As together they reviewed their expectations concerning the social calendar, religious practices, money management, and a host of other topics, they began to realize that they had taken a lot for granted in getting married; that they really did not know that much

# Worksheet No. 2
## Marriage Wish List

Instructions: Fill in what you wish would happen in your marriage and what you would like your spouse to do in each category:

|  | I would like to: | I would like my spouse to: |
|---|---|---|
| 1. Socializing |  |  |
| 2. Recreation |  |  |
| 3. Money management |  |  |
| 4. Sexual intimacy |  |  |
| 5. In-law relations |  |  |
| 6. Children |  |  |
| 7. House |  |  |
| 8. Religious practices |  |  |
| 9. Job or vocation |  |  |
| 10. Other topics: |  |  |

Adapted from John Narcisco, Ph.D.

about each other's thoughts and wishes. When they found a number of differences—some of them major—Tom and Julie now set aside time to discuss their feelings and ideas in depth so each could further understand the partner's side and could see where some "give and take," or some negotiation, was needed.

Before this exercise, Tom and Julie had usually expressed their wishes in vague generalities such as "I just want to be happy" or "I just want us to do things together." Now the statements became "It makes me happy when we talk together and listen to what each other says," and "what I like to do best is for us to go to either a musical play, a sporting event, or a movie together." This clarification of values and expectations now gave them some areas around which they could design their marriage activities and improve their relationship through better planning. Different expectations no longer needed to cause them such marital pain.

## A Major Myth About Marriage

A major myth exists about marriage. We think, "If my spouse really loved me, he or she would know what I am thinking and feeling and do it." Or we may say to ourselves, "If I have to tell him or her everything, it just can't be true love." These statements are not only untrue but also are generally damaging. Your spouse may love you dearly and yet be unaware of your wants and needs unless you make them clear. To add the dimension of "hide and seek," however, or to play "guess what I would really like you to do for me," adds unnecessary challenges to any marriage. The earlier worksheets were designed to be a catalyst to help you verbalize and share your expectations and ideas. Remember, you can differ on many issues and still be friends. Where differences exist, changing, redefining, or understanding expectations through negotiation can provide needed resolution of those differences.

## Negotiation

Negotiation in marriage is simply making the effort to come to an agreement on how something should be done, or deciding who can best handle a specific area of marriage so that all is fair and equitable within our power to make it so. Marriage gives us practice in negotiation, an art that must be a part of every close relationship. Our mutual desires and needs don't always match and we need to "work things out." We generally do not need a third party. We can do it ourselves, if we will, because we have made a commitment to each other to function as independent, yet dependent companions, in the context of marriage. Here are some suggestions for working through differences that are sure to arise in marriage.

1. *Set aside a specific, convenient time to discuss aspects of your marriage and evaluate elements of marital satisfaction.* It is especially crucial in the early stages of marriage that each couple take time to explore a variety of marital issues. Perhaps this could occur on date nights, after family home evening, after the children are in bed (when interruptions are less likely), or during intimate times together. In our modern, fast-paced world, most couples do not make or take sufficient time to really stay in touch with each other. This often causes a divergence from mutual goals, resulting in each making assumptions about the other that are not true.

It is important that we check in with each other periodically. We would not run a business without doing this. What proprietor would not stop at the end of a day, or certainly of a week, to review procedures, expenses, costs, and profits, and to check employee morale through some method of feedback. This review does not have to be profound or heavy; it is simply a time in which to determine whether our marital satisfaction is where we want it to be. We need such time in order to discuss various facets of our marriage, share feelings, indicate personal needs or wishes, check our calendar and schedules, pray together, and express appreciation for each other. This process ensures that a couple is talking and staying current on important things in each other's world.

Now answer these questions about your own marriage: "When do my spouse and I talk together about our marriage and family?" "When is the last time we examined our own expectations and assumptions and checked our own marital satisfaction together?"

2. *Each spouse must be able to share his or her own personal feelings about what is needed and wanted in the marriage.* This suggestion assumes that the marriage climate allows for both partners to share and risk with each other—something that encourages further communication.

No one likes to express personal feelings and ideas with another who is quick to judge, criticize ideas, ridicule feelings, or supply a "better solution." Such a smothering, suffocating environment violates our being; it is a domination of our spirit which is stifling to our character.

Also, we should avoid vague generalities, such as "I would like greater closeness." That is too broad. More specific statements might be, "I would like us to eat dinner together at least four times each week," or "I would like to spend time discussing the day's events each evening with you before we go to bed." These sharing sessions are not gripe sessions, for that is not wholesome. We would not look forward to being together if that was our objective. Rather, these are opportunities to reinforce our goals and exchange our feelings and ideas about life in general and our progress as a couple toward a celestial marriage.

Now, ask yourself these questions: "How comfortable am I in discussing, risking, and sharing topics and ideas with my spouse?" "What about my spouse—how easy is it for him or her to risk with me?" "Do I fill the role of a therapist for my companion?" "What topics seem to be off-limits for us because we become angry or otherwise emotional when the subjects arise?"

3. *State what you would like to have happen, not what you don't want to happen.* Focus on encouraging behavior, not on placing blame. For example, one could say, "It is helpful to me when you tell me something that you would like me to do"; whereas, "I want you to stop picking on me" might provoke an argument. Avoid black-and-white judgments. *Never* use terms like "You never . . ." or "You always . . ." Consider differences for what they are—differences—and be charitable in dealing with those that bother you. It is *your* problem if it frustrates you, and you may need to change. It is a good idea to discuss differences with your spouse. By doing so, both of you can grow from understanding their origins, which may be differing family backgrounds.

Ask yourself these questions: "Are there things in my marriage over which I take offense?" "Do I use 'you never,' or 'you always' with my spouse and children?"

4. *Do not negotiate feelings.* Only behavior can be negotiated, and only those behaviors that do not compromise a person's integrity are open to this process. People should not change emotions through bargaining, for some things are not open to negotiation: "Okay, I agree to be happy about your shouting at me" just won't work.

Now ask yourself: "Do I try to manipulate my spouse through emotional bargaining?"

5. *Be patient.* The Lord gives us a number of years to be married. Inevitably there will be differences along the way. Because most of our beliefs are deep-seated, or deeply ingrained in our makeup, it may take a while for either one of us to adjust our thinking or allow a new idea to sink into head and/or heart. It may take some time to see things as the spouse does, and vice versa. Like fruit that is ripening, a number of discussions and feedback sessions will be needed before maturity comes—even on what sometimes appear to be insignificant issues. The process of negotiation is the mechanism for resolving differences so that couples can unitedly move forward.

Ask yourself these questions: "Have I changed much from when we were first married? If so—how?" "Were the changes good or bad?" "What about my spouse, and how has he or she changed?" "How has he or she made an effort to meet my expectations during our years of marriage?" "Have I acknowledged that to him or her?" "What have I done to be a better companion to my spouse?"

## Marital Termites

Marital termites plague most marriages in one form or another. Even when we discuss and agree upon our expectations, human nature and personal tendencies plague us. In my twenty-three years of practice as a therapist, I have observed the following areas which seem to me to eat away at many relationships.

1. *Selfishness.* President Spencer W. Kimball stated, "Every divorce is the result of selfishness on the part of one or the other or both parties to a marriage contract" (*The Teachings of Spencer W. Kimball,* Edward L. Kimball, ed. [Salt Lake City: Bookcraft, 1982], p. 313). Selfishness develops when we focus on ourselves and our own needs rather than on our opportunities to enrich and strengthen our spouse. We use terms like "me" instead of "we." Our focus is skewed toward what we want or should *get* rather than what we can *give;* on *rights* rather than on responsibilities. Marriage is designed to be an exclusive relationship in which both partners commit to be their best selves. They give themselves to each other in trust and confidence with the assumption that the other will reciprocate. Power struggles— *who* is right—should be replaced with a desire to do *what* is right. It is obedience to the Lord's will that brings happiness and peace, not the need to prove oneself right at the other's expense. We frequently see things in a "right or wrong" context. Often this leads to power and

control issues rather than cooperation and a willingness to see another side to an issue.

2. *Lack of communication.* Another marital termite that destroys so many relationships is the lack of effective communication between husbands and wives. This includes the sending of verbal and nonverbal messages to each other and our ability to listen to these messages with both heart and soul. The worksheet exercises discussed earlier were designed to help couples communicate their expectations as to what they would like to have happen in their marital roles by monitoring nine basic areas of their "wish list." Communication is enhanced when we use words that are kind, charitable, clear, and that describe behaviors and events. Because we communicate to share information, our communication must be understandable.

Our nonverbal cues must correspond to our verbal cues if communication is to be effective and believable (we tend to trust nonverbal messages more than verbal messages). If we say one thing and do another, our mixed message will be confusing. For instance, we may say we don't mind staying home and missing the function (verbal), but then we pout all night to punish the spouse (nonverbal).

It may be a new experience to share personal and intimate thoughts and feelings with another person if you grew up in a family that discouraged sharing by their criticism or negative comments. It has been my consistent observation that one of the major complaints of most women is that their men need to be able to better express their feelings. Men, ask your wives if that is true in your case.

Listening is another trait essential to successful communication. Effective listening is dependent on our being more interested in hearing and understanding the other's message than planning our own response. Perhaps this well-known simple reminder will help: the Lord has given us two ears and one mouth; the anatomical design of our creator warrants our effort to listen twice as much as we speak. Our goal should be to really understand the messages of the sender, both verbal and nonverbal.

3. *Physical intimacy.* In today's world, so many view sexual relations as recreation. However, the Lord intended sexual relations as an expression of love between two married people, designed *only* for a man and woman within the bonds of marriage. The commands of the Lord are designed to bring two inexperienced people together in a discovery of their sexual natures, to uncover the meaning of the Lord's

command to multiply and replenish the earth. How much better it is for a newly married couple to learn from each other how to satisfy and please each other than for one or both to be experienced sexual partners who already are acquainted with the intricacies of sexual pleasure. Suspicion and mistrust of each other often stem from premarital promiscuity.

Some say that physical intimacy with the same partner becomes boring in time as the novelty and thrill wears off; that variety is the spice of life. Often this becomes an excuse for immoral behavior, for looking elsewhere for selfish gratification. When physical intimacy incorporates unselfish sharing and communication, it becomes something given and shared, not taken. There must be integrity in intimacy if trust is to develop. Marriage does not give ownership of one's body to the spouse. If one partner desires to do something sexual that is uncomfortable, embarrassing, or detrimental to the other's self-esteem, that act should be avoided. The greatest sensitivity to the needs and desires of one's spouse should be exhibited in this dimension of marriage. In the sexual aspects of marriage, not everything goes. Years ago, Elder Mark E. Petersen, a member of the Quorum of the Twelve, warned:

> If sex is as sacred to us as it should be, then it deserves that status both before and after the wedding ceremony. "Anything" does not go in marriage. Decency is as important for married people as for the unmarried. Perversions are perversions whenever indulged in, and the marriage ceremony cannot take away their stain.
>
> When indecency, indignity and unnatural practices are thrust upon a good woman by a lustful man, can she be blamed for resisting? Can any woman retain her self-respect or her regard for her husband if he insists upon and she submits to unnatural practices? . . . It is the unnatural, the extreme and the indecent which sickens self-respecting women. (*Marriage and Common Sense* [Salt Lake City: Bookcraft, 1972], pp. 94–95.)

President Spencer W. Kimball said: "If it is unnatural, you just don't do it. That is all, and all the family life should be kept clean and worthy and on a very high plane. There are some people who have said that behind the bedroom doors anything goes. That is not true and the Lord would not condone it." (*The Teachings of Spencer W. Kimball*, p. 312.)

Decency between a husband and wife are requisites to retaining the Spirit of the Lord.

4. *Money management.* All of us face economic pressures, and it behooves us to plan and budget monies wisely. The Lord counseled, "Thou shalt be diligent in preserving what thou hast, that thou mayest be a wise steward; for it is the free gift of the Lord thy God, and thou art his steward" (D&C 136:27). In a marriage there should be no such thing as "your money" or "my money." It is "our money," regardless of whose name is on the paycheck. Decisions about expenditures should be based on careful joint planning and budgeting. Purchases should reflect needs and not simply wants. Once needs are met, wants can be considered. Satisfying wants should be the result of joint decision-making.

If your budget permits, "mad" money is therapeutic to any marriage. This is money that represents discretionary spending for each spouse, spending money for which one does not have to account. For newlyweds it may be a small amount each week or month. For those with greater income, it could be much more. Each spouse should have some money to spend as he or she wishes.

5. *In-laws.* Many parents struggle with how to relate to their offspring once their children are married. Parents can provide a tremendous resource to married children if their intentions are in harmony with the couple's goals. Advising parents on their in-law role in a specific marriage usually becomes the responsibility of each child. This should keep parents from feeling that their relationship with their own son or daughter is being dictated by the new partner. I suggest that the in-law role be thought of as a consultant role, the consulting being done only upon request!

## Keys to a Happy Marriage

Relationships require conscientious effort on the part of both spouses if they are to be happy. It has been my experience that it takes two people working overtime to make a marriage work well, whereas only one person who will not make any effort can break up a marriage. I have listed below some areas that will assist any couple to strengthen their marriage.

1. *Continue your friendship.* Most couples fall in love as a result of spending time together in meaningful courtship activities. Continuing

dating patterns after marriage will ensure the growth of marital friendship. Having fun and enjoying each other is not limited to the premarital period. Weekly couple planning sessions where a weekly date is calendared strengthens the bonds of friendship. A mini-honeymoon at least once a year, or a get-away every four to six months—even if only for a night or two—helps retain the spark of marital desire and keep perspectives fresh and new.

As the marriage progresses we find out new things about each other. That is the way it should be. Trust is developed and maintained as we overlook differences and focus on the positive things our spouse does. You might think of it as "catching each other being good," rather than looking for things to criticize. Peace is experienced as you serve each other. Nothing controls selfishness more than mutual service. The Scout motto, "Do a good turn daily," is a good motto for all marriages.

2. *Demonstrate your love.* Love is a divine gift from Heavenly Father. It is nurtured when service and sacrifice have been a consistent part of the marriage relationship over the years. Love too is developed through mutual service. Love is a verb requiring action. Common courtesies of politeness such as opening doors are always appropriate. Other gestures of love include nonsexual touching (hugs and hand-holding), love notes, phone calls during the day to each other, flowers, and so forth. Our behavior should leave no doubt that the commitment we made at the altar is one that we intend to keep. We are to create an environment in our relationship that is emotionally safe, meaning that we can easily approach each other with concerns or appreciation without fear of ridicule or criticism. This is done by not taking each other for granted, by daily reassuring each other of our love and devotion by what we say and do.

3. *Make an effort to understand the expectations of your spouse.* As mentioned earlier, happiness in marriage is often explained by one's expectations being met or not being met by the spouse. Therefore the constant communication of wishes, wants, and other expectations is important to the successful flow of the marriage. The two worksheets were provided to help you find out how to improve your relationship. Every six months would be a good time frame for a thorough review, perhaps writing on these worksheets at first and then gradually moving to simply verbal sharing as you become more experienced at it.

4. *Learn to communicate well together.* Emphasized in every book

and article written on happy relationships, communication clearly is essential to building a great marriage. Healthy relationships have an open and effective communication system that works for them. This includes the ability to approach each other, share feelings, and listen with respect to what one's partner has to say. This kind of communication is enhanced by both partners being open, honest, and willing to risk personal ideas, thoughts, and feelings. Friendship is thereby enhanced, trust grows, and commitment is reaffirmed when we communicate with each other in kind and charitable ways. Those who were raised in an environment where sharing thoughts and feelings did not come easy will need a spouse who is understanding and helpful in establishing an environment where risk can occur. Nothing is more reassuring than a good marital relationship in which lines of communication are open and uninhibited.

5. *Develop mutual interests.* The continued development of mutual interests removes the threat of boredom that afflicts many relationships. We learn best from feedback, by checking in with each other, by sharing our feelings and ideas on a multitude of subjects. Be sure that each has a chance to be involved in the planning of activities and events. For example, one week the husband may plan the Friday night date; next week, the wife. Surprises always add excitement to any relationship—flowers for the husband or wife, a trip to the store, or a movie together, and so on.

With school and job opportunities, where we live and what we do may change from time to time. Use these situations as opportunities to try new adventures, new hobbies, new foods and cultures, to begin new family traditions. Life has many exciting experiences to offer you if you will do them together. Incorporate those experiences that continue to cultivate your interests and thus avoid the monotony that plagues too many marriage relationships.

6. *Be committed to each other.* We live in a day and age in which if we don't like something we trade it in for a newer or better model. Happy marital relationships are not based on trading partners, but are based on covenants made with one another in holy temples. We promise—without any clauses of "if convenient" or "if I can," or "I'll try." The covenant of marriage is not to be taken lightly. Reflect these promises in your priorities. If your spouse is the most important person in your life, he or she should know this by the time and energy you put into strengthening that relationship. We enter marriage as a couple.

We should make every effort to maintain the sacredness of this relationship. To compromise the relationship is to invite unhappiness and pain into your life.

Infidelity is becoming much too commonplace in our society and has no place in a healthy marriage. I give this caution: Do not rationalize yourself into believing that just because your relationship with someone else is not physical it is all right. To flirt and become emotionally attached—even if short of physical involvement with anyone else—is grossly inappropriate. Emotional and physical infidelity are, and always will be, a compromise to the sacred covenant of marriage and are sins.

7. *Make your intimate times enjoyable for both of you.* Sharing physical and emotional intimacy is designed by the Creator as a bond that enhances and strengthens marriage. The consistent dimension in intimacy helps reassure us that we are loved and appreciated. Unfortunately, some couples live as "married singles," in quiet desperation, or more like roommates because of the superficial shallowness of their marriages. What human being does not need to be loved? needed? thought important? valued? The marital relationship should provide that safe emotional haven where such personal needs are met. A healthy intimate relationship creates a peaceful setting in which two souls can find safety and fulfillment.

The sexual urge is a God-given gift, but one that must be exercised only within the bounds the Lord has set—marriage. Intimacy must be a free gift from one spouse to the other. It cannot properly be taken, or demanded.

8. *Keep your covenants.* Marriage is a covenant made by two individuals with God, indicating that they desire to spend an eternity as married companions. This contract becomes a contract between the husband and wife and God to ensure that all blessings associated with this compact will be theirs if they are true and faithful. The Lord has promised us that all he possesses will be ours if we will be obedient to his laws and commandments (see D&C 84:38). He has outlined in specific ways what we must do in this life to qualify for exaltation. Daily prayer and scripture reading, regular temple attendance where possible, church attendance, and service to one another are just a few examples. The Lord has promised that when such laws are faithfully obeyed his Spirit will remain with us so that we will not be led astray or persuaded to falter because of worldly temptations.

Never before in the history of the world has the smorgasbord of temptations looked more enticing to so many, but these telestial activities do not bring peace. Often so-called intellectuals would have us believe that the gospel is complex and thus difficult if not impossible to live. Actually the Lord has made his plan simple: keep his commandments and all that he has will be ours.

9. *Husbands, righteously fulfill your assignment to preside.* Priesthood holders have a special assignment as they preside over their families. To preside is not to control or dictate. The patriarchal order is an order of leadership by example. Men should be humble enough to change where and when it is needed. There is no room in a happy and healthy marriage for egotism, pride, or dictatorship. Marriage is an opportunity to serve one another, and indeed we reap as we sow.

To men, priesthood is a sacred stewardship, a gift from God to bless the lives of others. Priesthood is the power to act for God. Each husband must ask himself: How would God want me to care for his daughter—my wife? Each wife must ask herself: How would my Heavenly Father want me to treat one of his noble sons—my husband? The answer, of course, is: The same as *he* would! With love unfeigned, patience, and forgiveness.

## Conclusion

As for Tom and Julie, they quickly discovered that a couple's ability to adjust to the challenges of married life are the core of what makes a successful marriage.

Our trust is in the Lord and his plan, for he has promised us that he will not leave us alone if we will have faith in him. King Benjamin explained it best when he counseled:

> And moreover, I would desire that ye should consider on the blessed and happy state of those that keep the commandments of God. For behold, they are blessed in all things, both temporal and spiritual; and if they hold out faithful to the end they are received into heaven, that thereby they may dwell with God in a state of never-ending happiness. O remember, remember that these things are true; for the Lord God hath spoken it. (Mosiah 2:41.)

The great plan of happiness is designed to bring all men and women back into God's presence. The way is clearly defined. Marriage is an essential and beautiful part of that divine plan.

**David T. Seamons** *was born and raised in southern California. He attended Brigham Young University, where he obtained his B.S., M.A., and Ph.D. in psychology, school psychology, and clinical psychology, respectively. While at BYU he met and married the former Ann Finlayson. Along with their five children and son-in-law, they enjoy skiing, tennis, and horseback riding together. He served as an LDS missionary in the Alaska Canadian Mission. He has served as a bishop and stake president, and is presently serving as a regional representative. For the past twenty-three years he has been practicing professionally in the field of marriage and family therapy and is currently in private practice in Provo, Utah.*

# 9

# TALKING ABOUT
# SEXUAL INTIMACY
*Emily M. Reynolds*

According to the first chapter of Genesis, the first recorded utterance of God to Adam and Eve was in the context of a blessing: "And God blessed them, and God said unto them, Be fruitful, and multiply, and replenish the earth" (Genesis 1:28). Although there are variations among the scriptural accounts of the Creation, this theme is found in all of them. We are left to wonder to what extent, while God walked and talked with Adam and Eve in Eden, they talked about the begetting of children and the relationship that would make that possible.

From such tender and sacred beginnings, the conversation of human beings about their sexuality has unfolded in a wide variety of ways. Stand at the grocery store checkout and read the teasers on magazine covers. You will be hard put to find a single one that doesn't say something about sex. You will also be hard put to find a single one that still has God in the conversation.

I point this out to make plain a real and pervasive problem that we face as Latter-day Saints. There are many available conversations about human sexuality and sexual intimacy. (I am using the word *conversation* very broadly here so that it takes in not only things we say but also things we do and see and hear and feel.) It is as foolhardy as it is impossible to avoid participating in these conversations in some way. We marry and enter into covenant relationships. We bear children, and bear also the responsibility of conveying, whether intentionally or unintentionally, an understanding of covenant relations.

The ways we talk about these things have profound relational consequences. So an unavoidable question arises: How shall we talk about, and thus involve ourselves in, sexual intimacy?

At this point one wishes for a more detailed account of the walking and talking in Eden. How and what did God teach Adam and Eve about these things? What did he want them to understand as they set out to be fruitful and multiply? Unfortunately, however, it is usually the records of other conversations about sexuality that are most detailed and most available to us. Various religious and ethnic traditions, scientific and psychological theories and data, the unremitting deluge of the media, our own experiences and the experiences of those around us—all offer perspectives that must be sifted and sorted as we consider what sort of conversation we ought to carry on.

Sometimes the sifting and sorting are easy. For example, most Latter-day Saints, when confronted with the rhetoric of the gay and lesbian movement, have little difficulty in seeing that there is something deeply wrong with that perspective. The same is true for stories accepting or encouraging adultery and fornication. Often, however, the ways of understanding sexual intimacy that are actually getting in the way of our relationships with each other and with God do not involve blatant sin and are not so easily recognized.

We are reminded in Moses 4:5 that "the serpent was more subtle than any beast of the field." The text implies that this is why Satan chose the serpent as his representative with Eve. Subtlety is essential in leading astray those who are striving to obey the commandments of God, because invitations to what is obviously sin will never persuade them. Nowhere is this truer than in the arena of human sexuality, where subtlety and nuance get so much play. What this means is that recognizing what is wrong with a lot of conversations about sexuality simply requires a level of discrimination which most of us have not had occasion to develop. Often conventional wisdom seems borne out by our own experience and we never think any further than that.

The point of this essay is to "think further than that," to look more closely at some important aspects of our most common ways of talking about human sexuality and see what may be wrong with them. I think this is worth doing because I am deeply convinced that traditional ways of talking about sexuality bear little resemblance to the conversations in Eden and that our common cultural conversation concerning these things works directly against the relationships ordained by the

Lord's plan of happiness. A necessary corollary is that if we are to be able, as Latter-day Saints, to establish Zion and, more immediately, to engage in family relationships that are sustainable for eternity, we must recognize and turn from the distortions and misunderstandings of sexuality that are part of our culture. As this happens, we will be able to teach our children a conversation about sexual intimacy that has our relations with God and with each other at its heart.

I should note here that such a conversation requires both clarity and delicacy in a balance which is far more difficult to achieve in writing than it would be face to face. I will do my best, but I freely acknowledge my dependence on your thoughtfulness and reverence as a reader. In talking about a subject as intensely sacred as this one, I understand better the Prophet Joseph's statement that he taught correct principles and the people governed themselves. In the spirit of that idea I will talk about ways of talking about sexuality. It will be up to you to understand how those ways of talking may inform your own life and understanding.

## Sorting Out the Subtleties

I am going to begin with some generalizations which I hope need no more support than your everyday experience. The first is that we usually speak of sexuality as having its origins in our biological makeup. We frequently hear the phrase "sex drive," a term intended to convey a kind of necessity about human sexuality, a force that ensures the perpetuation of the species. Closely connected to this is the fact that when we speak of sexual morality it is nearly always a matter of controlling this drive, which would otherwise, by most accounts, run devastatingly out of control. If all of this seems very comfortable and familiar, then what follows may be uncomfortable, because what I want to do now is try to point out how such a view may lead us astray if we take it seriously.

The idea that sexuality is essentially biological reflects a philosophical stance called reductionism. Characteristic of most of science until the last few decades, reductionism involves taking a complicated phenomenon (and human sexuality certainly qualifies) and *reducing* it to something simpler, something that causes the complex phenomenon to happen. In the case of a biological reduction, we take the whole range of feelings, actions, and results that might be termed sexual and reduce them to the workings of a causal biological system of hormone secretions, neuron firings, genetic imperatives, and so forth. Having identified these biological causes of sexual behaviors, the next step is to conclude that what's *really* going on is the hormone secretions, neuron firings, and the playing out of genetic imperatives. Anything else that can be said is, in some sense, extra and doesn't really contribute anything to our understanding. Sex is just sex, no matter where you find it, and any talk of anything beyond the brute biological facts is superfluous.

Other kinds of reduction are possible, but what all reductionist theories have in common is that they assume that if certain causal things happen, sexual behaviors of various sorts will follow inevitably. Put that bluntly, it may sound absurd, but when dressed in the everyday language of our culture it's an assumption that seems to make perfect sense to most of us.

Consider, for instance, the tension that can be built in a television scene when a man and a woman who should not be sexually involved with each other are left alone. That tension is based on the assumption that certain unavoidable biological reactions are occurring and that only remarkable self-control (which almost no television characters seem to possess) will prevent the inevitable. Though we may not think of ourselves as having any theories about this, we are often willing to take at face value this kind of representation of sexual relationships. We do not object to the idea that sexual arousal just happens, that there is a chain of events which, once set in motion, will result in sexual activity, even if that activity is confined to our thoughts. We may believe that we can exercise control, but masked by that control is a cause and effect reaction that we take to be immutable.

Reductionism of this sort has been rather severely criticized in the last few decades' work in philosophy of science, but only one of its failings needs attention here and a person needn't be a philosopher to understand it. The problem centers around the way we think about causes. At one time the notion of causality had a richness and variety (many examples of which are still in the dictionary) that is largely lost to us today. One definition has come to predominate in common usage: A cause is whatever *makes* an event happen.

In part, this predominant usage is a result of the rise of science in the past century or so. For a scientist, the necessary operation of causes is important because it means that once the cause of a phenomenon or events is found, it is certain that it will happen that way every time. No other outcome is possible; if the cause operates, the effect will follow. We use the phrase "cause and effect" as shorthand for that understanding, and it encapsulates our rationale for trusting the world to keep turning, flowers to keep blooming, and, at a more personal level, the basic life functions of our bodies to keep functioning. Thus doctors often assume they have found the cause of an illness when they make a diagnosis and effect a cure. Geologists can discourse at length on what caused certain land formations to come into existence. Chemistry students in labs the world over drop soda into vinegar, fully expecting that the soda will cause the vinegar to foam every single time.

It is worth a little reflection to realize that this way of talking only works because we don't expect land formations to mean anything to other land formations, or chemicals to engage in relationships with each other. The same cannot be said, however, of our expectations of human beings, and this is where the problem shows itself.

In brief, causality precludes meaning. Things that have to happen don't mean anything; they just are. So if sexual behavior is caused, whether by hormone secretions or psychological drives or anything else, it too is meaningless. Put another way, if people engage in sexual relations because of, for example, a Darwinian imperative to procreate that is written in their genes, the vocabulary available for talking about sexuality is very restricted and the words we use to describe the meaning of our actions virtually disappear. Words like *covenant* and *love* can't even be given definitions in such a system. At best they are only disguises we use to create sexual opportunities. And chastity can only be defined as being seriously out of touch with reality. On this view, no matter what the relational context, to abstain from sexual relations is just plain silly. It goes against nature.[1]

---

1. An even more insidious twist arises if, in an attempt to reconcile science and religion, we say that the drive we experience is not Darwinian but God-given. I counseled with a young woman who, confronted with this problem, asked, "What kind of a sadist would God have to be to create his children with this urgent, life-dominating need and then command them never to fulfill it except with one person to whom they are married?" Good question.

At this point it should begin to be clear that it's not just meaning that disappears if we pursue this view to its logical conclusion. Morality goes as well. Returning to the land formations and chemicals of the earlier example, how much sense does it make to ask whether a mountain is right or wrong? Or whether soda has a moral obligation to avoid making vinegar foam? It makes no sense at all. Things that operate by cause and effect, that have to be as they are, can't be right or wrong. They just happen, and if we think about their moral significance at all we usually conclude that, since things couldn't be otherwise, they must be right; e.g., "Of course that mountain is supposed to be there; after all, it *is* there." So in the end the idea that things can't be right or wrong usually means only that nothing can be wrong and everything ends up being right.

Putting human sexuality in this same category makes nonsense of sexual morality and moral responsibility. If sexual behavior operates on principles of cause and effect, then whatever behaviors happen to occur must be all right. Perhaps you recognize this argument from the rhetoric of the gender revolution that I referred to earlier. It is common for homosexuals to claim a right to their lifestyle, with all it entails, because they are simply living out the demands of their biological makeup. But they do not have a corner on the use of this argument. Many acts of adultery, fornication, and even inappropriate relations between marriage partners have been justified in this way, as well. Whatever seems urged upon us by our biological drives is taken to be acceptable and we needn't feel any moral responsibility for it. It's like the line from a song that became popular in the early nineties: "It can't be wrong when it feels so right." The whole dimension of righteousness and sin just disappears.

Following the logical consequences of our traditional views to this point is sobering enough, but Lehi teaches us that we're only part of the way to where this argument ultimately leads. His words read, in part: "If ye shall say there is no sin, ye shall also say there is no righteousness. And if there be no righteousness there be no happiness. And if there be no righteousness nor happiness there be no punishment nor misery. And if these things are not there is no God." (2 Nephi 2:13.) Perhaps when we started out saying that sex is a drive we didn't mean to end up saying that there is no God, but that is, in effect, where we do end up if we take the idea of sex as a drive to where it leads. Like all the teasers on the popular magazines, we end up talking about sex in a way that leaves God out of the conversation entirely.

Losing meaning, morality, and even God would seem to provide ample reason to consider alternative ways of looking at sexual intimacy, but before we leave our explorations it is important to see one other relational consequence of thinking of sex as a drive.

We live in a time when individualism has virtually become an art form. We are met on every side by advice to improve our self-esteem, get our needs met, love ourselves, be assertive, and just generally "look out for Number One." The care and feeding of the private individual self has become the focus of a great deal of personal and cultural attention, and the idea that sex is a drive is deeply embedded in this world view.

A drive, like anything else we define as necessary, has the potential to be a very divisive and individualizing thing. It replaces the lost dimension of righteousness and sin with a single imperative: getting what I want. It is private and compelling and, because of its presumably basic and primitive nature, it influences or even dictates our perceptions. Thus the person whose behavior is driven by the need for sex (and if sex is a drive, then that's all of us) may begin very quickly to see other people only as possible means to fulfillment. If you are over there with your drive and I am over here with mine, it may be that the best we can hope for is some kind of negotiated settlement whereby you keep my needs met and I do the same for you.

The potential for conflict in this scenario is virtually unlimited. Probably every married couple on earth has experienced times when one partner was interested in sexual intimacy and the other was not. And this is only the beginning. Issues of timing, technique, frequency, and so on, all make for unavoidable discrepancies between partners. How are such situations to be resolved if we believe that our desires are simply the manifestation of a biological drive, that they have the status of needs, that we have a right to have them fulfilled—and to the exact specifications dictated by our biological makeup? In a culture that generally accepts the notion of a sex drive, is it any wonder that sex always makes the list of leading causes of divorce?

As sexual promiscuity is more and more accepted, the problem I am describing is less and less acute for many people because the scope for finding sexual fulfillment is very broad. But what of the Latter-day

Saints, for whom chastity is a deeply cherished virtue? In this setting the problem takes an ironic turn. To put it plainly, believing that sex is a drive drives us apart. In a marriage, it makes our partner into a potential enemy who may, for whatever reasons, fail to provide what we need. In our relationships with others, belief in a sex drive drives us away from every person of the opposite gender to whom we are not married, fearful of what we might do to one another, unable to sustain friendship because of what it might "lead to." And as the gender revolution gains momentum, we may find that we are increasingly wary of same-gender friendships, as well.

Some of what I have described might be dismissed as the extreme theoretical case. In real life, of course, the theoretical consequences of an idea don't always show up, because each idea has its place in a complex mix with a lot of other ideas, some of which we embrace more completely than others. We don't always see the self-contradictions in the particular mix we live with. So even though we accept the notion that sex is a drive, it may be possible to go on feeling that our sexual acts are deeply meaningful, keeping our covenant of chastity as if it mattered, knowing God is still there, working out disagreements about sexual intimacy with our spouses, and sometimes even managing cross-gender friendships. But perhaps we shouldn't be surprised if traditional ways of talking about sexuality get in the way, confusing things and sometimes blocking our ability to do what is right completely.

## Starting Over

Once we see some of the problems with traditional views, we ought to ask the question again, How shall we talk about, and thus involve ourselves in, sexual intimacy? I think the answer begins, as might be expected, at the beginning, with God blessing Adam and Eve and saying to them, "Be fruitful, and multiply, and replenish the earth." Recall that this utterance, although given at the beginning of Adam and Eve's earth life, already had a rich context. The earth which they were commanded to replenish had been created to provide a place for the sons and daughters of God to learn to be like him. The relationship on which they were about to embark was fraught with covenants and promises which bound them to all the rest of us, us to them, and all of us to God. Already enmeshed in this vast network of relationships, Adam and Eve undertook to be fruitful and multiply.

And it is no different with us. We, too, are enmeshed in that network of relationships that is fraught with covenants and promises, and have been so since before mortal birth. Our sensitivity to our covenantal context can be blunted by sin, self-deception, conformity to culture, or even simple lack of awareness (and when that happens we often behave very badly), but nothing makes the covenants, or the relationships they solemnize, go away. We are children of God whether we acknowledge it or not, and we are always already in a shared context in which every act is meaningful and every deed has moral significance.

If this is where we begin our conversation about sexual intimacy, the idea that sex is biologically driven is as out of place as meaning and morality were on the traditional view. In fact, everything shifts. There is only time and space in this essay to examine a few particular shifts, and even those don't divide up neatly, but I hope to get you started in your own pondering of the difference an understanding of the restored gospel can make to these issues.

## The Salience of Relationships

Traditionally, explanations of sexual activity have reduced it to biology. I would suggest instead, given the starting point I have just described, that our understanding of sexual intimacy arises out of our understanding of our eternal relationships. In fact, sexuality cannot be understood without the context that a knowledge of those relationships provides, which is why it is so little understood in our current culture.

Notice also that I did not say that sexuality reduces to relationships. This is because talking in terms of relationships is not a reduction. It is, rather, an augmentation, bringing into the conversation many things that would otherwise be left out. Understanding our relations with each other takes in everything about our world. Perhaps this is because our world was created expressly as a setting in which to learn Godlike relationships.

## Possibilities Rather Than Necessity

As we saw earlier, the view that sexuality is biologically driven assumes a necessity about all sexual behavior. Sex happens because genes or hormones or some complex interaction of things *make* it happen. By contrast, within the context of the covenants that give form to our participation in the plan of salvation, the command to multiply and replenish the earth does not *make* us do anything, rather it opens possibilities, eternities of them. Like all of the commands of God, it provides us with an understanding of how to live if we desire to fill the measure of our creation—to become like God and live eternal life as he lives it.

We are taught that the elements of the earth, the plants and flowers, the birds and animals, obey the commands of God (see Matthew 8:27; Jacob 4:6; Abraham 4:25; Moses 1:25). Sometimes, like many of our Christian friends, we think that they "obey" because they have no option. God simply becomes a necessary cause. I think, however, that we need to take seriously the agentive connotations of the word *obey*. Consider the possibility that what compels us—and the rocks, plants and animals—to do as God commands is not the impossibility of doing otherwise but rather the possibility of being in a covenant relationship with him and making his work our own.

It is, as John teaches us (John 8:32), the truth that makes us free, that makes our choices free, that makes choices leading to eternal happiness possible. God teaches us the truth unfailingly, whether by his own mouth, by the mouth of his prophets, or by the gift of the Holy Ghost. It is by this process that he literally gives us our agency— not just the right or ability to choose but also the light of truth in which to see our options for what they are so that our choices are meaningful and genuine (see D&C 93).

## The Gift of an Eternal Context

The direction we receive concerning our sexual behavior is just part of God's counsel concerning every aspect of our lives. Taken together, what this instruction does is to put in context all of the possible ways of having our sexuality so that we can see how they fit in an understanding of our relationships to each other, both on earth and through eternity. Suddenly other details besides the biological ones become important and we see immediately that, contrary to the traditional view, sex is not just sex wherever you find it. In fact, sexual acts that may seem to be biologically identical are clearly not the same at all when performed in different contexts. To use a common and not at all subtle example, this is how we distinguish lovemaking from rape. It is the context, and in particular the relational context, of the physical act that defines it or gives it meaning. Traditionally, context simply makes no difference, but on this view context is everything and makes all the difference. Context is what makes meaningfulness possible.

The context that God offers us is, as we have already seen, a richly relational one, and this is what brings morality back into the picture. Once we begin to think in terms of our eternal familial connections to one another, it is clear very quickly that some ways of having our sexuality are true to our relations with God and each other while others are not. This recognition provides us with a moral framework within which all of the possibilities can find their proper place.

The differences between the sexual union of a couple under covenant and other sexual acts such as fornication, incest, adultery, homosexuality, and so forth, become almost overwhelming against the backdrop of the plan of salvation. Sexual intimacy between marriage partners is an important part of participating in God's work among his children. The same cannot be said of other kinds of sexual activity, and that necessarily means that they work directly against God's purposes.

We should note along the way that this view turns on its head the conventional conclusion that whatever happens in fulfillment of a person's sex drive must be all right. In fact, if we think through the sexual acts that we are commanded to do and how they differ from those we are commanded not to do, a pattern begins to emerge that would suggest that exactly the opposite is true. Sexual acts that acknowledge and affirm a covenant relationship (i.e., marriage or possible parenthood within marriage) tend to be right, while those which result primarily from the desire of one or both partners to get sexual fulfillment tend to be wrong.

### Biology as an Endowment

Contrary to the oft-quoted traditional view that biology is destiny, in this setting we can see that our biological makeup is an endowment, part of what makes the blessings of earth life possible. Note that, on the long view, sexual relations are just as imperative in this context—but morally imperative, not biologically imperative.

Brigham Young taught concerning the way we have children that "there is no other process of creation in heaven, on the earth, . . . or under the earth, or in all the eternities, that is, that were, or that ever will be" (*Journal of Discourses* 11:122). It is clear that God's plan requires sexual intimacy, but he didn't create us with compliance built in biologically. Instead he gave us a body like his, with all of the possibilities which that entails. Our physical bodies are thus gifts, not givens.

## Morality as Truthful Response

Recall that if sex is a drive, the only way to talk about morality is in terms of controlling that drive, preventing what would otherwise happen. From this perspective, then, control becomes the central issue of moral discourse. It has always seemed to me that this view should make anyone familiar with the story of the Council in Heaven very nervous. In that setting, morality as control was at the heart not of God's plan but of Lucifer's, and we know that he was a liar from the beginning. We also know that our Father, and we, rejected that plan, which would suggest that we ought to think of morality in some other way.

One way that fits with God's plan is to talk about morality as truthful response, simply responding in ways that are in harmony with the truth. This kind of response is something you do with your whole soul; you cannot experience it just by doing right actions, all the while longing to do something wrong. The scriptures remind us repeatedly that the man who "looketh on a woman to lust after her hath committed adultery with her already in his heart" (Matthew 5:28; 3 Nephi 12:28), and that those who let such things enter into their hearts "shall deny the faith" (D&C 42:23; 63:16). What the Lord requires, and what there is real joy in giving, is "the heart and a willing mind" (D&C 64:34); in short, our all.

In this, as in everything else, Christ was a perfect exemplar. The New Testament accounts of his life give us several glimpses into situations which, for a mortal of our generation, might seem to be laden with potential entanglements. The woman at the well or the woman taken in adultery might have tempted one whose heart was not as it should be. The Savior, however, responded with love and compassion, holding nothing back, for there was nothing amiss in his feelings for these women. He was therefore free to bless and minister to them.

This, I believe, is the point of the covenant of chastity which we make in the temple. It is telling that we make that covenant in the endowment, not as part of the marriage ceremony (see *Encyclopedia of Mormonism* 1:266; 2:455). Often we think of chastity as an issue of fidelity to one's spouse, but everyone who receives the endowment, whether they ever marry in this life or not, makes this covenant. To me, this indicates that it is a covenant we make, in a sense, with the whole community. And if virtue is not just a matter of avoiding wrong acts, but also wrong thoughts and feelings, then chastity requires that, until we have chosen a spouse, the question of sexual involvement simply doesn't ever come up, even in our hearts and minds. It isn't something we do, it isn't something we want to do, it isn't even something we think about. We simply expect that when we marry, and not before, our spouse will become the one and only exception.

This seems very important to me. Where the old view drove us apart, fearful of what we might do to one another, our covenant of chastity, if we take it seriously, draws us together, faithfully acknowledging the whole constellation of covenants that bind us as a community. Chastity enlarges our understanding of what it is to be in relation with God and leads us to him together. It frees us to respond truthfully and openly to one another, giving and receiving Christlike love. It gives substance to the hope of becoming a people who are of one heart. As I understand the prophecies concerning our day, only this way of being together will enable us to withstand the evil that increasingly surrounds us.

One caveat is necessary if we are to speak of morality in these terms. The fact is that many, perhaps most, people experience their sexuality in the traditional way, as something that happens, not as something they do. As long as that is true, there will be an important place for self-control and avoidance of tempting situations. If our impulses are wrong, it is certainly better to control them than to act on them. But it is better still to become pure in heart (as well as in deed) so that we can respond freely to each other with all of the energy of our souls.

The etymology of the word *respond* is inspiring to me in this connection. It comes from the Latin root *spend-*, which means "to make an offering, perform a rite, hence to engage oneself by a ritual act," and from "respondere, to promise" (*American Heritage College Dictionary*, 3d ed., p. 1617). If we are looking for a word to describe how we should be with each other in a community of Saints, it seems good to have one that has such covenantal connotations.

## Layers upon Layers of Meaning

If we find a meaningful way of talking about sexual intimacy in the discourse of God, it should come as no surprise, since God is a god of abundance, that sexual intimacy turns out to be not just meaningful but also richly significant and symbolic. Jeffrey R. Holland has spoken of sexual intimacy between a husband and wife as "a symbol of total union: union of their hearts, their hopes, their lives, their love, their family, their future, their everything." He goes on:

> As delicate as it is to mention, I nevertheless trust the reader's maturity to understand that physiologically we are created as men and women to form such a union. In this ultimate physical expression of one man and one woman, they are as nearly and as literally one as two separate physical bodies can ever be. It is in that act of ultimate physical intimacy that we most nearly fulfill the commandment of the Lord given to Adam and Eve, living symbols for all married couples, when he invited them to cleave unto one another only, and thus become "one flesh." (Genesis 2:24.) (In Jeffrey R. and Patricia T. Holland, *On Earth As It Is in Heaven* [Salt Lake City: Deseret Book Co., 1989], pp. 189–90.)

Jeffrey Holland also points out the sacramental nature of this divinely ordained intimacy, suggesting a symbolic union of the man and woman, not just with each other but also with God. Once we come to see sexual union in this way it can take a sacred place in the marriage relationship, providing opportunity for the renewal of the covenants that bind us as husband and wife.

## Sexuality as a Family Matter

The only context in which sexuality makes complete sense is a family. Day in and day out, and through all eternity, our covenants with each other as members of families give sexual intimacy its meaning and make sexual morality sensible. We should not expect our children to understand their sexuality if it is presented to them in any other context. And we must acknowledge that what they learn about sexual intimacy in the family context, whether it is explicitly taught or not, can have eternal consequences.

Sometimes sexual matters seem difficult to talk about, but I think that may be entirely a result of the struggle we often feel with the worldly views which bombard us. There is much in traditional accounts of sexuality that is awkward and embarrassing and offends our tenderest sensibilities. It is my experience, however, that as we sort out and embrace a perspective on human sexuality that is wholly dependent upon the gospel of Jesus Christ, awkwardness and embarrassment simply disappear. Within a loving family circle parents can, and must, teach their children about these sacred things, saying, in effect, "This is how we got to be us!"

This, I think, is what happened in Eden: a loving father, the Father of us all, walked and talked with two of his children, imparting sacred understanding of what it would mean to be a family here on earth. If I am right about this, that is where conversation about sexual intimacy began. It is that conversation that we must carry on.

**Emily M. Reynolds** *and her husband, Mark, live in Provo and are the parents of seven children. In addition to being a homemaker, Emily holds a master's degree in psychology and is a part-time instructor in that department at Brigham Young University.*

# 10

# TRUE DOCTRINE AS MARITAL THERAPY

### S. Brett Savage

A wonderful LDS couple—I'll call them Bill and Martha— wrote me with this problem:

> My wife and I have a strong temple marriage built upon love, divine covenants, and a desire to serve one another. It is troublesome to us, however, that we so often fight over issues that in the final analysis seem trivial and not worth fighting about! Why do we do this? Why do we blame each other and have so much contention in our relationship and in our home when we want so much not to quarrel or fight? The hurt feelings that come when we argue sometimes linger on in our hearts for weeks, only to resurface with the next fight. We have committed to each other many times to stop all this pettiness and arguing, but it seems that the harder we try to fix our problems the more we argue about them. We will sometimes condemn ourselves for our lack of inner strength to overcome our contentiousness—this, in turn, becomes another issue to fight over and feel guilty about. We feel we are setting a terrible example for our children, and this makes us feel even more guilty. Is there a way out of this self-defeating cycle of contention? We have tried everything, but nothing seems to work for very long. We want so much to have a lasting change.

Here are two people, married in the temple, who outwardly are active and strong in their commitment to the Church, yet they can't seem to avoid constant fighting and bickering. Unfortunately, this is not an uncommon problem. We all know more than we *do*. We are much better at telling other people how to solve their problems than we are at resolving our own; often better at applying the gospel in others' behalf than we are ourselves. A gospel-based solution, of course, *is* the answer to this couple's dilemma and is the only way they can end the contention in their relationship. They must try "the virtue of the word of God" (Alma 31:5), for it is in the doctrines of the gospel that we learn the "good news" of how to "be" in relationships with each other so that we can resolve problems as they arise.

This chapter will "bring to light" some of the doctrines that can make a permanent difference in our marriages, doctrines that bring about a mighty "change of heart" (see Alma 5:26). This change or formulation requires that we be "brought to the knowledge of the truth" and be "led to believe the holy scriptures [and] the prophecies of the holy prophets" which will lead us to "faith on the Lord, and unto repentance, which faith and repentance bringeth a change of heart" (Helaman 15:7). We'll need some background to understand how Bill and Martha can change their relationship through the principles of the gospel of Jesus Christ. That will necessarily come from scriptural and prophetic counsel, for the Lord has said many things that can strengthen our marriages.

Much of the Lord's instruction in the Doctrine and Covenants is directed to working out relationship problems. His approach is this: If we will strive to understand and live doctrinal principles, we can be effective in our relationships with others—especially our married partners. Referring to the doctrine in the Book of Mormon, the Lord said:

> I will also bring to light my gospel which was ministered unto [the Nephites], and, behold . . . [the gospel] shall bring to light the true points of my doctrine, yea, and the only doctrine which is in me.
>
> And this I do that I may establish my gospel, that there may not be so much contention; yea, Satan doth stir up the hearts of the people to contention concerning the points of my doctrine; and in these things they do err, for they do wrest [twist or distort] the scriptures and do not understand them.
>
> Therefore, I will unfold [reveal] unto them this great mystery;
>
> For, behold, I will gather them as a hen gathereth her chickens under her wings, if they will not harden their hearts;
>
> Yea, if they will come, they may, and partake of the waters of life freely.

Behold, this is my doctrine—whosoever repenteth and cometh unto me, the same is my church. (D&C 10:62–67.)

To "establish" and "bring to light" "true points of doctrine" from the scriptures and the prophets can help us heal troubled relationships and repair any damage that occurs when we sin against one another and create a "spirit of contention" (see 3 Nephi 11:29–30) within ourselves and with others (see 1 Nephi 15:14; Helaman 11:22–23; 3 Nephi 21:6). This is why faith in the Lord and repentance bring about a change of heart that is so necessary because it is sin that creates contention in the first place.[1]

## Bringing to Light and Building Up True Points of Doctrine

At one point, as a group of Nephites were sinfully rebelling against the doctrines of the Church, they began to experience personal, emotional, and social problems. Many had such hard and contentious feelings towards each other that they were ready to go to war. The prophet Alma lovingly sought to help them, not by force or coercion but by preaching to them. The record says: "And now, as the preaching of the word had a great tendency to lead the people to do that which was just—yea, it had had more powerful effect upon the minds of the people than the sword, or anything else, which had happened unto them—therefore Alma thought it was expedient that they should try the virtue of the word of God" (Alma 31:5).

---

1. This article is greatly influenced by the work of C. Terry Warner, and many of the concepts, including some terminology, come directly from his writings. Brother Warner's work not only has given me a faithful framework for academic endeavors but also makes possible an interpretation of scriptural meanings I might have otherwise overlooked. An academic statement of C. Terry Warner's work is "Anger and Similar Delusions," in Rom Harré, ed., The Social Construction of Emotion (Oxford Basil Blackwell, 1986). Very helpful articles of Brother Warner's published in LDS-related sources include "What We Are," BYU Studies 26 (Winter 1986): 39–63, and "Feelings, Self-Deception, and Change," a lecture presented at the convention of the Association of Mormon Counselors and Psychotherapists (AMCAP), 2 October 1981, published in the AMCAP Journal 8 (April 1982): 21–32. Also very helpful is Brother Warner's talk "Repenting of Unrighteous Feelings," a Ricks College devotional address given 1 March 1983.

The word of God was more powerful than "anything else." The people who received the doctrines of the gospel preached by Alma were greatly blessed with peace. The Zoramites who did not accept the "virtue of the word of God" experienced no peace but instead became "angry against the people" who believed in Alma's words (see Alma 35).

It is no different in our day. If we are experiencing troubled, angry feelings in our relationships with others, it is because we are not benefitting from the "word" or doctrines of the gospel. In other words, do you think Bill and Martha consistently understood and practiced the doctrinal principle that there is to be no contention in our homes? Did they understand that contention results from sin? While they blamed their arguments on many things, they did not see it as sin. Consequently they did not apply correct doctrines to their specific situations so that they could find peace in their relationship. This is why the arguments continued to go on.

Following is an example of how doctrine can bring about a change of heart, a change of attitude, and consequently of one's behavior. Bob (I'll call him) attended a Sunday School class where the doctrines of the gospel were taught and the discussion centered on how to apply the principles—faith in Christ, repentance, and forgiveness—to marriage in order to bring about healing and to establish healthy marriage and family relationships. He wrote several weeks later of the effect of that experience on his life:

> The gospel truths taught and the healing effects of the Spirit were more than I have experienced in any one or combination of meetings—ever! My life has changed! I do not have off and on feelings of anger anymore. Before I understood these principles I was living a constant, intense life all the time. My feelings of self-protection and my aggressive actions to secure my personal share of what I conceived as a scarce source and limited supply of various resources kept me constantly driven! My undeviating and selfish pursuit for personal gratification kept me from appreciating the close love of my wife, Susan, and my children. I did not know the love and simple truths of living a pure life through following the teachings of our Father in Heaven and his son Jesus Christ. My heart was so impure and my mind so blinded as to the damage I was doing to myself, my family, friends, and more so, as to how I was separating myself from God.

My heart became so hardened in my sins that I was seeing scriptural instructions as severe and imposing interferences to my life. The scriptures were not open to me for instruction, rather they were merely textbooks for information to answer questions in Sunday School class or as common writings for discussions between myself and others. I felt I needed to know the scriptures only to keep up a social pace with others, to look good in their eyes. I did not perceive or use the scriptures as writings emanating from our Father in Heaven, or as a spiritual guide for us that was filled with simple truths to walk us through our daily tasks and associations with family and friends. . . .

I now realize how I have harbored and fostered feelings of anger and resentment and confinement within myself. I have always thought my feelings of frustration and impatience were caused by others. Many times I have blamed my children, and my wife, for the feelings. I now feel sorry for the pressure I put on them and the accused feelings that I, through the years, have put upon my family members. . . . I do not have to be angry—nor is it good to be angry—nor is it fair to be angry and blame it on others, especially the ones I love so dearly—my family.

I've asked Susan for her forgiveness for the things I have done in the past and have told her how sorry I am for the hurt that I have brought to her and our children. I love my wife and our children and appreciate them more now because of the change in my heart. I am so thankful for being brought to the scriptures. . . . What a wonderful blessing to be able to finally work with my wife rather than compete against her, to love and serve her rather than being concerned that I'm getting my fair share of the marriage [deal] and maintaining my position as "head of our house." Now I am the "father of our home" working to serve my wife and our children . . . there is a true, sweet spirit that fills me . . . and a peace so strong. Understanding the scriptures has helped me to forget about myself and love others.

Bob and Susan were blessed by his change of heart. Neither of them is perfect now, but learning and living the word of God has made a mighty change in their marriage relationship; they have been freed of many of the burdens of sin that troubled their relationship in the past.

Living the doctrines of the gospel can be especially helpful when we have longstanding problems, problems in our adult relationships that may stem from our childhood. The doctrines of repentance and forgiveness can heal our hearts of resentment, guilt, and pain even when a burden of sin has been "visited upon the heads of the children." Sometimes childhood abuses show up in adult relationships as repeated cycles of negative emotions and attitudes (see Exodus 20:5, 34:7; Ezekiel 18:2). Elder Boyd K. Packer explained the therapy that is available in forgiving:

> To you adults who repeat the pattern of neglect and abuse you endured as little children, believing that you are entrapped in a cycle of behavior from which there is no escape, I say: It is contrary to the order of heaven for any soul to be locked into compulsive, immoral behavior with no way out! It *is* consistent with the workings of the adversary to deceive you into believing that you *are*. I gratefully acknowledge that transgressions, even those which affect little children, yield to sincere repentance. . . .
>
> To you *innocent* ones who have not transgressed, but were abused as little children and still carry an undeserved burden of guilt, I say: Learn true doctrine—repentance *and* forgiveness; lay that burden of guilt down!

In that same speech Elder Packer said: "True doctrine, understood, changes attitudes and behavior. The study of the doctrines of the gospel will improve behavior quicker than a study of behavior will improve behavior. . . . That is why we stress so forcefully the study of the doctrines of the gospel." ("Little Children," *Ensign*, November 1986, pp. 17, 18.)

The true doctrines of the gospel can heal troubled relationships and improve "attitudes and behavior" that have application to all men and women through the world. Elder Spencer W. Kimball taught the importance of doctrine when he said: "In the seven two-hour sessions [of general conference], . . . truths were taught, doctrines expounded, exhortations given, enough to save the whole world from all its ills—and I mean from *all* its ills" (*In the World but Not of It*, Brigham Young University Speeches of the Year [Provo, 14 May 1968], p. 2).

At another time, he said: "There is only one cure for the earth's sick condition. That infallible cure is simply *righteousness, obedience, godliness, honor, integrity*. Nothing else will suffice." (Spencer W. Kimball, *The Miracle of Forgiveness* [Salt Lake City: Bookcraft, 1969], p. 321.)

What are these true points of doctrine that can save us? We need to understand what they are. Once we know what they are, we need to actually implement them in our lives and not just "know of" or "read about" them, as Bob had done for so many years. To live according to these principles requires us to abandon our sins and pride and come unto the Lord. In order to heal relationships, we may need to repent of some of our attitudes and emotions as well as some of our behaviors. We may need to repent or "give up" our excuses that serve to rationalize or justify what we do, that convince us we are right to have contentious feelings towards others.

To illustrate, here are some insights a friend of mine shared with me after realizing that her own sins and offenses were the cause of her present contentious attitude and behavior, both in marriage and with others:

> For me personally, the most meaningful concept or key to healing troubled relationships is to stop feeling offended. Not long ago, I doubt that these simple words would have had much power or significance for me, but I am now at a time in my life when achieving peace of mind and living in harmony with others is more important than maintaining what I now realize was . . . false pride.
>
> I have spent much of my life feeling as though I had to prove myself against a critical and grudging world, that I had to constantly protect myself against the thoughtlessness and malice of others. Little by little, I have come to realize that this is an incredibly distorted and crippling attitude, but I always found what I thought were compelling reasons to justify myself and hang onto them.
>
> Amazingly, some insightful part of me has always known that by taking offense, by lashing out or nursing a grudge, I do harm to myself. I have finally formed the conviction that there is no value whatsoever in feeling offended. On the contrary, I now see it for the poison it has been in my life. Those simple words—stop taking offense—are tremendously liberating in that they represent permission to drop a heavy load from my back. They allow me to unlearn a sorry lesson brought from my childhood—that if I did not take offense at the least provocation, I was somehow a victim. But, irony of ironies, I was actually victimizing myself and others every time I took offense.
>
> I am not so naive as to think I will never backslide, but I am certain that I will never feel obligated to waste so much thought, time, and energy in taking offense for any reason. For this I feel a profound sense of relief.

## Satan Doth Stir Up the Hearts of
## the People to Contention

Contentiousness is a sinful emotion or attitude that must be abandoned in order for one to start living righteously. We must repent of feelings of anger, resentment, animosity, and bitterness we hold for others. The teachings of the scriptures and of living prophets make this remarkably clear. Elder Russell M. Nelson of the Quorum of Twelve voiced this concern in an address: "My concern is that contention is becoming accepted as a way of life. From what we see and hear in the media, the classroom, and the workplace, all are now infected to some degree with contention. How easy it is, yet how wrong it is, to allow habits of contention to pervade matters of spiritual significance, because contention is forbidden by divine decree." ("The Canker of Contention," *Ensign*, May 1989, p. 68.)

The forbidding of contention of which Elder Nelson speaks is contained in the decrees of God found in the scriptures and renewed by the Lord's servants. Through them we are reminded that contention, anger, and malice in our relationships with others is sin. For example, in the Old Testament we read: "Thou shalt not hate thy brother in thine heart" (Leviticus 19:17). A footnote to this verse says, "Though you may reprove a neighbor and not tolerate his sin, do not hate him."

In his epistle to the Ephesians, Paul counseled:

> Can ye be angry and not sin; let not the sun go down upon your wrath:
> Neither give place to the devil. . . .
> Let no corrupt communication proceed out of your mouth, but that which is good to the use of edifying, that it may minister grace unto the hearers. . . .
> Let all bitterness, and wrath, and anger, and clamor, and evil speaking, be put away from you, with all malice.
> And be ye kind one to another, tenderhearted, forgiving one another, even as God for Christ's sake hath forgiven you. (JST, Ephesians 4:26–27, 29, 31–32.)

The Book of Mormon teaches doctrinal precepts with regard to our relationships with others. The Lord's precepts or teachings in the Book of Mormon about contention voice a similar prohibition against holding feelings of contention or malice:

And again, the Lord God hath commanded that men should not murder; that they should not lie; that they should not steal; that they should not take the name of the Lord their God in vain; that they should not envy; that they should not have malice; that they should not contend one with another; that they should not commit whoredoms; and that they should do none of these things; for whoso doeth them shall perish (2 Nephi 26:32).

The Lord personally instructed the Nephites on contention. He forbade them to have these feelings toward one another and commanded them to repent and do away with contentious feelings.

And there shall be no disputations among you, as there have hitherto been; neither shall there be disputations among you concerning the points of my doctrine, as there have hitherto been.

For verily, verily I say unto you, he that hath the spirit of contention is not of me, but is of the devil, who is the father of contention, and he stirreth up the hearts of men to contend with anger, one with another.

Behold, this is not my doctrine, to stir up the hearts of men with anger, one against another; but this is my doctrine, that such things should be done away. (3 Nephi 11:28–30.)

Again, he taught the Nephites:

I say unto you, that whosoever is angry with his brother shall be in danger of his judgment. And whosoever shall say to his brother, Raca [a word suggesting contempt], shall be in danger of the council; and whosoever shall say, Thou fool, shall be in danger of hell fire. (3 Nephi 12:22.)

The Prophet Joseph Smith said the Book of Mormon was "the most correct book of any book on earth, and the keystone of our religion, and a man would get nearer to God by abiding by its precepts than by any other book" (History of the Church 4:461). It is well worth considering that through that book we might also "get nearer" to our companions and children.

Latter-day prophets have spoken out against contention, anger, and similar accusatory feelings. President Brigham Young taught: "Now I charge you again, and I charge myself not to get angry. Never let anger arise in your hearts. No, Brigham, never let anger arise in your heart, never, never! Although you may be called upon to chastise and to speak to the people sharply, do not let anger arise in you, no, never!" (In *Journal of Discourses* 14:156.)

On another occasion he instructed:

> In our daily pursuits in life, of whatever nature and kind, Latter-day Saints, and especially those who hold important positions in the kingdom of God, should maintain a uniform and even temper, both when at home and when abroad. They should not suffer reverses and unpleasant circumstances to sour their natures and render them fretful and unsocial at home, speaking words full of bitterness and biting acrimony to their wives and children, creating gloom and sorrow in their habitations, making themselves feared rather than loved by their families. Anger should never be permitted to rise in our bosoms, and words suggested by angry feelings should never be permitted to pass our lips. (In *Journal of Discourses* 11:136.)

Elder Marvin J. Ashton, a modern Apostle, told the Saints: "Resentment and anger are not good for the soul. They are foul things. Bitterness must be replaced with humility. Truly, bitterness injures the one who carries it. It blinds, shrivels, and cankers." ("While They Are Waiting," *Ensign*, May 1988, p. 63.)

Anger, resentment, malice, bitterness, contention, wrath—all such are attitudes and emotions forbidden by divine scriptural and prophetic decree. We are commanded to repent of these emotions so that contention will not harden our hearts nor linger in our attitudes as blame for others and self-justification. We are commanded to repent and replace them with humility, because these negative emotions are not the result of what others are doing *to us* but what *we are doing to them.* This is why the Lord commands "such things should be done away." Often we are taught that negative emotions are the result of mistreatment from others or are perhaps caused by difficult or trying circumstances. But if negative emotions *are* "caused" by trying circumstances or what others do to us, there could be no "doing away" of them, at least not for very long, because eventually we would experience a greater difficult circumstance, or another person would surely do something to "offend us." If that were true we could not be held accountable by the Lord for those feelings, because they were "caused" *in us* by *others*—by people who "made us feel this way." Thus the other people would be accountable, not us.

Sometimes we blame the devil for tempting us and thus "making us have contentious feelings." The Prophet Joseph Smith "observed that Satan was generally blamed for the evils which we did, but if he was the cause of all our wickedness, men could not be condemned. The devil could not compel mankind to do evil; all was voluntary. Those who resisted the spirit of God would be liable to be led into temptation. God would not exert any compulsory means, and the devil could not." (*Teachings of the Prophet Joseph Smith*, sel. Joseph Fielding Smith [Salt Lake City: Deseret Book Co., 1938], p. 187.)

Years ago, Elder Sterling W. Sill remarked:

> In denying our own responsibility, we frequently blame Satan for much of the misery that we are bringing upon ourselves. Satan has no power over us except as we give it to him. And temptations without imply desires within; and rather than say, "How powerfully the devil tempts," we might say, "How strongly I am inclined." God never forces us to do right, and Satan has no power to force us to do wrong. As someone has said, "God always votes for us and Satan always votes against us, and then we are asked to vote to break the tie." It is how we vote that gives our lives their significance. ("Our Temptations Upward," *Improvement Era*, June 1970, p. 45.)

There are times when others can do things to us and we can take offense; yet we are accountable, not them, for our contentious emotions because we *opted* to take offense. It is ironical that we experience contentious emotions not as our own sin but as if they were "caused" in us by others. We do not say to ourselves, "I feel angry because of my sin or offense"; rather, we feel our emotions as mere reactions to some threat or provocation from others. As we commit this sin of resisting the Spirit, the very quality and meaning of our negative emotions feel like we are being hurt by someone, that we are emotionally a victim of that person's actions or the circumstances in which we find ourselves. This is perhaps why we so often blame others, or argue with them and try to get them to admit to the wrongs against us. We want them to see they are to blame for our hurt feelings; that we are innocent while they are guilty.

The truth is, we are "self-deceived" in our emotions and beliefs that others are to blame for our negative feelings.[2] In other words,

---

2. This term *self-deceived* comes from C. Terry Warner. See *Bonds of Anguish, Bonds of Love* (unpublished manuscript, 1990).

when we feel negative emotions swelling up in our hearts, we believe that others are to blame—perhaps because the emotions came at the time another person did some action; but neither our emotions nor our belief about their being caused by others is true. The scriptural words that describe this kind of self-deception are *hard-hearted* (Alma 9:5; 15:15), *stiffnecked* (Jacob 4:14), *minds have been darkened* (D&C 84:54), *eyes blinded* (1 John 2:11).

In order to have negative emotions and then feel like blaming others for them, we must first "take offense" ourselves. Again, when we "take offense" we do not say, "I'm sinning right now" or "I'm responsible for these feelings of offense." Instead we say, perhaps only quietly in our hearts but on occasion out loud, "You offended me," or "It really hurts me when you say or do such and such." To believe this about ourselves is equal to saying we are innocent for what is happening, and that we are not sinning ourselves but being sinned against. Wrote the Apostle John: "If we say that we have no sin, we deceive ourselves, and the truth is not in us" (1 John 1:8). In other words, we create these blaming emotions by taking offense when we refuse to love others and to do what is right by them. To do this is to sin, and as with all sin we become blind to the truth, or in other words, "the truth is not in us." Again, when we sin in this way we claim not to have sinned at all but to have been sinned against. We blame others for our emotions.

President David O. McKay spoke on this:

> I wonder how long it will take us to realize that in matters of temper [quarrelsomeness] nothing can bring us damage but ourselves—we are responsible for what helps us and for what injures us—that the harm that each one sustains he carries about with him, and never is he a real sufferer but by his own fault. I think you get that thought, and yet the tendency of each one is to blame somebody else, the wife blaming the husband, the husband blaming the wife, children finding fault with the parents when the fault lies with themselves. ("Something Higher Than Self," *Improvement Era*, June 1958, p. 407.)

In more recent times, Elder F. Burton Howard counseled:

> When faced with the consequences of transgression, rather than looking to ourselves as the source of the discomfort which always accompanies sin, many of us tend to blame someone else. . . . We fault our neighbor for our pain and try to pass it on. . . .

If we are so hedged about by pride, rationalization. . . . we then may not even know of our need to repent. We will have no idea whether the Lord is pleased with us or not and may become "past feeling" (1 Nephi 17:45). But all men, everywhere, must repent (see 3 Nephi 11:32). . . .

To excuse misconduct by blaming others is presumptuous at best and is fatally flawed with regard to spiritual things, for "we believe that men will be punished for their own sins, and not for Adam's transgression" (Articles of Faith 2). ("Repentance," Ensign, May 1991, p. 13.)

The following caution comes from Elder Hugh W. Pinnock:

Brethren and sisters, we are living in a strange time. It has been called the space age or computer age. However, it seems to be the age of blaming everyone and everything for any unfavorable condition. We blame acquaintances, parents, the Church, spouses, teachers, neighbors, the area where we dwell, or even the weather for our problems.

This is wrong. It is not God's way. It is not part of his great plan. . . . Of course . . . accidents can happen that can inflict terrible pain. . . . But to judge, blame, and not forgive always intensifies the problem. . . .

It is time to . . . take personal responsibility for [our] actions. Now is the time to stop blaming others, the government, the Church, or our circumstances for what might disturb us. ("Now Is the Time," Ensign, May 1989, pp. 10–12.)

But just what kind of "sin" is this—refusing to love others? The Lord taught that the two greatest commandments are to love the Lord and to love our neighbors, to not speak evil of them nor "do them any harm" (see Matthew 22:37–39; D&C 42:27). Often we feel to love others and do righteous acts for them when our conscience, the Lord's Spirit, prompts us. Because we have agency we can choose to bless others when that conscience prompts. Camilla Kimball, wife of President Spencer W. Kimball, said, "Never suppress a charitable impulse." As moral agents, however, we can suppress or go against our summons of conscience and can thereby sin against the light or the Spirit of Christ (see Moroni 7:16–19). When we refuse this inspiration, we sin. As James taught, "To him that knoweth to do good, and doeth it not, to him it is sin" (James 4:17).

Elder Bruce R. McConkie quoted Elder Orson F. Whitney's comment on this verse by James: "Sin is the transgression of divine law, as made known through the conscience or by revelation. A man sins when he violates his conscience, going contrary to light and knowledge—not the light and knowledge that has come to his neighbor, but that which has come to himself. He sins when he does the opposite of what he knows to be right." (*Doctrinal New Testament Commentary*, 3 vols. [Salt Lake City: Bookcraft, 1965–73], 3:267.)

When we sin in this fashion we always suffer consequences, for as Paul taught, "the wages of sin is death" (Romans 6:23). In this case death means that the true meaning of our emotions, actions, and circumstances becomes clouded in sin. In that sin we interpret circumstances as the cause of our discomfort, and we "die" to what is true about others. This "death" as to the true meaning of people and circumstances consists of being hardhearted, and having darkened minds. When we "refuse the light" we sin against others and twist the meaning of our relationship with them. It then becomes impossible to know the truth about them in our heart and mind because we make other assumptions—negative assumptions. This "death" is manifest in our feelings that accuse others of being the problem as well as in the rationalizations we make that hold them solely responsible for our misery. Just how distorted this "meaning" can become is illustrated in this vignette:

> I was just dying to know what was in the little purple journal that my wife kept hidden in her dresser. At first I had the clear feeling, "I wouldn't want her going through my private journal without asking," but I quickly pushed the feeling aside, remembering how she had refused to let me read it even when I did ask her. In inquiring, I only wanted her to share her life with me so we could be even closer. I very quickly thought to myself, "After all, if it's that private, she shouldn't have written it down in the first place." This seemed to reassure me.
>
> I opened the dresser, pulled out the diary, and opened it to May 14, 1989, her 36th birthday. As I read, tears formed in my eyes. I could barely read her words: "I am so blessed to have a husband as caring and faithful as John. I love him so much for his integrity and goodness." I quickly thought to myself, "Who asked you? I didn't ask you to think of me that way!" Anger swelled up in my heart; I couldn't believe I had fallen for such a stupid trick. I just knew that she had only written those words so that I would feel guilty if I read them without her knowledge. I threw the journal back into the drawer and stormed out of the room, angry at my wife for setting me up by writing all that nonsense! (I know now of course that all this was my doing. I should never have stolen a look in the first place. I knew better.)

John had felt that first prompting, but he overrode it. He knew to do good and did it not. He sinned by refusing to follow the directive of the Spirit/conscience, opening the journal anyway. He immediately experienced the consequences of his sin: rationalization, excuse making, guilt, contentious emotions, and blame for his wife who genuinely loved him. Her guileless expressions of love were twisted by him; in his sinful frame of mind they were not expressions of love but a "trick." When we go against the light of Christ, even the true expressions of a loving wife are seen in a distorted and self-deceived way. Death or distorted meaning comes when we resist the Lord's voice (see D&C 108:2). Perhaps that is what Paul meant when he said we are guilty of speaking "lies in hypocrisy" having our "conscience seared as with a hot iron" (JST, 1 Timothy 4:2).

## Repent of Contentious Feelings

Elder Russell M. Nelson explained "true points of doctrine" on how contentious feelings, and what I have called the death that comes with them, can be done away. If we have contentious feelings, the solution is not to learn to own them, to accept or cope with them by developing some form of self-control, as many in the world would teach, but instead to repent of them and love the Lord. Repentance and faith on the Lord will change not only our behavior but our hearts as well. Elder Nelson said:

> The ultimate step lies beyond . . . control of expression. Personal peace is reached when one, in humble submissiveness, truly loves God. Heed carefully this scripture: "There was no contention in the land, because of the love of God which did dwell in the hearts of the people" (4 Nephi 1:15).
>
> Thus, love of God should be our aim. . . .
>
> [The] healing begins with a personal vow: "Let there be peace on earth, and let it begin with me." . . . This commitment will then spread to family and friends and will bring peace to neighbors and nations.
>
> Shun contention. Seek godliness. Be enlightened by eternal truth. Be like-minded with the Lord in love and united with Him in faith. Then shall "the peace of God, which passeth all understanding" (Philippians 4:7) be yours, to bless you and your posterity through generations yet to come. ("The Canker of Contention," p. 71.)

A story from Church history sheds light on how, if we are to know the truth about ourselves and others, we must repent of contention and replace it with the "love of God." The Prophet Joseph Smith and his wife, Emma, were living in cramped quarters with the Whitmer family in New York while Joseph and Oliver Cowdery were finishing the translation of the Book of Mormon. David Whitmer later told of an incident between Joseph and Emma:

> [Joseph] could not translate unless he was humble and possessed the right feelings toward everyone. To illustrate so you can see: One morning when he was getting ready to continue the translation, something went wrong about the house and he was put out about it. Something that Emma, his wife, had done. Oliver and I went up stairs and Joseph came up soon after to continue the translation, but he could not do anything. He could not translate a single syllable. He went down stairs, out into the orchard, and made supplication to the Lord; was gone about an hour—came back to the house, and asked Emma's forgiveness and then came up stairs where we were, and then the translation went on all right. (Quoted in Lyndon W. Cook, *The Revelations of the Prophet Joseph Smith* [Salt Lake City: Deseret Book Co., 1985], p. 24.)

Elder Boyd K. Packer counseled parents with wayward children that the change of heart must first come from them. (This may also suggest that any problems in the parents' marriage must be resolved and repented of before they can effectively resolve problems in their relationships with their children.) He said:

> I speak to the parents of wayward and lost children. . . . [fathers and mothers who ask,] What have we done wrong? What can we do to get our child back?
> Even parents with the best intentions—some who have really tried—now know that heartache. . . . [of] losing one.
> Parents, can we . . . consider the most painful part of your problem? If you want to reclaim your son or daughter, why don't you leave off trying to alter your child just for a little while and concentrate on yourself. The changes must begin with you, not with your children.
> You can't continue to do what you have been doing (even though you thought it was right) and expect to unproduce some behavior in your child, when your conduct was one of the things that produced it.
> There! It's been said! After all the evading, all the concern for wayward children. After all the blaming of others, the care to be gentle with

parents. It's out! It's you, not the child, who needs immediate attention. Now, parents, there is substantial help for you if you will accept it. I add with emphasis that the help we propose is not easy, for the measures are equal to the seriousness of your problem. There is no patent medicine to effect an immediate cure.

And parents, if you seek for a cure that ignores faith and religious doctrine, you look for a cure where it never will be found. When we talk of religious principles and doctrines and quote scripture, interesting, isn't it, how many don't feel comfortable with talk like that? But when we talk about your problems with your family and offer a solution, then your interest is intense.

Know that you can't talk about one without talking about the other and expect to solve your problems. Once parents know that there is a God and that we are His children, they can face problems like this and win.

If you are helpless, He is not.

If you are lost, He is not.

If you don't know what to do next, He knows.

It would take a miracle, you say? Well, if it takes a miracle, why not? ("That All May Be Edified" [Salt Lake City: Bookcraft, 1982], pp. 137, 139.)

## If They Will Come, They May

Elder Packer lovingly counseled that blaming others does not help; instead we must concentrate on ourselves first. The Lord himself teaches this principle in scripture. He indicates that when we are accusing and condemning others we see only *their* faults and not our own even larger fault, the fault in blaming and condemning them for their faults (see D&C 64:8–10). If we want to help them, we must first willingly give up our contentious and blaming attitudes. The Lord commanded, "First cast out the beam [our condemning and contentious accusation of them] out of thine own eye; and then shalt thou see clearly to cast out the mote [the other's faults, which are small] out of thy brother's eye" (JST, Matthew 7:8). Notice that the Lord does not say we will not see others' faults (motes) if we quit blaming them; just the opposite—removing our own blaming "beam" will allow us to "see [their motes] clearly." Repenting first of our contentious feelings will end our own self-deception, blaming attitudes, and hardness of heart (see D&C 64:34). We will then, and I believe only then, be in a position to help others repent (remove their motes) and be free from their sins and self-deceptions.

The Lord has said, "Behold, this is my doctrine—whosoever re-penteth and cometh unto me, the same is my church" (D&C 10:67). Our willingness to give up our contentiousness by repenting first and coming unto the Lord is perhaps the best thing we can do to invite others to be willing to repent and come unto the Lord and be healed (see 3 Nephi 9:13). This willingness to repent and come unto Christ, is, I believe, what the Lord meant when he said, "Yea, if they will come, they may, and partake of the waters of life freely" (D&C 10:66).

A story from a friend of mine will illustrate the truth of Elder Packer's counsel to first make changes in oneself. This man and his wife were experiencing troubles in their relationship with their teenage daughter. Both were working to repent first in order to be free of their self-deceptions and sins, to be "one" in their marriage. He was a student working on an assignment to "remove the beam from your own eye" first. He told his experience:

> Recently I noticed that my oldest daughter and I had been having confrontations on an almost daily basis. She is the oldest child in the family and has a younger sister and two younger brothers. She is also a very conscientious student and is busy with homework and practicing the flute for band; not to mention that at thirteen, clothes, boys, and friends are becoming the most important things in her life. In the midst of all this she has become extremely hard-headed and argumentative lately, and it has really started getting on my nerves. Our confrontations are hardly yelling matches or name calling, but it just seems like every time we talk I am trying to "straighten her out." This has been going on for probably two to three weeks and has been quite troubling.
>
> A problem developed the other day when something arose without any preliminary discussion at all. Suddenly we were speaking in harsh and accusing tones. I felt myself become so angry I wanted to tip the couch upside down with her in it. I walked into the other room, wonder-ing "What's a father to do with a child like this?"
>
> As I write this story, trying to see the situation without sin-filled eyes, I now see a beautiful young girl's teenage years (and perhaps life) ruined by an accusing and domineering father. Her accusing attitude to-wards me, I decided, was provoked by my constant accusing attitude to-wards her. After receiving this assignment, I realized I could never re-move her "motes" without first removing my own beam.
>
> Then, the other morning, while shaving, I was pondering this as-signment and the scriptures we had been discussing in class, trying to

just be loving with others. Just then Julia, my daughter, came in the bathroom. "Would you hurry up? I've got to get ready too, you know!" she said in *that* tone of voice, ready to start the whole thing over again. But almost as if I were someone else, I heard myself in a calm and concerned voice say, "Oh, I'm sorry, I didn't realize I was taking so long. I'll hurry and get out of your way." Her response was immediate. Instead of saying, "Well, next time have a little more consideration," or something like that, she softly said, "Oh . . . it's okay, Dad, I'm sure I'll have plenty of time."

Later I . . . realized that the mote I had seen in her eye was probably just the other end of the beam sticking out of my eye, the beam of constantly hovering over her trying to tell her all the things she was doing wrong. This assignment certainly gave me a good lesson as to what life for others is like when I'm willing to first give up my sins and offenses.

## Whosoever Declareth More or Less Than This

Elder Packer also cautioned us that we must not search for "easy cures" to our relationship problems, trusting in "patent medicines" that may ignore faith and religious doctrine. Too often, in my opinion, this is what many of us as members of the Church inadvertently do. In a search for answers to our personal, marriage, and family struggles, we sometimes try to "find ourselves" by looking for patent medicines or cures that are not founded on true points of doctrine—repentance and coming unto the Lord. Sometimes these "cures" include religious language and may even have a "form of godliness" (see Joseph Smith—History 1:19), but they often end up creating a dependence in the person so that he or she must "continue the cure," sometimes for weeks, months, or even years in order to "stay healed." This dependence on the cure often gets very expensive and sometimes results in creating other more difficult problems. Ultimately, the "cure" does not heal, or invite one to repent and come unto Christ, but rather causes one to stay beholden to the "cure." I believe this is what the Lord warned against when he said, "Whosoever declareth more or less than this [repentance and coming unto Christ], the same is not of me, but is against me; therefore he is not of my church" (D&C 10:67–68).

This declaring "more or less" than repentance takes many forms. Many members go to meetings, study the latest books, or attend seminars that claim to have the solution or the cure for their problems. Some do come away feeling better, but they often do not have the change of heart that comes only with repentance and faith. Many do behave differently for a while, but in time they find their problems have only changed style—the beam is still in their eye, they are still self-deceived in sin. And while many may outwardly behave differently or be able to communicate their accusing feelings better, their contentious and accusing feelings remain, their hearts are still hardened. Church leaders have given warning concerning such "solutions" and "groups."

> The following is from the Church Bulletin, 1993–2:
> There is increasing concern regarding Church members' involvement in groups that purport to increase self-awareness, raise self-esteem, and enhance individual agency. Many of these groups advocate concepts and use methods that can be harmful. Some falsely claim Church endorsement, actively recruit Church members, charge exorbitant fees, and encourage long-term commitments. Some intermingle worldly concepts with gospel principles in ways that can undermine spirituality and faith. Although participants may experience temporary emotional relief or exhilaration, old problems often return, leading to added disappointment and despair.
>
> Church leaders and members should not become involved in self-awareness groups or any other groups that imitate sacred rites or ceremonies. Similarly, members should avoid groups that meet late into the night or encourage open confession or disclosure of personal information normally discussed only in confidential settings.
>
> Church leaders are not to pay for, encourage participation in, or promote such groups or practices. . . . Local leaders should counsel those desiring self-improvement to anchor themselves in gospel principles and to adopt wholesome practices that strengthen one's abilities to cope with challenges. Members are invited to consult with their bishops or stake presidents when seeking appropriate sources of counseling. ("Caution Concerning Self-Awareness Groups," *Ensign*, March 1994, p. 80.)

The following story may help to illuminate how "finding oneself" comes through living gospel principles and not from something "more or less" than gospel principles. This man had attended a family relations class that stressed "true points of doctrine." During one of the sessions he shared the following:

> I have had the opportunity, through both business and personal interests, to attend several different seminars on "relationships" and self-

help. I was impressed with the enthusiasm and the energy of the presentations and felt temporarily uplifted following each experience. I felt especially motivated by one seminar in particular that I believed changed my life and helped me to understand many of the feelings I was having about myself and others and how those feelings reflected in my behavior.

In this one seminar we were taught to get into each other's heads, to better understand the feelings our spouse was having and therefore have a better understanding of our "relationship" and why it did or didn't work. I was feeling fairly comfortable with this skill and experienced a sense of accomplishment as headway was being made in the understanding I had of others' feelings and emotions. I was really quite proud of my ability to "stand back" and see what was "going on in others' heads."

Through all this I still did not feel the "peace of conscience" I desired, because although I felt I had a satisfactory way to communicate my negative feelings and emotions, the negative feelings still existed in me and in my relationships with others. I had only changed my behavior. After all the skills, practice, coping techniques, and "communications" I felt even more convinced that I was feeling rotten because of the mistreatment I was receiving from others. I still blamed others for my pain.

Then I attended a marriage relationship class where the scriptures and prophets were being taught. As the class progressed I was more and more impressed with the stories, ideas, and wise counsel from the scriptures and the prophets. Everything seemed to ring true with me.

In the back of my mind I was continually comparing gospel principles with the many principles from the self-help seminars I had attended. As I was listening to the comments and questions going on around me, a thought came to me in an instant that almost literally knocked me off my chair! It created a big enough disturbance to be seen by others, because the discussion immediately stopped and I was asked if I was all right. I told the class that at that moment I realized that although I had become very proficient at understanding, expressing, and communicating my negative feelings, thoughts, and emotions to others, those feelings, thoughts, and emotions were not representations of the truth but rather of my own sins and offenses against others. I was amazed at this revelation.

All the other seminars had taught, basically, that we are all stuck in our negative emotions, stuck in our lies forever with no hope of ever feeling differently—that's why communicating them is all you've got. They teach that all feelings just come—that it's okay, even good, to feel anger, bitterness, impatience, frustration, even hate against others.

How could I have been so blind? Actually, I believe now that my ability to see the truth was clouded by the sins and offenses in my own life (however small or large they might be). I see now why I felt an attraction to those other seminars; they implicitly convinced me that others were to blame for all my frustrations. I felt a kind of "ego boost" attending them, coming out with more tools and techniques to "understand," "diagnose," and "know" myself and others. After the self-help seminars I still had a "disposition to do evil," and sadly, I never felt to genuinely love others, truly ask forgiveness of them, or repent of my sins against them.

Now as I follow the promptings of the Spirit, ask forgiveness, and "feast upon the word of God" the sinful blaming feelings disappear and the right thing to do and feel is all that's left. I'm not perfect with this, so don't get the wrong idea. I have a long way to go yet, a lot of repenting and yielding yet to do.

This man experienced what I would call a mighty change of heart (see Mosiah 5:1–4; Alma 5:5–14). That change came by his repenting and coming unto Christ—no more, no less. His "beam" of hard, blaming emotions was removed by repenting and afterwards having his heart filled with the love of God. He learned the difference between the "philosophies of men" and the "peace of God, which passeth all understanding" (Philippians 4:7).

The Lord promises to send peace to those who come unto him, but it is a different peace from what the world has to offer. He said: "Peace I leave with you, my peace I give unto you: not as the world giveth, give I unto you. Let not your heart be troubled, neither let it be afraid." (John 14:27.) The Lord's peace touches our hearts and deeply changes us, not just our behavior. His peace brings rest to our souls and comfort to our lives, for he said: "Come unto me, all ye that labor and are heavy laden, and I will give you rest. Take my yoke upon you, and learn of me; for I am meek and lowly in heart; and ye shall find rest unto your souls. For my yoke is easy, and my burden is light." (Matthew 11:28–30.)

It would seem that if our yoke and burden are not easy and light, we are not yoked in Christ. We have a yoke and burden (responsibilities, commandments, covenants) in Christ, but if daily we are living faithful to true points of doctrine we will not experience our trials and afflictions as unbearable. If we do not sin or take offense at others we will be spared the burdens of negative, accusing feelings. However,

life will nonetheless present trials and afflictions which we must endure faithfully.

President Marion G. Romney spoke of the Lord's succor to the
faithful in their afflictions: "If we can bear our afflictions with . . . understanding, faith, and courage . . . we shall be strengthened and comforted in many ways. We shall be spared the torment which accompanies the mistaken idea that all suffering comes as chastisement for
transgression. . . . I have seen the remorse and despair in the lives of
men who, in the hour of trial, have cursed God and died spiritually.
And I have seen people rise to great heights from what seemed to be
unbearable burdens." ("The Crucible of Adversity and Affliction,"
*Improvement Era*, December 1969, pp. 68–69.)

## Endureth to the End

Just as the man in the story said he was not perfect but only better
at living the principles of the gospel, we too will not reach perfection
in this life. The Prophet Joseph Smith taught: "When you climb up a
ladder, you must begin at the bottom, and ascend step by step, until
you arrive at the top; and so it is with the principles of the Gospel. . . .
It will be a great work to learn our salvation and exaltation even beyond the grave." (*Teachings of the Prophet Joseph Smith*, p. 348.) Our
earthly duty, then, is to seek perfection with all our heart as the Lord
has commanded: "Therefore I would that ye should be perfect even as
I, or your Father who is in heaven is perfect" (3 Nephi 12:48). This
"perfection seeking" will not drive us ceaselessly, but will be a daily,
lifelong endeavor, an "enduring to the end" (see 1 Nephi 22:31). As
we daily endure by living the gospel, having faith in Christ, repenting
of our sins, our lives will be marked with a trust in the Lord, and we
will be directed by him (see Proverbs 3:5–6). We will undoubtedly experience hardships as the last days wind down, but we will also be
comforted and protected by him. "And now, behold, whosoever is of
my church, and endureth of my church to the end, him will I establish upon my rock, and the gates of hell shall not prevail against
them" (D&C 10:69).

President George Q. Cannon explained what it means to endure
to the end:

> The Lord our God had sent us here to get experience . . . so that we
> may know the good from the evil and be able to close our hearts against

the evil. . . . It is true that some have greater power of resistance than others, but everyone has the power to close his heart against doubt, against darkness, against unbelief, against depression, against anger, against hatred, against jealousy, against malice, against envy. God has given this power to all of us, and we can gain still greater power by calling upon Him for what we lack. If it were not so, how could we be condemned for giving way to wrong influences?

There could be no condemnation for our doing what we could not help; but we can help doing these things. We can help yielding to wrong influences and being quarrelsome and selfish. . . . When Satan comes and assails us, it is our privilege to say, "Get thee behind me, Satan. . . . I will not listen to you; I will close my heart against you. . . ."

Whenever darkness fills our minds, we may know that we are not possessed of the Spirit of God, and we must get rid of it. When we are filled with the Spirit of God, we are filled with joy, with peace and with happiness no matter what our circumstances may be; for it is a spirit of cheerfulness and of happiness. (*Gospel Truth*, Jerreld L. Newquist, ed. [Salt Lake City: Deseret Book Co., 1987], pp. 16–17.)

Nephi expressed in this way our need for righteous enduring:

And now, my beloved brethren, after ye have gotten into this strait and narrow path, I would ask if all is done? Behold, I say unto you, Nay; for ye have not come thus far save it were by the word of Christ with unshaken faith in him, relying wholly upon the merits of him who is mighty to save.

Wherefore, ye must press forward with a steadfastness in Christ, having a perfect brightness of hope, and a love of God and of all men. Wherefore, if ye shall press forward, feasting upon the word of Christ, and endure to the end, behold, thus saith the Father: Ye shall have eternal life.

And now, behold, my beloved brethren, this is the way; and there is none other way nor name given under heaven whereby man can be saved in the kingdom of God. And now, behold, this is the doctrine of Christ, and the only and true doctrine of the Father, and of the Son, and of the Holy Ghost. (2 Nephi 31:19–21.)

## Remember His Words

The Lord's counsel to his Saints is: "Remember the words of him who is the life and light of the world, your Redeemer, your Lord and your God" (D&C 10:70). The words or doctrine of Christ will liberate us from the bondage of sin and self-deception in our marriage and in all other relationships. We can get out of the vicious cycle of blame and self-justification and experience harmony, oneness, and peace with our spouse if we will repent of our sins against him or her, ask the spouse's forgiveness and the Lord's, and come unto Him for strength. We need to endure to the end by repenting to the end—meaning, the end of our mortal probation. In this way the Lord can put into us a "new spirit," a soft "heart of flesh," and remove the hard "stony heart" of contention (see Ezekiel 11:18–20; 36:24–28). We then become "new creatures," (2 Corinthians 5:17) and experience a mighty change of heart, "love one another," (John 13:34) and seek perfection with all our hearts through the gift that we received at our new birth into the kingdom—the Holy Ghost.

President George Q. Cannon remarked:

> If any of us are imperfect, it is our duty to pray for the gift that will make us perfect. Have I imperfections? I am full of them. What is my duty? To pray to God to give me the gifts that will correct these imperfections. . . . If I am an angry man, it is my duty to pray for charity, which suffereth long and is kind. . . . No man ought to say, "Oh, I cannot help this; it is [just] my nature." He is not justified in it, for the reason that God has promised to give strength to correct these things, and to give gifts that will eradicate them. (*Millennial Star*, April 1894, p. 260.)

The following story from one of my married students demonstrates our need to "rely wholly" upon the Lord and his points of doctrine as we endure to the end. This husband, after studying the scriptures and doctrines of the restored gospel, concluded:

> There has been one very serious relationship I've worked to heal—my relationship with my wife. I went at it with the attitude that I would completely follow the Spirit of the Lord and end my self-deceptions. I hoped I could have the "change of heart" instantly and stop the feelings of blame and antagonism toward her. Here is what happened: As long as I yielded to the feelings of the Spirit I had no feelings of antagonism towards her and we simply did not argue or fight about anything. It was freedom, we had arrived. But . . . I didn't always act on what I knew to be right. It wasn't a one-shot thing where I did it and that was it. One day I'd do great—the next day I wouldn't follow those spiritual feelings and Boom! all of those old traps and bad feelings were right back in my face. We would fall headlong into arguments and contention, threatening one another, provoking one another.

When I followed the Spirit we got along so well, no deceptions, and I didn't experience any lingering feelings of contention. But when I'd fail to follow the spirit of love, the accusing feelings were right back as if they had never left. Is that how it's supposed to be? I don't know, but I do know how good it felt when we could be as one, and I like doing what is right. So, I do have to work at "hearkening to the voice of the Spirit." Surprisingly, there is no sacrifice in this and it's becoming easier.

That can be true for all of us if we will simply follow the pattern the Lord has outlined in the scriptures and given us through his servants. Then we can achieve the peace and happiness we all sought when we tied the knot.

Fortunately, Bill and Martha, whom I discussed at the first of this chapter, came to this peace and happiness when they "tried the virtue of the word of God." Here are their own words:

> It has not been easy to admit that we created our marriage problems because of sin and our unwillingness to forgive each other and "come unto Christ." We tried everything but the doctrine of the restored Church. We called our problems every name but sin—no wonder our hearts remained hard. We even thought that the doctrines of the gospel didn't really apply to marriage or relationship problems; just to issues of spiritual salvation. But spiritual salvation and marital salvation are not two different things. We do not see eye to eye on every matter, but we no longer argue about the differences, either. It took a few trips to the bishop and several long, teary, "broken-heart" discussions to come to see our sins and grudges, but we feel new again and love each other so much. We would not go back to the contention and fighting again for anything. We feel so grateful for the gospel, for the Atonement, for Christ. Being with each other for eternity now sounds like a very attractive possibility.

*S. Brett Savage is very happily married to the former JaLee Deaton, his college sweetheart ("My life began when I first saw her in class"). They have six children—two sons, four daughters. Brother Savage is currently a management consultant with The Arbinger Company, and is the assistant director of outpatient therapy for the Anasazi Foundation, a residential treatment program for youth and their families. He has also been a part-time faculty member in the department of Ancient Scripture for three years at Brigham Young University. Having received a bachelor's degree in child and family studies from Weber State University, a master's in family life education from BYU, he is currently a doctoral candidate in theoretical philosophical psychology at the latter institution.*

# 11

## LIVING GOSPEL PRINCIPLES STRENGTHENS LATTER-DAY SAINT HOMES
### Ted L. Earl

One autumn Sunday afternoon I was about to leave my bishop's office to return home after a very hectic day when I received a desperate call from a couple in my ward. I decided to stay and meet with them. When they arrived, the wife had been crying and the tension between the two was obvious. They had been married two years and now they wanted to end their marriage. We talked for a while and identified a few areas which were giving them some problems. Finally, they consented to meet with me regularly to see if the three of us could straighten out some of their marital kinks.

Later that same week another couple with similar problems called. As I greeted them in my office I could see that the wife was very emotional and her eyes were swollen and red. They both agreed that after twenty-five years of marriage and five children, they were ready to call it quits. Their love for each other was gone, leaving only hurt and anger to fill the void. They too had decided that they didn't want to be married any longer.

I spent considerable time with both of these couples. It mattered not that one couple had been married two years and the other twenty-five. To me, their problems were similar—they had lost the vision of what marriage could be in the context of the gospel of Jesus Christ. After many talks together, emotional ups and downs, sharing personal feelings, and much repentance, both of these couples were able to restore their marriages by humbling themselves, strengthening their testimonies of marriage, and reestablishing their connection to eternal truths.

I wish all the unhappy stories I hear in my office could have a happy ending. Many times I see couples struggling with each other, allowing petty arguing, selfishness, competition, and defensiveness to eat away at their fragile relationships and strangle the love they once felt—neither one willing to repent and make needed changes.

On the other hand I have witnessed numerous beautiful marriages, where love, tenderness, peace, courtesy, and a partnership with each other and with God was the pattern. There is nothing more wonderful than to see a couple in love, honoring each other as eternal companions, finding life challenging but grateful for the opportunity to be together and to be the parents of a number of Heavenly Father's spirit children.

Over the years that I have observed LDS couples as an instructor and a counselor, I have noted a number of issues that seem to recur in troubled relationships. Following are some basic principles that are imperative if we are to succeed in this profound relationship.

## Becoming the Right Person

We often hear the expression that marriage is not so much a matter of finding the right person as it is of being the right person. As Church members our individual responsibility in preparing for marriage is to focus on becoming increasingly like our Exemplar, Jesus Christ. This can best be accomplished as we develop in our character the same attributes he exhibited in his earthly ministry, which will enable us to make our marriage relationship what God intended for married couples. Christlike principles make us lovable and trustworthy and ensure our success as marriage partners.

## Christlike Traits

It was the Savior who asked his disciples the question, "What manner of men ought ye to be?" He then answered his own query: "Even as I am." (3 Nephi 27:27.) Clearly this should be the goal of all Latter-day Saints, both male and female. President David O. McKay taught this important truth: "What you sincerely in your heart think of Christ will determine what you are, will largely determine what your acts will be. No person can study this divine personality, can accept his teachings without becoming conscious of an uplifting and refining influence within himself." (*Gospel Ideals*, [Salt Lake City: Improvement Era, 1953], p. 34.) What traits did Jesus exhibit that were so important that incorporating them into our natures would make us better husbands and wives, mothers and fathers? Here are a few examples from his life:

| Event | Reference | Trait He Manifested |
|---|---|---|
| Raised Jairus's daughter | Luke 8:41–56 | Compassion |
| Forgave a sinful woman | Luke 7:36–48 | Forgiveness |
| Healed a nobleman's son | John 4:46–53 | Blessed others |
| Calmed the storm | Mark 4:35–41 | Power over elements |
| Blessed children | Mark 10:13–16 | Loved children |
| Socialized with friends | Luke 10:38–42 | Not a recluse; socially outgoing |
| Suffered in the Garden | Luke 22:41–44 | Submissive to God the Father |
| Washed feet of Apostles | John 13:3–17 | Humble |
| Chose apostles | Luke 6:12–13 | Dependent on God |

My point is simply this: If we were to make these and other attributes and traits of the Savior a part of our personality and character and applied them to our marriage and family relations, our spouse would be thrilled to be our companion and our children would be honored to be our posterity. Jesus set the example for us. As Christians we have a perfect being to emulate, and we are under covenant to follow him.

## Individual Righteousness Through Obedience

Once we understand that the principles and ordinances of the gospel are to teach us how to develop these Christlike traits, our life's goals become easier for us and we understand what we must do to succeed. We have a standard to measure our performance by: What would the Savior do if he were in my place? Therefore, individual righteousness is simply obedience to eternal principles and covenants. Covenants extend power to our lives because if we are faithful the Godhead can fulfill any promise made in those covenants. President David O. McKay explained how we could influence the entire world:

Many years ago—a Chinese philosopher expressed the thought that I am trying to give you, and the result of individual righteousness as follows:

> "If there is righteousness in the heart
>     there will be beauty in the character.
> If there is beauty in the character
>     there will be harmony in the home.
> If there is harmony in the home
>     there will be order in the nation.
> If there is order in the nation
>     there will be peace in the world."

God helps us to bring about that peace in the only way that it can come, and that through obedience to the gospel of Jesus Christ. (*Improvement Era*, June 1953, p. 390.)

A marriage worthy of the celestial kingdom begins with an individual's desire to emulate the Creator and Redeemer. Satan has labored to convince us that being Christlike represents some kind of fanatical worship or practice, but in truth, becoming like the Savior brings a solid, rational, feet-on-the-ground, head-on-our-shoulders, commonsense, gospel-oriented approach to life. And when we obey the Lord's commandments, all of our family members feel the Spirit in their lives. Our children want to adopt our attributes, our virtues, our values, because their experience with present-day cultural values involve so many negatives—selfishness, greed, divorce, abuse, stimulant dependency—with subsequent misery. Character traits develop from our conscientious effort to be true disciples.

No one wants us to succeed more than our Heavenly Father does, who authored the plan of salvation. When our lives are in harmony with that which God asks of us, insights and discernment in our roles as husband and wife will solve or eliminate many troubles and difficulties and will strengthen our marriage and family relationship.

## Applying the Scriptures to Oneself

The scriptures become an important key by which to learn what our Father would have us do. They apply to each of us in most cases, so one helpful key that has influenced my own behavior over the years has been to place my name in the scriptures, as if the Lord were directing all his comments to me, to make them more personal and provide greater perspective for my own obedience. For example, Doctrine and Covenants 18:8 contains a promise from God that we can live with him forever if we are obedient. Notice how it reads when you put your own name in:

And now, marvel not that I have called him unto mine own purpose, which purpose is known in me; wherefore, if he shall be diligent in keeping my commandments he shall be blessed unto eternal life; and his name is [Ted]—[substitute your own name here].

This scripture is a promise of eternal life if we are obedient. Have you experienced what Elder John Groberg meant when he said: "Nothing, absolutely nothing in this life, is worth the cost of not fully keeping the Lord's commandments—not fatigue, not sickness, not personal convenience, not the honors (or scorn) of men, not the pressure of peers, and not the lure or lusts of worldly things" ("Honorably Released," *Ensign*, April 1991, p. 21).

Did not the Lord give us classic counsel when he said: "I, the Lord, am bound when [Ted] does what I say; but when [Ted] does not what I say, [Ted] has no promise" (see D&C 82:10). Here are several more examples:

And now, verily, verily, I say unto thee, [Ted,] put your trust in that Spirit which leadeth to do good—yea, to do justly, to walk humbly, to judge righteously; and this is my Spirit.

Verily, verily, I say unto you, [Ted,] I will impart unto you of my Spirit, which shall enlighten your mind, which shall fill your soul with joy;

And then shall ye know, [Ted,] or by this shall you know, all things whatsoever you desire of me, which are pertaining unto things of righteousness, in faith believing in me that you shall receive. (D&C 11:12–14.)

For by my Spirit will I enlighten [Ted], and by my power will I make known unto [Ted] the secrets of my will—yea, even those things which eye has not seen, nor ear heard, nor yet entered into the heart of [Ted] (D&C 76:10).

But the Comforter, which is the Holy Ghost, whom the Father will send in my name, he shall teach [Ted] all things, and bring all things to your remembrance, [Ted,] whatsoever I have said unto you.

Peace I leave with you, [Ted,] my peace I give unto you: not as the world giveth, give I unto you. Let not your heart be troubled, neither let it be afraid. (John 14:26–27.)

## The Value of the Atonement to Us Now and Later

While most Christians are grateful for the Savior's mission of remitting sins if we will repent, Latter-day Saints see further blessings, blessings that pertain to marriage and family life that stem from Christ's ultimate sacrifice:

1. A remission of sins—all Christians accept this concept.
2. Restoration of our physical bodies—the resurrection is a free gift to all.
3. Restoration of male or female attributes and characteristics that allow us to continue our wonderful functions as masculine and feminine beings.
4. Relationships entered into by priesthood power (the authority of an eternal rather than a mortal being) persist beyond death if we are faithful in this life.
5. All covenants entered into and sealed by the Holy Spirit of Promise will be valid beyond mortality.

Would it not be a shame if we came to earth, received a physical body, married in the temple, were assigned a number of God's spirit children to rear and teach, only to be found unworthy to have these relationships continue beyond this life? Wouldn't it be a shame if we came so close—temple marriage, children, ordinances and covenants—only to lose out because we were careless in our application of the laws of the gospel?

## Personal Revelation

God has not left us on the earth without direction, without inspiration. As Latter-day Saints we receive the gift of the Holy Ghost at baptism, a gift that can provide us with revelation to succeed in our most important stewardships—marriage and parenting. Why would any rational person try to go it alone when he or she has access to Deity, who has promised rich blessings if we will tap this divine source of all knowledge and power? When we use this gift properly we learn, through the Atonement, how to refine our character into a being who is more like Christ. "The gift of the Holy Ghost," said Parley P. Pratt,

> quickens all the intellectual faculties, increases, enlarges, expands, and purifies all the natural passions and affections, and adapts them, by the gift of wisdom, to their lawful use. It inspires, develops, cultivates, and matures all the fine-toned sympathies, joys, tastes, kindred feelings, and affections of our nature. It inspires virtue, kindness, goodness, tenderness, gentleness, and charity. It develops beauty of person, form, and features. It tends to health, vigor, animation, and social feeling. It invigorates all the faculties of the physical and intellectual man. It strengthens and gives tone to the nerves. In short, it is, as it were, marrow to the bone, joy to the heart, light to the eyes, music to the ears, and life to the whole being. (*Key to the Science of Theology*, [Salt Lake City: Deseret Book Co., 1978], p. 61.)

Who would be so foolish as to ignore this divine assistance? Is it not reasonable that if each of us exercised our gift of the Holy Ghost we would be spiritually healthy and able to cope better mentally and physically? What wife or husband should not be satisfied if we exhibited these traits in our character?

I came to a realization years ago that everything that matters in this life is centered in our ability to listen to and respond to the Spirit of the Lord. I am convinced, as Alma said, that if we do not neglect the small and simple means, great things will come to pass (see Alma 37:6). Let us each ask himself these questions:

1. Because I have been baptized and received the Holy Ghost, I am eligible for inspiration. What has the Spirit of the Lord been trying to tell me lately?
2. What have I done with the inspiration I have received from my Heavenly Father through this wonderful personal gift?

Don't ignore or dismiss the experiences and feelings you have as the Lord teaches you through his Spirit. Presumably you have had revelations already, for Joseph Smith said, "No man can receive the Holy Ghost without receiving revelations" (*Teachings of the Prophet Joseph Smith* [Salt Lake City: Deseret Book Co., 1938], p. 328).

Consider this point: If you do not take time to find out what the Holy Ghost is trying to tell you, what makes you different from a person who doesn't have the gift of the Holy Ghost? Do you think God wants you to fail in your marriage and family relations? Your children are his children! He has a great interest in your success. He is anxious to entrust you with more and more information and wisdom by which to rear his children, to support you in your marriage covenants—if you will let him. Said Elder Neal A. Maxwell: "The greater our sensitivity to the Spirit, the greater our response to beauty, grace, and truth in all their forms as these exist about us. Our righteousness opens us up like a blossoming flower to both detail and immensity. Sin, on the other hand, closes us down; it scalds the tastebuds of the soul." ("Creativity," *New Era*, August 1982, p. 7.)

The connection this statement has with the marriage relationship is obvious. When we bring the Spirit into our life our marriage union will reflect the sensitivity, tenderness, courtesy, love, forgiveness, trust, loyalty, kindness, happiness, and commitment that is so desirable and so necessary for the success of the two partners. We will see and feel the growth, the nourishment, and the blessings of the Lord in our marriage. In simple daily ways, the Spirit will prompt us and teach us what to do and how to carry out our roles more effectively. We will feel his power and influence as he influences our total companionship.

You will also experience true peace. Speaking in an LDSSA conference at Brigham Young University, April 16, 1986, Elder Marion D. Hanks stressed the following: "Satan cannot duplicate a peace of heart and a peace of mind. He can imitate most everything else, but not this kind of peace."

## Prayer

It always amazes me how many Church members will not pray consistently as individuals, as couples, as families. It is as if they are too proud to take the time to pray. Or perhaps too busy. Martin Luther is reported to have said, "I have so much to do today I must spend twice as much time on my knees."

Prayer will bring great strength and comfort. Individual prayer and husband and wife prayer should be a high priority for every couple. One key to successful prayer that has helped me is to commit to the

Lord one small, special thing that is easy to keep during that day. Then at night I report to him on how I did with that small, special thing. For example, not displaying any temper toward any family member or brother or sister. "By small and simple things," Alma said, "are great things brought to pass" (Alma 37: 6). Prayer is certainly one of those simple yet powerful things we often fail to do.

Another dimension of prayer is the opportunity to express appreciation. That expression alone softens the heart and makes us more pliable to righteous inspiration. In a general conference address Elder Richard G. Scott observed: "I have saved the most important part about prayer until the end. It is gratitude! Our sincere efforts to thank our beloved Father generate wondrous feelings of peace, self-worth, and love. No matter how challenging our circumstances, honest appreciation fills our mind to overflowing with gratitude." ("Learning to Recognize Answers to Prayer," *Ensign*, November 1989, p. 32.)

Gratitude must be a part of our home life. As a favorite hymn teaches us, we should count our many blessings, name them one by one. A beautiful spirit of peace is associated with being grateful. Courtesies will abound in a marriage when gratitude is frequently expressed.

Learning to offer meaningful prayers is only part of it. Learning to listen to the answer is another. It may come immediately, while we are still on our knees, as a very strong impression or sense of peace. It may come to us later as we study and meditate, or as we are reading scripture or other inspired writings.

Many times the Lord reveals answers to our prayers through another person. It could very well be our spouse or our children. "The woman has natural intuitive light, listen to her," counseled Marion D. Hanks. "The Lord will reveal, often, through the wife to the husband." (LDSSA Conference, Brigham Young University, April 26, 1987.)

I remember being stranded in the Nevada desert late at night. My family of ten was in a dangerous situation because I had not listened to my wife's promptings. She had insisted we did not have enough gas to get to our destination, and we ran out of gas five miles short. My daughter, in her sweet, innocent voice, said to the Lord in her prayer: "Heavenly Father, Dad has done it again. Please don't let us all suffer because he wouldn't listen to Mom." Prayer is our communication link with the presiding officer of the universe. Besides, he is our Father; he cares about us, our marriages, and our children.

## Priesthood

The priesthood is a divine gift, a divine investiture of authority, so to speak, to act in his behalf. This means we can act in behalf of the Lord when we perform ordinances. Because of the sacredness of this great power we are obligated to act in a responsible and righteous manner. The Lord warned his sons:

> That the rights of the priesthood are inseparably connected with the powers of heaven, and that the powers of heaven cannot be controlled nor handled only upon the principles of righteousness.
>
> That they may be conferred upon us, it is true; but when we undertake to cover our sins, or to gratify our pride, our vain ambition, or to exercise control or dominion or compulsion upon the souls of the children of men, in any degree of unrighteousness, behold, the heavens withdraw themselves; the Spirit of the Lord is grieved; and when it is withdrawn, Amen to the priesthood or the authority of that man. . . .
>
> We have learned by sad experience that it is the nature and disposition of [Ted and] almost all men, as soon as they get a little authority, as they suppose, they will immediately begin to exercise unrighteous dominion.
>
> Hence many are called, but few are chosen.
>
> No power or influence can or ought to be maintained by virtue of the priesthood, only by persuasion, by long-suffering, by gentleness and meekness, and by love unfeigned;
>
> By kindness, and pure knowledge, which shall greatly enlarge the soul without hypocrisy, and without guile—
>
> Reproving [correcting with love] betimes [within the proper time frame—usually immediately] with sharpness when moved upon by the Holy Ghost [all of the husband-wife correction may fit exactly the marriage manual rules, but if done without the Spirit it is not of God]; and then showing forth afterwards an increase of love toward him [her] whom thou hast reproved, lest he [put your spouse's name in here] esteem thee [husband or wife—put your name in here] to be his enemy.
>
> That he may know that thy faithfulness is stronger than the cords of death. (D&C 121:36–44.)

Paul instructed that the husband is to be the head of the house even as Christ is the head of the Church (see Ephesians 5:23, 25, 28–29). The Savior led by example and service rather than by coercion and force. He gave his life for mankind. Someday as husbands we will stand before the Lord to be judged concerning our family stewardship. We will then have to give an accounting of our efforts to lead our family in righteousness. Were we willing to truly serve them? Were we willing to give our lives for them? The extent to which we gather our children together to teach them the principles of the gospel, to administer the ordinances to them, to prepare them for missions, marriage, and the temple through family home evenings, individual instruction and attention, and prayer—all this will no doubt be reviewed.

As you think about it now, is there an atmosphere of love in your home because of the example you set? We are not to use fear or guilt to preside there, but love, tenderness, gentleness, and obedience in such a way as to bring the Spirit of the Lord into our home life.

Every priesthood leader in the home would do well to listen to his counselor—his wife. N. Eldon Tanner remarked: "Behind every good man there is a good woman. . . . In the Church when men are being considered for new priesthood offices, the question is always raised about the worthiness of the wife and whether or not she can give him full support." Then, quoting President Hugh B. Brown, he continued: "What man can match a woman who is really converted to the gospel! Women are more willing to make sacrifices than are men, more patient in suffering, more earnest in prayer. They are the peers and often superior to men in resilience, in goodness, in morality, and in faith." ("No Greater Honor: The Woman's Role," Ensign, January 1974, p. 8.)

## Developing Our Divine Nature

A few years ago I was counseling a fine couple who had major deficiencies in their marriage. Because their hurts were so deep, they wanted to end their marriage instead of trying to find a solution. We had one last meeting scheduled, and I had prayed that I might find the key to help them be more positive in their relationships. They were destroying each other through their negative attacks.

I was late in leaving home to meet them. On my way I got caught behind a large bus and became very annoyed that it was in front of me. After realizing that I was not able to pass it, I settled in behind it, admitting my stupidity for leaving so late. It was then that I noticed an advertisement on the back of the bus that was the very key I was looking for. It was sponsored by one of the local hospitals which had mental health services. I had time to scribble on a notepad as we plodded along. The signboard read "101 Ways to Praise," then it listed those ways. Many of the expressions shown were more appropriate for children or youth, but one's marriage partner would surely be happy to hear some of the others at the right times: Nice work; You made my day; Good for you; Terrific; You're precious; You're sharp; and so on.

Being positive brings a great spirit into the home. This concept and a lot of hard work changed the critical attitudes of the couple I counseled that evening and contributed to the improvement of their marriage. Being positive and praising your spouse will bring not only an added dimension of love to your marriage but also blessings from our Heavenly Father.

I question whether there is such a thing as "constructive criticism." The words *constructive* and *criticism* seem to me to be incompatible.

## The Home Is a Temple

Home is to be a place where one is loved, accepted, understood, and appreciated. It is a place where feelings, hopes, and dreams may be shared without risk. It is to be a place where joy is multiplied and sorrows divided. Our homes, if they are to serve all of us well, must be holy places, even as temples. They must be our refuge from the storms of life. A modern revelation counsels us to stand in holy places and be strong in living the standards of the gospel. "Wherefore, stand ye in holy places, and be not moved, until the day of the Lord come; for behold it cometh quickly, saith the Lord" (D&C 87:8).

Pictures, music, videos, behavior, manners, language, dress, cleanliness, media, reading materials, and courtesies are all part of making our home a temple. Certainly, considering the filth that abounds in our world, our guide must be the thirteenth article of faith: "If there is anything virtuous, lovely, or of good report or praiseworthy, we seek after these things."

"Have you the courage to keep out of your home some television shows that are filled with suggestive sexual conversation—and even experiences?" asked Elder H. Burke Peterson. "Have you thought lately how effective these shows are in piercing even the strongest spirits? Brethren, we must not feed ourselves a diet of trash!" ("Purify

Our Minds and Spirits," *Ensign*, November 1980, p. 39.) "There can be no genuine happiness separate and apart from a good home," said President Ezra Taft Benson. "The sweetest influences and associations of life are there." (*The Teachings of Ezra Taft Benson* [Salt Lake City: Bookcraft, 1988], p. 493.)

I know that when I come home late at night from teaching or counseling or "bishoping," I feel refreshed as I enter my home. The peace and comfort I experience reaffirms the great blessings the Lord pours out upon me as my family tries to make our home a temple of the Lord.

Home is a place where family members learn to work hard, and work together. One of the things the Lord dislikes is idleness. "Let every man be diligent in all things. And the idler shall not have place in the church, except he repent and mend his ways." (D&C 75:29.) The old adage that "idleness is the devil's workshop" is especially true in our day, with so many leisure pursuits available to us. Our children need to learn how to work, and to work well. Too many mission presidents are having to spend time with missionaries who do not know how to work hard. That is properly the task of parents, whether they live in the city or the country. If children are given the gift of learning how to work, they can avoid much of the trash of our day. However, caution must be given against workaholics, those who chase after money so that they can heap upon themselves the material trappings of our day. It is important to keep our priorities right—God, marriage, children, home, church, and work. Any other order can "lead us into temptation."

Home is a place where unity and harmony should abound. Building unity in a marriage should be a top priority for making home a temple. How do you build strong husband-wife relationships? Certainly the basics: dating, husband-and-wife prayer, common interests and hobbies, vacations, family home evenings, husband-wife councils, reviewing goals, parenting as partners, intimacy, building family traditions, and helping each other achieve individual and family goals. The strength of a marriage cannot be measured by looking at the house, its spaciousness, the cars, or the bank account of the inhabitants. The true measure is the feelings of love within the hearts of each partner, their commitment to God, and their actions toward each other. When strands of rope are woven together, there is strength. When horses are equally yoked together, there is synergism.

When people are of the same mind, spirit, and heart, there is Zion. "And the Lord called his people Zion, because they were of one heart and one mind, and dwelt in righteousness; and there was no poor among them" (Moses 7:18).

Strong marriage relationships begin with the commitment to be one. "I say unto you, be one; and if ye are not one ye are not mine" (D&C 38:27). When wood is glued together it strengthens by the mathematical formula for squaring. If three pieces are laminated together they have the strength of nine. This process begins at marriage and continues as children are added to the family circle. Every couple must bind themselves to each other with a holy love that is eternal in its nature.

Home is a place where people truly care about each other. As a married person, you should be sensitive and aware of how your spouse feels about life and your family. This means knowing not only what they are doing but what they are thinking, what concerns them, and what problems they are struggling with, what encourages them, and what you can do to bless him or her. Time together is such an important element in strengthening the marriage. Be sure you:

—Have weekly dates together.
—Take time to be genuine friends; friends make better lovers.
—Plan and take time to read together: scriptures, conference reports, and uplifting materials.
—Have morning and evening prayer—they are essential to your spiritual health.
—Have regular family home evenings that are uplifting and enjoyable for all family members.
—Hold husband and wife councils.
—Make mealtime a special time for the family. Share the day's events and successes.
—Do things for each other.
—Work together.
—Get away together for an overnight adventure at least quarterly.
—Use your best manners and courtesies with each other.
—Take time to listen to the counsel of the Spirit of the Lord regarding the operation of your home and your family relationships.

Home is a place where peace abides. The Spirit of the Lord can be in our homes when we speak softly. It cannot abide harsh, loud, even abusive retorts. "A soft answer turneth away wrath." Elder Boyd K. Packer explained:

> The voice of the Spirit is described in the scripture as being neither "loud" nor "harsh." It is "not a voice of thunder, neither . . . [the] voice of a great tumultuous noise." But rather, "a still voice of perfect mildness, as if it had been a whisper," and it can "pierce even to the very soul" and "cause [the heart] to burn." . . .
>
> The Spirit does not get our attention by shouting or shaking us with a heavy hand. Rather it whispers. It caresses so gently that if we are preoccupied we may not feel it at all. . . .
>
> Occasionally it will press just firmly enough for us to pay heed. But most of the time, if we do not heed the gentle feeling, the Spirit will withdraw and wait until we come seeking and listening and say in our manner and expression, like Samuel of ancient times, "Speak [Lord], for thy servant heareth." (1 Samuel 3:10.) ("The Candle of the Lord," *Ensign*, January 1983, p. 53.)

Home is a place where miracles are wrought by small and simple things. Wrote Alma: "Now ye suppose that this is foolishness in me; but behold I say unto you, that by small and simple things are great things brought to pass; and small means in many instances doth confound the wise" (Alma 37:6). In this day of sophistication, we are often tempted to ignore what we too often consider the "little things."

Reading the Book of Mormon daily as an individual and as a family is one of those simple things. Listen to this promise from President Marion G. Romney that surely every spouse and parent would desire to generate in their homes: "I feel certain that if, in our homes, parents will read from the Book of Mormon prayerfully and regularly, both by themselves and with their children, the spirit of that great book will come to permeate our homes and all who dwell therein," he said. Then he outlined the blessings that would follow: "The spirit of reverence will increase. . . . The spirit of contention will depart. . . . Righteousness will increase. Faith, hope, and charity—the pure love of Christ—will abound in our homes and lives, bringing in their wake peace, joy, and happiness." ("The Book of Mormon," *Ensign*, May 1980, p. 67.)

President Ezra Taft Benson reaffirmed these blessings after quoting President Romney's statement: "These promises—increased love and harmony in the home, greater respect between parent and child, increased spirituality and righteousness—are not idle promises, but exactly what the Prophet Joseph Smith meant when he said the Book of Mormon will help us draw nearer to God." ("The Book of Mormon—Keystone of Our Religion," *Ensign*, November 1986, p. 7.)

When you do the daily simple, little things—reading scriptures, having prayers, observing the sabbath, having family home evening, holding husband-wife councils, showing courtesies, respecting each other, and so forth—the Spirit of the Lord will come into your life to a greater extent than you thought possible.

> Closeness to our Father in Heaven and a constant spirituality in our lives is our greatest need as individuals and as a people. A true Latter-day Saint home is a haven against the storms and struggles of life. Spirituality is born and nurtured by daily prayer, scripture study, home gospel discussions and related activities, home evenings, family councils, working and playing together, serving each other, and sharing the gospel with those around us. Spirituality is also nurtured in our actions of patience, kindness, and forgiveness toward each other and in our applying gospel principles in the family circle. Home is where we become experts and scholars in gospel righteousness, learning and living gospel truths together. (Spencer W. Kimball, "Therefore I Was Taught," *Ensign*, January 1982, p. 3.)

"Build traditions of family vacations and trips and outings," counseled President Ezra Taft Benson. "These memories will never be forgotten by your children." ("To the Fathers in Israel," *Ensign*, November p. 51.) "Develop family traditions," urged Elder James E. Faust. "Some of the great strengths of families can be found in their own traditions, which may consist of many things: making special occasions of the blessing of children, baptisms, ordinations to the priesthood, birthdays, fishing trips, skits on Christmas Eve, family home evening, and so forth. The traditions of each family are unique and are provided in large measure by the mother's imprint." ("Enriching Family Life," *Ensign*, May 1983, p. 41.)

"Our family activities and traditions can be a beacon to the rest of the world as an example of how we should live to merit His choice blessings and live in peace and harmony until the day that He returns to rule and reign over us," was the counsel of another Apostle, L. Tom Perry. ("Family Traditions," *Ensign*, May 1990, p. 20.)

The implementing of traditions brings soft, warm feelings to your heart. A good idea would be to calendar at the beginning of the year all of the dates where traditions can be strengthened—birthdays, vacations, and special times together as a family. The difference between a wish and a goal is to write it down.

## Summary

What could be more important than building a righteous family kingdom here on earth? Where else could our time be put to better use? Think of the investment we all make in each other and in the children sent to us by the Lord and what our dividends will be in eternity if we perform well here. Our greatest happiness comes from a home life patterned after the principles of the gospel of Jesus Christ. Our homes must be temples, and our behavior consistent with that of a holy environment. We thus please our Heavenly Father and prepare our children to meet the challenges from a world "ripening in iniquity." The Lord has given us the challenge to bring our families back to him and it is within the power of all of us. It is the plain and simple things that in our sophisticated age we often refuse to incorporate into our lives and those of our posterity. We can be the "right person" through obedience, applying the principles of the gospel as they are taught to us in the scriptures and by living prophets, when we appreciate the practical implications of the Atonement in our lives, when we seek and receive personal revelation, are consistent in our prayers, honor priesthood principles, are positive, and make our homes temples where the Lord's Spirit may dwell. It is then that we can look forward to happiness in this life and immortality and eternal lives in the next as well.

*Ted L. Earl is married to the former Carol Liddell. They are the parents of four sons and four daughters, and have two granddaughters. Over the space of many years he has worked in various capacities in the Church's seminary and institute program, and has guided Church history and American history tours to the eastern United States. He is presently an associate director at the Orem Institute of Religion, which serves the Utah Valley Community College campus. He has served as a bishop and a high councilor and is currently serving as bishop of a singles ward at Brigham Young University. He holds a bachelor's degree in secondary education, with a major in psychology and a minor in math, from BYU, and has a master's degree in educational psychology in the area of counseling and guidance from that same institution.*

# 12

# LIVING SUCCESSFULLY AS AN IMPERFECT SPOUSE

*David and Marva Coombs*

Marriage is not easy.

Yet nothing can contribute to our personal happiness more than a great marriage. However, when couples naively expect their relationship to blossom into a great union without much effort on their part, marriage can be anything but heaven on earth. Perhaps it is an overworked cliché, but good marriages don't just happen.

Success in marriage requires work *and* realistic expectations. Young people today expect a great deal from marriage, perhaps too much in comparison with those of an earlier era. When we compare our comfortable life-style with that of our pioneer forefathers, maybe we take too much for granted. They married, bore children, worked hard, and were dependent on each other. They *expected* life to be tough and challenging, and it was. Disease could take any family member at any time, but marital differences or unmet expectations were not resolved by divorce.

Today married couples want it all—high income, perfect bodies, charm, spiritual experiences, leadership positions, education, comfort, communication, luxuries, health, and so forth. They don't want, nor do they tolerate, many difficulties. And many believe that obedience to gospel laws alone—paying tithing, for example—should bring material comfort and perfect health automatically. When they see other couples apparently getting what they want while they themselves are not, they may feel cheated or even betrayed by God.

Too many become intolerant and demanding of their partners. They expect their companions to meet *all* of their physical and emotional needs, and are disappointed when they don't. Have we lost (or did we ever have) the emotional toughness of our pioneer ancestors that could see us through the hard times and help us function more effectively in solving modern challenges?

This chapter shares ideas to help couples face marital differences and solve joint problems. These concepts and suggestions will help readers move from the present state of the relationship to a higher one.

When we marry, we obviously expect to be happy. After all, when we "fall in love" we think we have found the person who will heal any emotional wounds we may suffer. As we ride off into our honeymoon sunset together, we believe that we will never be alone or unhappy again. Sooner or later, though, the bloom on our new love gives way to painful reality. Neither one of us is perfect. Adjusting to each other becomes a lifelong process. At sometime after the wedding there are always a number who experience severe struggles that make them question their ability to sustain and maintain a long-term relationship; they question whether they were ever really "in love" in the first place.

The scriptures affirm that "marriage is ordained of God" (D&C 49:15). We must understand, therefore, that marital difficulties are a part of life and that we *can* work out our problems and *can* rekindle feelings of love that are bruised or damaged. We must never lose hope—we are committed not only to the principle of marriage but also to our individual relationship and the mutual growth that will enrich our particular companionship.

## Beginning to Heal

Assuming that almost all of us periodically have difficulties in relationships, what do persons do when they feel that their partners are not doing their share to contribute to the success of the marriage? Surely most of us feel that way at some time or another. Dismiss divorce. Reject other options that rarely work: demanding change, preaching repentance, nagging, and constant criticism. These prickly behaviors neither encourage change nor invite closeness. Would anyone want to hug a cactus? As the old saying goes, "We get more flies with honey than with vinegar." While we can talk together and strengthen our relationship, we do not have the right to demand change in our spouse to fit our preconceived notions. We do not have control over others—nor should we.

This means that we must begin the process of healing a troubled marriage in two ways: (1) looking inward and asking ourselves what we can do to enhance our marital relationship; and (2) turning to the Lord for help to love our spouse.

## Looking Inward

When Jesus told the Twelve that one of them would betray him, rather than accuse each other each one approached the Master and asked, "Lord, is it I?" (Matthew 26:22.) This ability to look inward, a willingness to accept personal responsibility for our actions, might be termed the "apostolic attitude." Couples in conflict generally do not take this approach. Each partner tends to blame and accuse the other, viewing the spouse as the culprit, the "imperfect one." Arguments intensify as each declare innocence, all the while gathering evidence to "prove" the other is the cause of the relationship's deterioration. So often marriage counselors hear disgruntled clients complain, "I'm OK, it's my spouse who has the problem."

Couples possessing an "apostolic attitude," however, ask themselves, "What part of our problem am I?" "What can I do differently to help resolve our differences?" It takes a mature, humble, and courageous person to acknowledge error, apologize, and initiate personal changes that will strengthen the relationship. Of all the couples seeking counseling, those who make the most progress in building a healthy relationship are those who humble themselves, take responsibility, and make changes in their own behavior that will lift the relationship.

As the babies were born, Sharon found herself working harder and harder. She was often tired and discouraged. She found herself yelling at her husband and children. He didn't earn enough money. He didn't fix things, or he didn't do them fast enough. When he cared for the children, they made messes that he was slow to clean up. Her complaints became increasingly biting.

One morning Sharon began yelling at Rob from the bathroom. At the same time that she yelled at him, she saw her face in the mirror—

ugly with anger—and her husband's face showing hurt and bewilderment. Painfully and slowly Sharon began to look at her own behavior and at what she was doing to her husband and consequently to her marriage. Wisely, she was honest enough and sufficiently humbled to repent, to apologize to Rob, and to make changes that resulted in healing their marriage.

## Turning to the Lord

As Christians we can gain much help from the Lord in developing a Christlike love for our spouse. Love is a gift of the Spirit that we receive from Heavenly Father. In order for us to love what we sometimes see as an "unlovable" spouse, we can seek help from the Lord. This is an important dimension. Our prayers might go something like this: "Dear Father, I know that thou dost love my spouse too. Help me to be more patient and long-suffering when we see things differently, to be willing for us to work together to become one. Help me to understand his (or her) feelings and needs, to gain a greater insight into them. Help me in being charitable so that I may love and understand my companion better. I want to be a good husband (wife) and build a great marriage."

Marriage and family life are actually the laboratories where we learn how to apply Christian virtues such as kindness, patience, repentance, forgiveness, and charity. The best marriages are those in which both husband and wife commit themselves to the gospel of Jesus Christ and apply its principles to their own relationship.

Heavenly Father understands that as mortals we will have difficulties arise that challenge our unity and our ability to get along with each other. He wants us to succeed. He stands ready to inspire, bless, and help us.

We need to realize that marriage will test our ability to apply the teachings of Jesus Christ. As his followers we must not allow our partner's weaknesses to interfere with our commitment to do what is right. While it may be a natural reaction for us, when hurt, to want to hurt in return, a better response than this is expected of us, for we are taught to return good for evil, to turn the other cheek, to go the extra mile. It is through an understanding of our eternal nature and potential (as well as our covenants with God) that we are enabled to do this. Remember, his challenge to us was to love our enemies; and, strange as it may seem, there are times when it appears that the spouse is a person's intimate enemy. We are to bless them when they are upset with us, return good when they are angry at us, and pray for them when they despitefully use us and persecute us (or misinterpret our actions or statements). (See 3 Nephi 12:44.)

The most obvious place for us to apply the principles of the Sermon on the Mount is in our marriage relationship. The Savior explained that it is easy to love those who love us, but he asked us to love those who are, at times, difficult to love (see Matthew 5:46–47). Many tense situations can be quickly defused by "agreeing quickly with thine adversary" (see Matthew 5:25), and repenting with a genuine: "I am sorry. It was not my intent to hurt. After listening to how you interpreted this whole thing, no wonder you were upset with me. I sincerely apologize."

The Savior, the master psychologist, taught us to turn a negative situation into something positive by returning good for evil. When our spouse is rude or insensitive and we do something kind and loving in return, we have immediately introduced the soothing balm that will heal the marital wound. By applying Christian principles to marriage we send a powerful message that, regardless of what has transpired, we love our spouse because we realize that behind the negative behavior is a person who is hurt, confused, or frustrated. If it has been provoked by something we have done, we can correct the problem by apology and appropriate behavior. And if we can continue to look past rude blasts and disappointments and respond with empathy and concern, we come closer to the ideal of being a disciple of Christ and move to a new plateau of Christian living.

Marianne and Doug had a good marriage and lovely children. All seemed perfect until Marianne joined the Church. She was a strong convert who would have faithfully walked with the pioneers across the plains. She was determined that her husband, Doug, would join the Church too. She preached, pushed, and demanded righteousness from him. The harder she pushed, the further he retreated and the more he set up roadblocks to the children's spiritual progress. At last, divorce seemed the only alternative.

Prayerfully Marianne sought help through counseling. Deep down she loved her husband and wanted her marriage to succeed. She learned how to restore her husband to the status of her "best friend." Initially she missed some church activities to be with him and, in return, asked his support for her church attendance. She stopped nagging and became more accepting of him as a person. He again became Number One in her life. Today the family is united in the faith.

## Choosing to Avoid Anger

Almost everyone chooses to become angry, but few have learned to express this emotion appropriately. Too often we speak crossly and hold grudges. Loud voices have sharp edges that cut deeply into hearts. It is angry words that destroy marriage relationships. "A soft answer turneth away wrath: but grievous words stir up anger" (Proverbs 15:1).

Angry words increase anger. Anger is habit forming—the more we express it, the more difficult it seems to look positively or gratefully at our lives and circumstances. Clinically, when we express anger toward others, our brain interprets it as self-directed, self-hate. On the other hand, our brain interprets our expressions of love for others as self-love. "Whatsoever ye sow, that shall ye also reap" (D&C 6:33).

As with Jesus, there are times when men and women, under inspiration, may act in righteous anger as they fight injustice and hypocrisy. While the rest of us would like to believe we have that same noble goal in the anger we express, we seldom qualify. We simply want things to go our way, and to do so *now*—a sign of selfishness and pride against which the prophets have warned us.

While most of us express anger too freely, there are those who refuse to acknowledge any emotional upset. They don't realize that feelings denied and buried may surface in unproductive ways at a later time. These denied feelings may cause overreaction, depression, lack of an ability to love, excessive eating, or even physical illness. Thus we should pay attention to what hurts us and our spouse and what leads to disappointment. How we respond demonstrates how well we have incorporated the gospel into our lives. The Spirit can guide us to know when and how to express our feelings in ways that can be healthy and constructive, or can let us know when we simply ought to forgive and leave things alone.

Becoming angry is our choice, but it is a secondary emotion. The first emotion may be hurt, fear, frustration, or disappointment at unmet expectations. Throughout our lives we develop patterns and habits that cause us to respond so quickly with anger that we convince ourselves we do not have a choice. But we do. We are not to be at the mercy of our emotions. Even if our choice is to express our feelings of hurt or frustration, it is neither righteous nor helpful to be cruel or unkind when resolving conflicts. The Apostle Paul asked, "Can ye be angry, and not sin?" (JST, Ephesians 4:26.) We *can* be upset, of course, without losing either self-control or the Lord's Spirit, just as we *can* disagree without being disagreeable.

The Lord's approach is to resolve conflict with persuasion, gentleness, meekness, and kindness (see D&C 121:41). Even when occasion requires us to "reprove betimes with sharpness" (D&C 121:43), we must do so with the clear intent to bless and draw closer to the person we reprove. The scriptures counsel that if our brother has "ought" against us we should go to him, and the two of us should talk together and be reconciled (see Matthew 5:23–24). We never have the right to become enraged (a sure sign of immaturity). Let us repeat that: *We never have the right to be enraged.* In translating the Bible, Joseph Smith left out the phrase "without a cause" in Matthew 5:22, making the verse read, "whosoever is angry with his brother shall be in danger of [the] judgment" (JST, Matthew 5:24). There is no cause that justifies losing control of our emotions. Nothing causes more damage in families than uncontrolled anger. When persons deal poorly with hurt or emotional pain, feelings are bruised and relationships damaged—often for lengthy periods of time.

We all want to develop the ability to be good communicators, to converse well, to say the appropriate things to others. Nephi promised that after we are baptized and have received the Holy Ghost and are feasting upon the words of Christ, we can "speak with the tongue of angels" (2 Nephi 32:2). This spiritual gift should allow us to communicate with each other in ways that build our marital bonding while helping us to appreciate the unique entities that individually we are.

Sometimes talking about spiritual gifts sounds impossible to those who grew up in homes where angry parents expressed their negative feelings habitually. For such persons, eliminating angry responses seems incomprehensible. However, in the spirit of Nephi's "I will go and do the things which the Lord hath commanded" (1 Nephi 3:7) we can repent and eventually eliminate destructive anger. And when family members repent, we can be as accepting as Nephi, who "frankly forgave" his brothers' grave offenses (see 1 Nephi 7:21). Temper tantrums seldom stop "cold turkey." But we can diminish their frequency and intensity as we dialogue with our spouse about our source of frustration and learn to substitute better communication skills for our past bad habits.

## The Little Things

Love, like the tide, may ebb and flow. There will be times when romantic feelings will be out like the tide. To bring it in, or restore them, we can initiate loving behavior. In other words, we consciously decide to do something we know will please our companion.

President Kimball's watchword was, "Do it." In our courting days we automatically looked for spontaneous ways to surprise and please each other. Why stop this behavior just because we are married? Little acts of kindness express our feelings, show that we care. "I want our marriage to work." "I love you." Or, what is often realistic: "I want to increase my love for you. I want the love feelings I had for you restored, and I will do my part."

Consider the power of gentle touches, hugs, squeezes, kisses, expressions of appreciation, endearing words, gifts, kind deeds, flowers, and thoughtful acts. Think of the message given when jobs are completed voluntarily and household projects are finished without our being reminded. When we daily spend couple time going for walks, sharing feelings, and appreciating each other, when we plan and execute weekly dates and occasional weekends together, we are continually feeding our relationship by communicating love messages. Certainly, too, we must voice the words. When we love each other, these "little things" are easy to do. When the heart-thumping love leaves, we do these things to ensure that the tides of romantic feelings return again and again to deepen and enrich our love. Such acts provide the spark and freshness we felt when we were courting, and, even better, they help us develop an enduring love which brings comfort and peace to our souls.

The Carlsons spent several fruitless sessions in counseling. They couldn't stop criticizing and demanding change from each other. Finally, in desperation their counselor turned to the husband and said: "Brent, it is up to you to make this marriage work. President McKay, when speaking to the brethren in a general priesthood session, said, 'We have too many divorces in the Church, and men, I think we are to blame for most of them—not all, but most of them' (in Conference

Report, October 1959, p. 89). If your marriage is going to work, you will have to take the lead, soften your heart and change. I want you to shoulder the responsibility of making this marriage work."

Brent responded angrily. "Don't you stick it to me. She has just as much responsibility for the problems in this marriage as I do. That is not fair." And he stormed out of the office.

The counselor wondered if Brent would ever come back. He did. In fact, when Brent and his wife, Kathy, returned a week later, they were holding hands and smiling.

The counselor inquired, "What happened to you two?"

Brent explained: "I was angry when you blamed me for our problems, but I could not get your thought out of my mind. I began to wonder if you were right. We have a counter in our kitchen where Kathy makes little piles to put away later. I hate those piles and I always yell at her when I find them. One day I came in from work and found several piles on the counter. I was about to launch into my usual yelling when I thought, 'Since I'm the one that is bothered by this, and since it means so much to me that this counter remain clean, then I can put this stuff away as well as she can.' So I took yesterday's paper to the garage, I put away our three-year-old's storybooks, and I put the clean, folded sheets in the linen closet. Kathy came in a few minutes later while I was reading the mail. She saw the counter and asked, 'Did you clean this off?' There were tears in her eyes as I said, calmly, that I did. She didn't say a thing. Our evening progressed nicely because it was free from conflict; in fact it was very pleasant. That night we made love for the first time in three months—her idea. Since then we've had a contest to see who could please the other the most. We've slipped on occasion, but we don't like slipping. We have learned that it's more fun to please each other than be grumpy all the time."

## Taking Time to Be Together

A vibrant marriage requires time—time on the part of both companions. Try reserving at least an hour a day for each other (about six percent of our waking hours, incidentally). That hour doesn't have to be one big chunk of time; it can be spread throughout the day. But this time commitment loudly proclaims, "I love you and I want to be with you." Every couple needs time to talk, share feelings, listen, make plans, solve problems, review schedules, work together in the home or yard, shop, or do errands together. Some couples walk during their daily couple time; others enjoy pillow talk early in the morning. Some couples, whose work schedules make them feel like ships passing in the night five days a week, discover that they can meet for lunch or even eat a sack lunch while visiting on the phone.

For this sacred time together, some set time at night after all the children are in bed. The Madsens set 9:30 P.M. for their couple time. Everything else is set aside. They chat as they get ready for bed; then he rubs her feet while she reads a chapter from the scriptures, or she rubs his back while he does the reading. Sometimes they discuss the chapter, or it serves as a springboard to discuss any number of things. They testify that reading the scriptures together—especially the Book of Mormon—has served to guide them in solving problems and making decisions as a couple. Around 10:00 P.M. they kneel in prayer, following this with a traditional kiss.

Circumstances and attitudes may influence the ease of our getting together. We show our love by our willingness to give up lunch with friends, the television news, Monday night football, phone calls, or whatever it takes to be together. Cherishing time as partners may take some planning or it may be somewhat spontaneous, but the investment brings wonderful returns.

The Brethren have counseled us to keep our courtship alive. One way to do this is through a weekly date together, away from the children. Occasionally the date might include other couples; however, most often couples need time alone to enrich the emotional intimacy we all need with our spouse. Those who come from dysfunctional homes—homes marred by alcoholism, abuse, divorce, or temper tantrums—may have learned as children that intimacy threatens one's emotional well-being. When they shared feelings with others during their growing years, they may have been mocked or belittled. Persons from that heritage may be uncomfortable with daily chats or dating designed to bring couples closer.

Often men become workaholics, both at work and at church, while some women spend inordinate amounts of time with children, church work, and community service—all to avoid emotional intimacy. Closeness frightens some people. If we recognize this defect in ourselves, we need to risk reaching out, patiently and courageously, to build an environment in the marriage that allows each to speak openly and freely. Trusting and sharing must be a part of every strong marriage, and we have the responsibility to foster that trust in our spouses. Professional counseling may also be needed to tear down these emotional barriers.

As marital dating partners, we ought to avoid the rut of repeating the same pattern every Friday night; we can be creative and make our weekly dates fun. The Bensons alternate responsibility for planning this special time together. It is not the activity that is so important, but it is critical that *we do something.* In one study of four hundred couples who had been married more than twenty years and who considered their marriages successful, the number one factor reported as contributing to their happiness was that their marriages were fun. The second factor was planning for time together to review problems without hurting each other. The third was non-sexual touching that often (but not always) led to satisfying sexual activity. The point is clear. It takes time with each other to develop a successful marriage.

Brad and Marilyn Benson use part of family home evening to calendar their week. They have learned that they must correlate their own calendars before calling a family council. This is their time to schedule marital dates, to determine who is responsible for obtaining the baby-sitter, and so on. They feel money need not be the most important factor. They suggest being creative. They trade sitting or other services with other couples. Their dates are as simple as a walk along the beach, a hike, or a walk through the mall eating an ice cream cone. One of their favorite dates is going to the temple; they always discuss inviting another couple to go with them, and sometimes do, though most often they are pleased to have the two hours' traveling time to be completely alone. They bear testimony that temple attendance has "armed [them] with righteousness and with the power of God in great glory" (1 Nephi 14:14). They attribute part of their increasing love for each other and their success with their children to regular temple trips.

Mike and Cheryl also schedule weekly dates. When it is her turn to choose their date, Cheryl often suggests walking in malls or drives in lovely housing tracts. One evening Cheryl wanted to walk through a model home.

"I don't want to go," Mike blurted.

Surprised she questioned him. He admitted that he saw these excursions as challenging his success as a wage earner. He thought his wife was not satisfied with what he could afford for her, and that she would want everything she admired and would expect that he would provide it. Since she explained she just likes "seeing what's out there," he is now able to enjoy these inexpensive dates. They discover ways to decorate their home that are within their budget and talents.

About every six months the Bradfords go on a "mini-moon" (away from children and out of the area overnight). They report: "Our children need us to be away occasionally so that they develop some independence; we need these retreats to refresh our relationship. Because the Church recognizes the need for biannual conferences to revitalize our spiritual commitment, we feel that we need mini-moons to revitalize our marriage relationship."

Just as some real estate developers put greenbelts around their subdivisions to beautify them, so in our marriages we need the greenbelts of weekly dates and occasional mini-moons to add interest and enjoyment. We need this time to review and perhaps rethink our goals and our commitment to each other and our approach to parenting.

John and Natalie plan a mini-moon every January. They take all of their calendars—professional, personal, school, stake, Scout, Young Women—with them and put all pertinent information on their calendar. Then they plan monthly temple trips, mini-moons, family vacations, and super-Saturdays. They have discovered that, just as they need greenbelts in their marriage, their children require special times too. Super-Saturdays are no-work-around-the-house days used for family hikes, biking, visits to museums, or exploring parks and other local interest spots.

Some people are afraid that if they plan and write things down it will threaten spontaneity. It doesn't need to. Calendaring simply means that adventures happen. Actually, those who plan couple and family activities are even more likely to spontaneously play. They like being together and watch for opportunities to enjoy one another.

Those who have not learned how to play well with others must accept the challenge to develop that ability. Learning to play means that we have given ourselves permission to enjoy life. Wives may enjoy the ballet, for example, while husbands prefer sports—or vice versa. As we support each other's interest by going as a couple to both the ballet and the sporting event, we give each other a special gift: true friendship.

## Communication

Many married couples develop poor communication patterns. All couples have differences—that is normal. But if we are unable to discuss them easily our problems are never resolved, or they are resolved temporarily and will show up again and again in the future.

Good communication means having the ability to say what we feel, at the time we feel it, while still being sensitive to the feelings of others. Critical statements and negative behaviors that devalue others are probably the biggest barriers to good communication. Many of us rarely argue or quarrel over the real issue. Most often an argument occurs when one or the other feels unloved or unappreciated. We interpret the behavior or comments of others as evidence that we are being discounted, put down, or rejected. As a consequence we often respond defensively with either an attack or a withdrawal—the fight or flight syndrome. But a third and better way exists. Instead of fighting or taking flight, we can move closer to each other and seek understanding. We can put aside our feelings for the moment and, instead of insisting that justice be done, empathically listen and give assurance that we do care and do value each other's feelings and ideas.

Empathic listeners ask questions like: "What did I do that made you feel that I didn't care?" "What would you like me to do differently?" "What did you expect me to do in that situation?" "What would you like me to do the next time this issue comes up?" Problem-solving statements that promote reconciliation are: "I really want to understand what you are thinking and feeling." "Let's keep talking until we both feel understood, and we can reach an agreement that allows both of us to feel loved and valued." Couples with good communication patterns are simply nice to each other. They seek to guard each other's self-esteem. Just as the rose opens in the warmth of the sun, so do they open to each other when it is emotionally warm and safe to do so.

## Sexual Intimacy

The misuse of sexual passion causes dreadful heartache. When we cross appropriate boundaries, we pay an exorbitant price. Yet when expressed within the bounds the Lord has set, our procreative capacity "is a sacred and significant power. . . . It is the very key to happiness." (Boyd K. Packer, "Why Stay Morally Clean," *Ensign*, July 1972, pp. 111, 113.)

Latter-day Saint doctrine manifests the procreative power as an eternal gift not limited to mortality. This sacred power continues in the resurrection for those who marry worthily in the temple and then qualify for the highest degree of celestial glory (see D&C 131:1–4; 132:19).

No wonder Satan wants to do all he can to degrade this sacred power. Most everything vulgar in our culture has reference to some dimension of our sexuality. Satan does not have a physical body; therefore, he cannot enjoy the gift of procreation. He does what he can to cause us to abuse our bodies and to misuse our sexual powers. If we do this and fail to repent, he will succeed in keeping us from obtaining our goal of attaining the quality of life our Father has—eternal life.

Victims of sexual abuse often struggle to accept their sexuality, and often need counseling to help them overcome the consequences of that abuse. But they can have healing. In fact, exploring our sexual natures is something every couple should anticipate and enjoy. Women need to be careful of making demeaning statements such as, "You know how men are" or "Look out, that's all men really want from you." Our sexual intimacy is private; and those who understand the value of this gift from God enjoy their sexuality, while those who don't, don't.

## Sex in Marriage

In his opening address of the April 1974 general conference, President Spencer W. Kimball, in emphasizing the importance of sexual morality, quoted Billy Graham: "The Bible celebrates sex and its proper use, presenting it as God-created, God-ordained, God-blessed. It makes plain that God himself implanted the physical magnetism between the sexes for two reasons: for the propagation of the human race, and for the expression of that kind of love between man and wife that makes for true oneness. His command to the first man and woman to be 'one flesh' was as important as his command to 'be fruitful and multiply.'" (*Ensign*, May 1974, p. 7.)

The prophets have consistently taught that we should be "pro-family," that we are anxious to bring children into the world. But the bearing of children only represents part of the need for healthy sexual intimacy. Latter-day Saints read the biblical call for sexual intimacy as a power to unite a couple physically, mentally, and spiritually. Marital sex can bond a couple together, powerfully cementing their love for each other.

A frequent question that arises has to do with family size. In an *Ensign* article Dr. Homer Ellsworth discussed gospel "family planning." He referred to First Presidency counsel that "the health of the mother and the well-being of the family should be considered," and suggested that this consideration should extend also to emotional well-being. (*Ensign*, August 1979, p. 24.) What concerns Church leaders is that couples may limit the number of children for selfish reasons. As couples seek heavenly guidance, their prayers will be answered and they will have the right number of children at the right time.

Another facet needs some attention in this area. Today, many couples pick up secular books that are designed to introduce sexual practices that are at least questionable. Elder Mark E. Petersen wrote of some of the problems that married couples face. Regarding the frequency of sexual intercourse in marriage he said: "There are two extremes which lead to difficulty: 'too much' and 'too little.' Both extremes breed discord in the home." In response to the question, "Does anything go in the bedroom?" he said: "If sex is as sacred to us as it should be, then it deserves that status both before and after the wedding ceremony. 'Anything' does not go in marriage. Decency is as important for married people as for the unmarried. Perversions are perversions whenever indulged in, and the marriage ceremony cannot take away their stain." (Mark E. Petersen, *Marriage and Common Sense* [Salt Lake City: Bookcraft, 1972], p. 94.)

Anything that offends the sensitivities of either spouse should be avoided. Kevin sought counsel from a member of the bishopric. He wanted to try some variety in his marital intimacy and had bought a book that suggested techniques new to him. To his dismay, his wife, Sandra, felt insulted by his proposals and wouldn't even look at the book he brought home.

"Look," he said to his bishopric friend, "there is nothing offensive about this. Is there anything here that you don't agree with?"

"It doesn't matter what I think," answered the counselor, pushing the book aside.

"Just take a look at it," Kevin said in a demanding tone.

"If the book and its ideas offend your wife, it isn't worth it. Making love includes making her feel loved. Forget the book and love your wife."

The important message we should want to convey to each other is mutual love and respect. Our sexual relationship can be beautiful when we do so.

## Non-Sexual Touching

This chapter discusses what might be labeled the three *T*s essential to a successful marriage: time, talk, and touch. When these three ingredients are present in a marriage, strong emotional bonds will develop and be reinforced between husband and wife. This is particularly true when time together is enjoyable and rewarding, when talking is mostly expressed in positive exchanges, when touching conveys worth and value.

It was proven years ago that if infants were not cuddled and held by another human being, they risked death or abnormal development. As we grow older, we do not lose this need for caressing and affection. One of the beautiful aspects of the marriage covenant is the freedom to touch and be touched. Nothing is quite so sweet and romantic as a gentle touch from our eternal companion.

When we were courting we were so in love we could hardly keep apart. We always wanted to be touching. Successful married couples keep that special emotional spark alive by maintaining this "contact comfort." The results of a survey reported by Ann Landers showed that if the women who participated had to choose between sexual activity and being held tenderly, seventy-two percent would prefer the latter. It was not Ann Landers's intent to diminish the importance of sexual contact, but rather to highlight the importance of non-sexual touching. Both are necessary in happy marriages. If, in marriage, our only contact with each other is sexual, then one or both will begin to feel devalued and emotionally, and perhaps physically, will shrink from all touching. In order for us to feel valued as partners, we must find a balance between touches that convey love and tenderness yet do not lead to sexual activity, and those that do.

# Summary

Living successfully as imperfect spouses begins with the realization that we are all imperfect and all stand in need of a Savior. That is Christ's mission. He saves individuals and he saves marriages, if we will let him. Wouldn't it help us to know that the Lord not only has ordained the institution of marriage but specifically wants you and me to be successful in *our* marriages? Armed with this assurance of divine support, we would all work harder, have more faith, and as a result be blessed with sweeter, eternal marriages.

Marriage can be difficult. But our investments of time for daily interaction, for weekly dates, and for mini-moons will be rewards with greater faith in and commitment to one another. Our efforts to share our feelings will tear down old barriers and increase closeness. An eternal perspective enhances our understanding that our sexuality is a divine gift to be honored and enjoyed within the sweet bonds of marriage. Through our diligent efforts and by the grace of God we come to know that marriage can be the most wonderful adventure of our lives—both here and hereafter.

*David Coombs and his wife, Marva, live in Tustin, California, have been married for thirty years, and have eight children. Dr. Coombs received his doctorate in educational psychology from Brigham Young University in 1974. He has a professional counseling practice and is currently supervising early morning seminaries for the Church Educational System. He teaches classes for the institutes of religion adjacent to California State University at Fullerton, and Fullerton College. He is a faculty member for the Know Your Religion series and BYU Education Days. He has written articles for the* Ensign *and the* Latter-day Sentinel. *He has served in a variety of Church callings, including high councilor, bishopric member, and Scoutmaster. Sister Coombs met her husband when they were students at the University of Utah, where they both graduated with their bachelor's degrees. Working as a team, they present seminars on parenting and couple communication. Sister Coombs is working on her master's degree in creative writing at California State University at Fullerton. Marva's service in the Church includes being a stake board member, a Relief Society president, and an early morning seminary teacher.*

# 13

# WAYS OF BEING

## Terrance D. Olson

W hat manner of men ought ye to be? Verily I say unto you, even as I am." (3 Nephi 27:27.)

"If we walk in the light, as he is in the light, we have fellowship one with another, and the blood of Jesus Christ his Son cleanseth us from all sin" (1 John 1:7).

I learned something the other day, not only about what manner of man I ought to be but also what manner of human it is possible to be.

I got on the elevator one morning, so absorbed in thumbing through the mail I had picked up that I did not notice that the elevator door had not closed behind me. My past experience with that elevator had been that you must jiggle the door slightly for it to close. I asked permission of the people in front of me to let me tinker with the door, and while I did so I explained to the riders the idiosyncrasies of this particular piece of machinery. As I did so, a rather authoritative voice from the back of the elevator spoke up: "It will close, if you will just leave it alone!"

I responded with the voice of experience, the voice of a teacher who wanted to educate those less familiar with the problem of this particular elevator. "No," I said, "I've found that if you don't wiggle this protector, we'll just sit here forever." Sure enough, my technique worked and the elevator door immediately closed.

I turned around and observed that the voice telling me to leave the door alone was that of an elevator repairman. I said nothing further. We traveled one floor and two people exited. The door, again, did not close. This time I busied myself sorting through my mail. We waited. And we waited. Some people left to seek a different elevator. But not me; I waited. Finally, the elevator door closed.

Before the elevator stopped again, I realized I had *enjoyed* the interlude when the doors had not closed. But in a few minutes I realized (perhaps by being willing to attend to a prompting) that my enjoyment was counterfeit. During the second wait for the door's closure, my "preoccupation" with my mail was simply hypocritical. It was feigned disinterest in the door (and I was deeply interested in that which I was pretending not to be interested in). I reflected further, and it became obvious to me that my "enjoyment" came from having "proof" against an expert, in this case the repairman, that I was right and he was wrong.

Sorting my mail while the doors remained open was not a genuine act on my part, even though, moments before, the very same act had been guileless. The second time, as the moments passed and we stood stranded, I was only *appearing* to sort my mail. In reality, I was savoring the evidence that I knew more, after all, than this fellow; this rude, unappreciative fellow. I was more interested in showing him that he had a problem than in helping to find a solution. I actually wanted him to be embarrassed, since he had earlier behaved toward me in a way I took as a rebuke. It became obvious to me that I was acting hypocritically, that I was a different person than I was when I was helping to move the elevator along. A synonym from the Book of Mormon that describes my hypocrisy is hard-heartedness.

When I became hard-hearted, the quality of my experience changed, but *I* had changed it. I realized that I really was not a victim of the elevator man's treatment of me. My attitude and feelings changed because of something I was *doing*. I was being an agent while experiencing life as a victim. Being hard-hearted creates contention and destroys charity. The hard-hearted not only take the truth to be hard as did Laman and Lemuel (see 1 Nephi 16:1–2), but take themselves to be innocent of the trouble they create.

In the beginning of my experience on the elevator I was genuine, honest, and unself-conscious. I felt that I knew how to solve the problem, and my only desire was to help all of us in the elevator reach our destination. To have done nothing, when I knew what to do and believed I should do it, would have been wrong on my part. Even when I was "commanded" by someone on the elevator to leave the door alone, my continued efforts to solve the problem were sincere. I saw myself as being helpful; after all, I was teaching people something they needed to know about this particular elevator.

But in an instant, probably as I turned around to see what I assumed was the irritated face of an elevator repairman, I changed into another being. I no longer was self-forgetfully helping my fellow humans. I had become self-centered, defensive, justifying—all symptoms of being hard-hearted. I had transformed the meaning of the earlier events into something different. Now I saw myself as having to defend myself against a supposed authority, an "enemy." I did this, of course, silently, by doing nothing as the elevator opened on the next floor, and I took great pleasure in the fact that the door gave no hint of closing before lunch!

My focus on my mail this time, however, was hypocritical. My interest now was not in being helpful but in being justified in my refusal to help. By my silent withdrawal from the call of my conscience, I had changed the manner of man I was. I was being in the world differently—very differently, and not positively—than I was moments before. Although I was the same person at the end of that elevator ride as I had been at the beginning, I had been, for a very brief span, two different people. My manner of being in one moment was compassionate and self-forgetful. The next moment I was resentful and self-concerned. The two ways of being are incompatible.

Although my experience involved a stranger on an elevator, my seeming choice between being helpful and being resentful applies even more intensely in marriage relationships, and with more drastic consequences. In relationships with people we love, we can also be hard-hearted. Our attitude when we are hard-hearted is like mine in the elevator when I quit trying to be helpful. We become resentful toward the very people we care about, and we simultaneously think our feelings are "their fault."

I believe that you and I cannot turn our backs (or hearts) on the people we love and on what we believe is right without simultaneously excusing and justifying ourselves in what we are doing. We live in the world differently when, as described by Terry Warner, we betray ourselves; when we act differently than we believe we should.[1]

---

1. I am indebted to C. Terry Warner for the framework of analysis I use to show the meaning of my examples and illustrations in this chapter. He has broadened and deepened my understanding of the law and the prophets, and his work is fundamental to my professional activities.

A woman whose husband was due home from another long-distance drive in his eighteen-wheeler was trying to have dinner ready so that she could create a moment of welcome and relaxation. She was behind in her preparations, and actually relieved that he too was late. She did not want him to arrive, tired and hungry, while the meal was not ready and see his disappointed look.

All too soon she heard the air brakes outside and realized that her deadline had come sooner than she wanted. Upon entering and seeing the incomplete preparations, he looked at her. When their eyes met he smiled and said, "Looks like I got here just in time to help." She was more than relieved. Neither one of them felt defensive, no one had to excuse himself, create rationalizations, or find someone to blame for a late dinner or a late arrival. Unity and cooperation were possible because of the ways they were being with each other. It took no particular communication skill or relationship strategy to avoid tension, argument, or disappointment.

With an honest heart, our desire is to be helpful rather than blaming. This couple experienced what I felt only part of the time on the elevator. They continued to "be" the same way with each other and worked together to make the evening a relaxed reunion rather than an antagonistic encounter.

Withholding our hearts or feelings from others, refusing to do for others what we believe to be right actions and service, produces what King Benjamin refers to as the "natural man" (see Mosiah 3:19). When I withdrew my heart from being helpful on the elevator, instead of putting off this natural man I put it on. I was now wearing the emotions, attitudes, thoughts, and feelings of one who was not true to what I, under normal circumstances, consider my "true being." Even my silence was a symptom of hard-heartedness. I had become a person who wanted those who didn't appreciate my efforts to suffer, to see that I was right—even if that suffering consisted only of the embarrassment of an elevator repairman who was a complete stranger to me! In contrast, the truck driver and his wife put off the natural man by being true to the love and compassion and charity they felt for each other. The obvious things to do to help were symptoms of an honest heart, of a couple who were willing to have their hearts knit together in unity and love.

This all-too-true tale should sound like a slice from everyday life—perhaps even your life. Most people would be able to identify with both "ways of being" I have described. Your experience may not have been on an elevator. You might have seen yourself as you were in heavy traffic last Wednesday. Or you might reflect on your relationship with the umpire at the Little League game. Perhaps your harshness was with your wife when you thought your cues to be intimate were somehow ignored and you felt rebuffed. Or an incident of hurt or being unappreciated by your husband or children comes to mind. Alternatively, perhaps you are able to recall your compassion, your genuineness along with that of other ward members when you helped the bishop's family during his surgery, or your swift "dropping of everything" to race your daughter to the library before it closed because she needed a book in order to meet a deadline.

Actually, we are haunted in our memories more by our hypocritical moments than by our genuine ones. That is in part because in our genuine moments we have no interest in keeping score; we are not tallying up our goodness. In our hypocritical moments, on the other hand, we are consumed by the insistence that we are not at fault for the feelings we are experiencing. "After all," I could have rationalized, "the repairman could have said what he said much more gently than he did." Or I might have thought smugly, "Ah, no good deed goes unpunished." Looking back on it, though, I see that I took offense at his tone of voice. My manner of being became that of a defensive victim rather than a giving neighbor. I became very self-conscious about how I was suffering because of my circumstance. I was not at peace.

Some people respond to my analysis of this example by saying, "Terry, what happened to you is just normal, everyday life. Do you have an overactive conscience which makes you feel guilty about trivial, everyday incidents? I mean, it would be exhausting to try to live every moment true to your conscience. You know the hazards of being a perfectionist, don't you?"

This seemingly gentle counsel actually illustrates how far astray from seeing ourselves honestly our culture has come. To do the right thing, to live in a manner which is true to conscience, is seen as unrealistic and burdensome—even as an expression of a fanatical, rigid personality. The message seems to be that if we try to live up to "impossible" standards of expectations we will be guilt-ridden, anxious, and humorless.

To see standards as impossible expectations which are burdensome already reveals more about us than about the standards. But we actually may relieve ourselves of exhausting pressures by doing the right thing as compared to trying to rationalize our wrongdoing. When we hold our standards honestly, without guile, we see what is possible to do and be. Which requires more energy, apologizing to a mate for our own unkindness or harboring extensive accusations as to why he or she is responsible for our bad behavior and feelings? Which is the greater burden, to ask for the Lord's help when facing the chronic illness of a loved one or to bitterly keep score about how unfair life is?

When we discount the possibility or benefits of living in a compassionate, forgiving manner, we have created a spiritually exhausting world indeed, because there is no balm of healing available in it. Once we excuse ourselves from being meek, humble, or charitable, or from offering love unfeigned, we partake of a spirit of bitterness which, all by itself, is exhausting. As a matter of fact, the hard-hearted are, in a way, prisoners of the past, for they must constantly remind themselves that what others have done to them, or "just the way the world is," justifies their discouragement or despair in the present moment.

The idea that we are psychologically trapped in the present moment by certain past events, or by the way others are treating us now, undermines the idea that we can change; that we can always have hope; that we can repent and forgive. The hard-hearted are blind to the fact that their attempts to excuse themselves from their moral responsibilities keep them in a psychological and spiritual prison where there is no escape from their burdens and feelings.

This kind of hampering perfectionism is not the lot of the obedient. From within the gospel, the present moment is not hostage to the past. When people give their best, they are learning, repenting, and forgiving. They do not see themselves as perfect, nor do they use the fact that others also fall short to excuse and justify their own mistakes or misdeeds. Those living charitably are confident, even in the presence of those who are faultless (see D&C 121:45). "A doubleminded man is unstable in all his ways" (James 1:8), and peace and grace are offered by the Lord to those who are humble and purify their hearts (see James 4:1–8). In brief, it is not our obedience to our moral feelings which creates our emotional pressures and problems, but rather our resistance to those feelings.

The only way to escape our hypocritical way of being is to repent. As long as we cling to the "lie" we sold ourselves that when we do wrong we are somehow justified in that wrongdoing, we will keep seeing others as our enemies. Remember, when I became offended at the elevator repairman I became a "different person," but in my mind so did he. Now he was someone I had to defend myself against. Now the elevator door was no longer the issue. I had made a morality play out of the situation. My helpfulness had been criticized, and I now had to prove I was right—even in my feelings—no matter that there might be a cost in personal agony.

We attribute the burden we experience while performing these actions as being caused by those about whom we complain. If we were to be honest in our assessment of ourselves (which is the same as saying, "If we were to repent of our refusal to do right") we would see that this manner of emotional suffering is self-produced. We would see how we make or "need" others to be enemies so as to justify our feelings against them.

Another way to express this same idea is to note that the natural man sees himself as a victim of situations, circumstances, and forces he thinks are beyond his control. Consider the proposition that Satan felt justified in his wrongdoing. He resented the Father and the Son. He was blind to the fact that he had become an enemy to them by his own acts. He then could be offended by their goodness, their godliness.

When we put off the natural man through repentance and obedience, through our acting on the ideas that come into our mind when we are guileless—and there are such times—we see our sins for what they were. In abandoning wrongdoing, we see an alternative way of being which, while we were sinning, seemed impossible for us to acknowledge or grasp. We even see, if we will shed the natural man, how rewarding it is to be compassionate and forgiving. In fact, we regret our own foolishness and wonder why we didn't repent earlier. We wish we could replay the same scene over again. Occasionally we even stand all amazed that we clung to our misery for so long.

Another aspect of this point has to do with others. If our relationships with others provoke or invite them to do to us what we were doing to them, then they also need us to be guilty of sins they can use to justify their feelings against us. When we repent, they may become angry. In their own justifying behavior they "need" us to be enemies just as perversely as we had needed them! If we seek to be reconciled with them they may accuse us of ulterior motives. After all, their fear of us is due to their past experience with us. From their point of view we were obnoxious before and probably always will be.

Alternatively, if we are true to the light within us when we are so accused, we sorrow. Our sorrow is not so much for ourselves as for them. We understand how they could mistrust us, based on earlier exchanges, and we may need to plead with them to forgive us and allow us another chance. The best way to bless them now, however, is to continue to be true, to continue to walk in the light. Our repentance is a powerful invitation for them to give up their defensiveness just as we have given up ours.

Before the elevator ride was over, I came to my senses. I became a different manner of man, walking in the light. I saw what I had been doing while hard-hearted and how it contrasted with my previous willingness to help. I turned to the elevator repairman, who seemed justifiably suspicious of my next move. I asked him, "Has it really been your experience that if you leave that door alone, it will close without having to wait forever?"

He was mildly startled by the question. "Well, yes," he said, "but I can see that the electric eye is out of alignment and I've got to adjust it."

I don't really know if, while he was on the elevator with me, he too had put on the coat of the natural man. But I felt my question to him, and his answer coming back, were genuine. I got off on my floor knowing I did not need to have, nor did I have, him as an enemy.

In brief, I can be genuine in my way of being or I can be hypocritical. I can be true or I can be false. I can love my wife and children as myself or place myself above or below them. I can act in their best interests or undermine them. I can joy in their success and mourn with them in times of their sorrow, or I can be jealous of their blessings and relieved that their sorrows are not so personally mine. Such ways of being with others are expressions of the quality of life and character I am living in the present moment. The most important question about my different ways of being with others does not involve the degree or intensity of my feelings or actions. It is not how damaging my hypocrisy is to them or how beneficial my compassion. The issue is one of being true or being false; being obedient or being disobedient to what I know is right. The quality of life I live is an expression, first, of morality, not personality.

The gospel suggests that, even for those who have been raised in darkness, "light and truth forsake that evil one" (D&C 98:37), and that by living by the light we have, in the present moment we can cast off what sometimes seems to be psychological chains produced in the past. When we honor our spiritual understanding by being obedient, examine our lives according to what is moral, and seek to distinguish between right and wrong, or good and evil, we see possibilities that we could pursue, line upon line.

The hope offered by the restored gospel is that we can put off the natural man and, through the atonement of Christ, become a saint—submissive, meek, humble, patient, and full of love (see Mosiah 3:19). Many philosophies and world views do not grant the possibility that we can become like the Savior. In some instances that is because the philosophies are actively hostile to the possibility of human change. In other philosophies, observers of the human condition see the impatience, resentments, and emotional troubles of everyday life and deem them normal, even typical—and certainly not escapable. Even the concept that change comes line upon line and day by day seems insufficient to benefit those suffering in the present moment. What good does it do for them to wait for the eternity necessary to perfect them or free them from their current miseries? And in some philosophies which disqualify the meaning of spiritual understandings, pessimism about human change is linked with a logical demand: What good is religion if the only benefits come after this life? Shouldn't the benefits of religion show up on this planet, now? But of course such philosophies grant neither hope nor progress, and they often consider human pettiness to be evidence of human nature, of "just the way we are."

Observers who are rational and logical about the human condition and also pessimistic about change can defend their view with the front page of any newspaper. The topics are greed, murder, deceit, destructive competition, vanity—such stories document "the way we are."

Latter-day Saints have evidence, however, that such a despairing view of humanity is not the whole story. First of all, we know that what is being observed is "natural man" at his or her "best" (or worst). Self-centeredness, jealousy, resentment, defensiveness—these are descriptors of self-destructiveness as well as of those who live as enemies to God. Our own experience suggests that altruism, compassion, forgiveness, charity, honesty, and sacrifice are also expressions of the human condition. That humans can be benevolent and empathic in one moment and harsh and hostile in the next is a mystery dissolved when we do not try to label a person's way of being in the world as "just the way they are." If we define a person's way of being with others as his or her "personality," and mean that is "just the way they are," we have denied either their power to change or their responsibility for having become as they are. Spiritually speaking, the Savior's offer to help one become a saint is available to all. Ultimately, whether we receive him is the measure of our progress, of our ability to change for the better, no matter what our "personality" might be.

## Application to Marriage and Family Relations

What this all means for everyday life is that solutions to marriage relationship problems are simpler than we often suppose, even though they are not necessarily easy. When Gretta discovers Garth has been spending beyond their agreed-upon budget, she raises the issue. He blames her for being hard and picky. She responds that he can't expect to be trusted if he violates their financial contract. She also points out that every month they overspend postpones their dream of moving from an apartment to their own home. He then accuses her of being materialistic, and reminds her that people have got to live once in a while or they'll go crazy. She responds that if she had known marriage was going to be like this, she wouldn't have consented in the first place. He then silently rehearses the idea in his head that she is demanding, emotional, and not what she seemed when he met her.

This is a dramatic but realistic escalation of what should be attempts to solve a financial disagreement. In a few short exchanges, the very identity of the other person and the foundation of their relationship is in jeopardy, at least psychologically.

If this scene could be rerun according to each person's willingness to be guided by conscience, by their personal moral commitments, it would unfold differently: Gretta discovers Garth has been spending beyond their agreed-upon budget, and she raises the issue. He admits he blew it. She asks what can be done to keep them on their financial targets—especially since they are trying to save the down payment for a house within the next twenty-four months. He admits he sometimes feels that their future goals have so financially constrained them that the present moment has been mortgaged. She asks if that means they should put off the home for another year. He admits he doesn't feel good about that, either. After a while she proposes that he accept homemade sack lunches instead of patronizing the corporate cafeteria, and that the money saved be placed in a "whims for us" jar to be used for doing crazy things together every month. Such a solution to this disagreement is not so much an expression of talent and creativity as it is of willingness, commitment, and restoration of the moral meaning of their financial boundaries.

Of course, some will think such a transformation from argument to mutuality is a bit forced, naive, and unlikely. Would that be because one party to such a discussion could continue to be hard-hearted? Gretta discovers Garth has been spending beyond their agreed-upon budget, and she raises the issue. He blames her for being hard and picky. She responds that she thought their financial plans and goals for purchasing a home were mutually agreed upon and voluntary. She asks if they can rearrange the budget categories to give him some "craziness" money, while keeping the future house money intact. He then accuses her of being materialistic, and reminds her that people have got to live once in a while or they'll go crazy. She asks if he sees a way to live in the present moment without mortgaging the future. He then complains that she is making him feel guilty. She asks what his own conscience would suggest as a starting point of solution. He accuses her of not playing fair, and of making him feel more guilty. She explains she does not want to be his enemy, but his partner.

At this point he finds it so difficult to keep complaining about her that he falls silent. At first his silence is a hard-hearted way of wordlessly saying to her, "You are impossible." She waits and then says, "Whatever we decide on this is less important to me than being one with you." His silence transforms to regret that he has been a hard person. He says: "Thank you. This argument really hasn't been about money, but about my own selfishness. I've just been making excuses to justify myself. Let's start over."

Of the three versions of this scenario, only the last one actually occurred between the real Gretta and Garth. Neither the total love unfeigned example nor the unresolved, mutually accusing one actually happened. But all three examples could have been real. Money matters, educational decisions, lawn care, distribution of allowances to children, the celebration of an anniversary, travel to the family reunion—we can use any everyday life task to create emotional distance and disharmony or unity and oneness.

When we are hard-hearted, we use temporal issues like these to prove that life or our marriage is a burden. We can literally argue about anything, because what we argue about is usually not the real issue. We can avoid our moral responsibility and feel victimized by others over anything we wish. We can huff and puff in self-righteous impatience. But, as the eighteenth-century philosopher George Berkeley once noted, such ways of being with each other are examples of how "we raise the dust and then complain we cannot see." To examine our hearts, to admit our faults, to search our consciences—these are starting points of solutions we refuse to consider when we blame others.

The way we are in the world, including the way we treat our companion and children, is something we help create. As agents, we have the ability, in every moment, really, to "choose liberty and eternal life," as Jacob teaches, or to "choose captivity and death" (2 Nephi 2:27). Our choices come down to acts of obedience or disobedience to the light and knowledge we possess. More specifically, the Spirit of Christ is given to everyone that they might know good from evil (see D&C 84:46). That which invites and entices us to do good and to believe in Christ is sent forth by the power and gift of Christ (see Moroni 7:16). People who behave in Christlike fashion, whether they ever heard of the Savior or not, are being true to this light. If they have not heard of the Savior they simply lack knowledge and ordinances.

In marriage, the quality of our companionship is related to both knowledge and obedience. We may have been exposed to a limited amount of light and knowledge by growing up in a dysfunctional family, but if we are true to whatever light and knowledge is ours, or that we may acquire, we will be given more, and so it is possible as we get older to get better also. If we have been raised in darkness we will be ignorant of the light and will need experiences with light, which is one of our purposes for coming to earth. Marrying a person who lives in the light is a way of assuring we will refine ourselves. Forgiving one another our dark moments keeps us on track for fulfillment and peace. Marrying someone who was raised in darkness and brings it forward is also an opportunity, for we can, by the manner of person we are, confront them with the light. Gretta and Garth are both capable of living in the light or betraying it. They can either create and magnify their own troubles or dissolve them. They can progress line upon line, but only when willing to be true to covenants, commitments, and conscience.

If we are to make sense out of our lives, we must grant the possibility of change and of our ability to see moral meanings. We do not always act according to the light we have, but to remember that we have had moments of living true to the light, or that we have seen others who have lived by the light, is fundamental to our progress. No doubt our way of being in the world determines what we learn; but we determine our way of being.

We live in a culture which often invites us to see ourselves as victims of, or trapped by, our previous experiences. But if we grant the possibility that we can always respond to light and truth, then we not only live in our world with hope but we also acknowledge and understand how the Atonement applies to us. We can appreciate how the Savior descended below all things and that we may cast our burdens on him.

Thus we live in the world in one of two ways: true or false. When we live true, we see others' needs, we understand light and truth, we can then honor our commitments, act in behalf of others, and bless the next generation. This is all consistent with the idea that obedience is the first law of heaven.

Moreover, should we live falsely, we see ourselves as victims. We then may rationalize bad behavior on our part as we blame others for our difficulties and thus call good evil and evil good. This amounts to wickedness, which, as Alma taught us, never was—or can be—happiness (see Alma 41:10).

When we take gospel principles seriously enough to realize that it is possible to live the commandments, and yet in spite of the light we thought we had acquired we engage in destructive behavior with others, it is not a sign of "the way things are" but is evidence that we are being in the world falsely. We are shunning the light; we are refusing to live true to our responsibilities and may even think it is a burden to try. Everything about our experience becomes twisted when we resist the light. That is true even with our emotions. They become expressions of the natural, unconverted man, and we then falsely think we can't help how we feel. After all, we really do feel frustrated, or helpless, and they are "our" emotions. But while we cannot change those feelings by a conscious act of will, we surely can give them up, because such emotions are symptoms, and not the cause, of our betrayal of the light, of what we know is right. The natural man is thus

produced by our own wrongdoing; it is a condition which is a consequence of sin. President David O. McKay noted:

> I wonder how long it will take us to realize that in matters of temper
> nothing can bring us damage but ourselves—we are responsible for what
> helps us and for what injures us—that the harm that each one sustains
> he carries about with him, and never is he a real sufferer but by his own
> fault. I think you get that thought, and yet the tendency of each one is
> to blame someone else, the wife blaming the husband, the husband
> blaming the wife, children finding fault with the parents when the fault
> lies with themselves. If in the dignity of manhood such a man [or
> woman] would cease to magnify his troubles; would face things as they
> really are; recognize blessings that immediately surround him; cease to
> entertain disparaging wishes for another; how much more of a man he
> would be, to say nothing about being a better husband and a more worthy
> father! A man who cannot control his temper is not very likely to con-
> trol his passion, and no matter what his pretensions in religion, he
> moves in daily life very close to the animal plane. ("Something Higher
> Than Self," *Improvement Era*, June 1958, p. 407.)

The solution to "animal plane" behavior is to give up our resistance to the atonement of Christ with its attending way of being in
the world. Then, behold, a new world opens to us. We see possibilities,
including the ability to act upon the environment and not be acted
upon. We become offspring of God in fact, in our daily living. We give
up guilt and experience love. We no longer look for how others are
creating problems for us, but we examine how our way of being could
invite solutions. We realize we can't demand that others change for us,
but given that *we* can change we now have opportunities open to us to
which we were blinded while living as a natural man. We no longer
find life a series of ups and downs on an elevator out of control. We
find nobody else can push our buttons without our collaboration. We
become sensible to our imperfections in a way that involves humility
instead of self-doubt. Our acceptance of the Savior's mission in both
attitude and action gives us confidence rather than fear and worry.

When we do all this, we are being in the world differently than
we were when we were living as natural man. Our way of being is an
expression of our wholeness, and of our true identity. We discover
that when we live this way, what we have given up was of little worth.

All we need to do in all of this is to be honest *in the present moment*. Honesty is not an external quality we seek outside ourselves. It is fundamental to a way of being which takes the mission of the Savior seriously and grants that light and truth forsake that evil one. This way of being is available to all.[2]

*Terrance D. Olson is chair of the Department of Family Sciences and a professor in that department at Brigham Young University. He served as an editor of the* Encyclopedia of Mormonism. *He has served on national committees addressing adolescent pregnancy and issues of character and citizenship in family life education. He received a Ph.D. in marriage and family living from Florida State University, and is the author of numerous articles for professional journals. He has taught at the University of New Mexico in Albuquerque. In the Church he has been a Cubmaster, high councilor, bishop, and stake president for a BYU married stake. He and his wife, Karen, have six children.*

---

2. For further reading, the following sources are suggested: *Teach Them Correct Principles: A Study in Family Relations* [manual] (Salt Lake City: The Church of Jesus Christ of Latter-day Saints, 1992); Warner, C. T., and T. D. Olson, "Another View of Family Conflict and Family Wholeness," *Family Relations: Journal of Applied Family and Child Studies* 30 (October 1981): 493–503.

# 14

# HAPPINESS FANTASIZED AND REAL

## C. Terry Warner

An individual obviously in pain comes to you for counsel. We'll suppose this person is a woman, though it very well might be a man. She tells you she feels deprived, even cheated, of nurturing, emotional sustenance from her husband. "Isn't marriage supposed to be sharing and communion, at least some of the time, so that the partners can have the support and the strength to meet the challenges and hardships of life? My husband gives me none of that. He's completely wrapped up in himself. I have given and given to him, while he carries on with a heart like flint, completely task-oriented and uncaring."

The argument underlying this lament is that marriage is meant to be an intimate union, a union distinguished from mere cohabitation by its spiritual and emotional quality. The partners have promised one another to become of one heart. They have committed themselves by covenant to give one another respect and unreserved affection. By that definition, this woman is contending, she has no marriage. She says she's done everything humanly possible to create one, but cannot because of her husband's hardness of heart.

She doesn't want a theoretical answer from you. She wants, or at least says she wants, practical advice, something she can do now to make a difference, but she is profoundly pessimistic about the possibility of finding it, for she has become convinced he will never soften his heart.

How do you assess this situation? I want in this paper to offer what will seem to many a radical and perhaps even shocking suggestion: This woman's heart has become hardened toward her husband. Many options exist for her that, in her hardness, she will not see. If she repents she will begin to discover them. I will share a story which illustrates some of these options, and which teaches that our salvation does not lie in a change of our circumstances but in a change of our hearts. This proposition will cease to seem preposterous, I believe, when we understand something of the extent and power of Christ's redemption.

The story is from a man I'll call Jeff. He put his experiences on paper in an effort to understand the process of repentance he was going through, and agreed to the publication of the following summary of his story with the excerpts I have included here.

As a newlywed, Jeff desired to live the gospel as best he could. He assumed he would be able to manage all the obligations that lay before him in life: to be a good husband, to provide for and nurture his family, to serve in the Church wherever he might be called, and to make whatever professional contribution he could. As his family grew and his Church responsibilities increased, he found himself often falling behind his co-workers. Whereas they would renew themselves by recreation in the evenings and take days off, he had only begun his day when he got home from work. He wrote that he spent no time regretting this circumstance; he and his wife, Linda, just did what they had to do, month after month, then year after year. Many Latter-day Saints know his story well, for it is their own.

The arduous tenor of his routine seemed to accumulate like plaque on the walls of arteries and veins. After a time it began to crimp his love of life and his spontaneity, and though it did not entirely staunch the flow of hope and of affection in his relationship with Linda, it slowed it down considerably. He wrote that though his marriage was never in danger, it lost some of its luster. Both he and Linda felt weighed down by more demands than they could meet.

Gradually Jeff began to think less in terms of the load they were bearing together, and to see Linda as the source of his problems. In his eyes, she would worry overmuch about maximizing every opportunity that opened up for their children, and about all the social and maintenance obligations Jeff was supposed to meet. He began to see her as overly demanding and lacking in sensitivity for his burdens. He says that looking back from the vantage point of the present, he can appreciate that she too felt deprived and neglected and would sometimes get discouraged, just as he would. Indeed, he wrote that he cannot comprehend how she did it all. "But at the time, in my clouded feelings, I sympathized much more with myself than with her."

One year there penetrated this somber setting a bright burst of light, as if springtime had returned following a depressing winter. Jeff's company had assigned him a project in a nearby city in which all his talents were brought to bear for the first time in his career. What is more, he found himself working with people who shared his interests and delights. He rediscovered friendship—not just friendliness, which had always been part of his and Linda's (mainly Church) social life, but friendship. The members of the project team simply had a joyous time together; they taught and enriched one another, and looked forward to their work with great anticipation.

So exhilarating was it all to him, in comparison with the overload life he shared with Linda, that he began to feel guilty for it. The guilt confused him, for he had done no wrong that he knew of. Far from it, he had been impressed that the project was a blessing prepared for him through the influence of heaven.

This dissonance precipitated a spiritual crisis. Though objective facts seemed far too ordinary to constitute a crisis, Jeff said, he could scarcely have been more tormented. "I was deeply troubled because I felt that even though I was not abandoning my duties at home, I had lost my commitment to these duties. I wondered how my heart could be so divided."

He entered a period of intense and desperate prayer, feeling his soul to be at stake. In the course of this odyssey he passed through several stages of understanding of his condition. This progression of understanding contains many lessons that may help others who find their marriages not completely fulfilling.

Initially, Jeff believed he was being required to sacrifice what he loved wholeheartedly in favor of doing his duty. He thought of himself as caught between two good things, one more obligatory and the other more desirable. It bewildered him that the desirable one seemed to have been given him as a blessing and now was being taken away. He could only suppose this was happening to make the sacrifice more painful and poignant. He wrote:

At the time I expressed in my journal these thoughts: We are told we will be required to sacrifice everything. This includes what we love most. We must be tried until we love God above all things. The trial comes where we can least bear it. Certainly not where we have planned for it. What I enjoy most and have the hardest time giving up, this must be required of me. What we are asked to sacrifice in life is probably not something evil. It is something worthwhile and valuable to us.

Why would I be required to make this sacrifice? Because the Lord wants to change me from a petty person troubled by unworthy desires into a person he can trust.

The only hope I have is to come unto Christ, listen carefully to his Spirit, and serve him with dedication. I don't think this will make the sacrifice less painful. But I think it will keep me from losing faith in the Lord. In the end, I know the Lord will heal the pain of this loss, though I cannot imagine how that is possible.

No sooner had Jeff arrived at this understanding of his situation than he came to a remarkable realization. He discovered that he himself had created his inner conflict! If he had done any wrong in this matter, it was not by becoming involved in the work or with the friends who graced it, but by his role in the burdened-down life he and Linda had forged for themselves. He wrote: "I could see, as I tried to think through the conflict I felt, that I was more responsible than anyone else for the problems I was discouraged about. I have added to the clutter, tolerated the hectic schedule, taken on too much, and procrastinated too much. I could have set my house in order, put first things first, trained the children better, and set aside time for using my talents, but I haven't done so."

The third stage of Jeff's self-understanding surprised him even more. He discovered this: *To the extent that he had allowed his life to become a drudgery, to that very extent he imagined that he could find emotional salvation in his work and in his friendships.*

I want to emphasize this point by suggestion that this is a case of a person's making part of his life (his work and his friendships) an object of fantasy. This is not to say he was imagining this part of his life, but rather that he was imagining that it would bring him happiness.

One of the elements of his fantasizing that troubled him most he expressed in these words: "I came to realize that depending on my new relationships for happiness was my way of finding fault with how things were at home. In a way, I was telling myself that if it weren't for my burdens there, I could be happy. I could tell myself that there *really* were too many demands, that life *really* can become overwhelming. Maybe this was so. But when I was really honest with myself, I knew I'd held back. I blew family pressures out of proportion so I could have an excuse for not giving my heart at home. It was like I asked myself, 'How can I be cheerful and at peace considering all I've got to do?' "

Fantasy of Jeff's kind is a flight from reality. By fleeing reality, fantasizers find fault with it. They are discontented with, resentful of, their present situation. "What I have is not enough" is the complaint of people who feel this way. In their mind, it is not possible to be happy given their lot in life. They live by the doctrine that happiness is circumstance-dependent. Their problem is not their desire for things to be different—there is nothing wrong with that—but their conviction that unless things are different, they can't be happy. Many joyful souls have labored long and faithfully to make the world a better place, our own pioneers included, but they did not refuse to be happy in the meantime.

It helps us appreciate the devastating quality of this sort of fantasizing to offer a few other, more blatant examples of how we human beings indulge in it. For instance, we fantasize about a rival's downfall, wishing her to get what she deserves. At the prospect of vengeance we salivate emotionally. Or we let our minds be dominated by an obsessive aspiration—for example, to lose 30 pounds or be named corporate vice-president or be accepted by a parent we feel has rejected or demeaned us. Or we dream of the day when a rebellious child (or domineering mother or inconsiderate spouse) will have a change of heart—then, we imagine, all our problems will be solved. Or we nurture a wayward affection, for a person or perhaps an exotic place, in whom or which we might escape the tedium and irritations of our present existence. Or we indulge morbidly and addictedly in greedy or pornographic or violent thoughts. Or we swamp ourselves in hopelessness, which consists of fantasizing coupled with belief that the fantasy can never be achieved.

This last option is the condition of the woman we imagined at the beginning of this article and of Jeff when he began to believe he needed to sacrifice his happiness. In cases such as theirs, the counterfeit "high" that accompanies the prospect of having what they wish for and the despondency that comes with doubting it will ever be theirs—these are twin sides of the single "dis-ease" I am calling fantasy.

In this kind of fantasizing, we are choosing the path opposite of faith in Christ. We refuse to believe that our present circumstance, our parentage or talents or body or appearance or opportunities, can ever become blessings to us. We reject the possibility that the Redeemer could ever turn them to our advantage. There can be no blessings for us, we are convinced, without a change of circumstance. Thus, to quote a famous anti-Christ, we assume that we fare in life "according to the management of the creature" (Alma 30:17), and that the more we can acquire of our fantasies the happier we will be. Fantasy, as you can see, is a pagan modality of existence, not a faithful one. (Realizing this, we can find new meaning in the Lord's admonition to Martin Harris: "Thou shalt not covet . . . ; nor seek thy neighbor's life" [D&C 19:25]—not only should we not *take* our neighbor's life, but we should not wish we had his life instead of our own.)

Think about this fantastic belief on which Jeff was operating. He believed he would be transformed by a change of his circumstances! He was pinning all his hopes on *magic*, which I define as a transformation of his life that involves no process of redemption.

Magic? Yes. For what in fact happens when the objective facts of a fantasy are realized? Everyone knows. We might experience a temporary rush, but with disappointing rapidity we adapt to the new situation and begin to reexperience the same kinds of discontents we thought we had escaped. (Anyone wanting to can find illustrations of this familiar story in the acquisitions of the super-rich or the liaisons of movie stars.) For though the circumstances change, we take who we are with us; we remain the same person—a person disposed to evade responsibility for his or her condition by finding fault with present circumstances. How could anything be different for Jeff until he himself underwent a transformation? Jeff believed in the impossible—or in other words, in magic.

Seeing how he had found fault with his circumstances at home helped Jeff see that his fantasizing had been more than a flight of his imagination. He had withheld his heart from Linda, found her less adequate as a companion in happiness, at least in the situation they shared, than his newfound friends. (How surprised he was to realize this!) When he came to this stage of understanding, he suddenly could see not only that Linda too had felt deprived—this he had long recognized—but that *he* was the person who had deprived her. In longing for more affection and nurturing for himself, he was refusing to care for and nurture his wife. "I was worried about me, not about her. I looked at her and wished she would change, but I was the one who needed changing. How could I not have seen this before?"

This humbling insight led Jeff immediately to solutions. It told him what faith required. It eschewed magic altogether. He had gone wrong not in giving way to the reawakening of friendship, as he had feared, or of joy in his work. He had gone wrong in disbelieving that the Lord could bless him, redeem him, in his present situation. He wrote, "I had failed to give myself with all my heart to the family which God had given me." It was his failure to cultivate his allotted portion gratefully that made another situation seem to promise him salvation.

Jeff's trust in magic, his wish not to be saddled with his lot, his capitulation to hopelessness, his refusal to take the bold steps necessary, with all holiness of heart, in order to cultivate his lot in life faithfully—all these were self-deceptions that arose from his rejection of the Redemption. This explains why without faith, faith in the power of the Redemption, it is impossible to please God. So Jeff's fantasizing, and with it the sense that the joy of friendship was tainted with selfishness, came from having indulged himself in fear or laziness with regard to the inheritance he was commanded to cultivate and enjoy. Sacrifice was required of Jeff—not sacrifice of the joys which had overtaken him, but of the way he was misusing these joys as an excuse for not tending to his inheritance wholeheartedly.

This at last was the sacrifice that, he felt, really was required of him—*a sacrifice of sin, not a sacrifice of happiness.* (How distorted life gets for the sinner!) And when he began to make that sacrifice, when he threw himself without reserve into the labors and for the people and with the talents given to him, he could write:

> Already the conflict I felt between "duty" and "happiness" is gone. What I have learned is that I need to tend my corner of the vineyard and "let God give the increase." Not putting my whole heart into my stewardship made it into a drudge. This lie colored everything and resulted in the conflict I felt.
>
> I know now that if I am not faithful in every way to my stewardship, the feelings of conflict will return. The Spirit whispers to me, "Cultivate your part of the vineyard, and if you do not, you will begin to be ungrateful and wish you were working elsewhere."
>
> My conflict is gone. My task is not choosing between happiness and duty, but between giving myself to Christ (and to others for his sake) and holding back.

I too have learned this in my experiences with the Spirit of God. Every situation can be redeemed and turned into exactly the preparation we require for a fulness of joy—to the extent of our faith in Christ's redemptive power. To that extent, the very circumstances we may have cursed will turn out to be our schooling for salvation. (And no words can speak the consolation this principle brings as I consider the sorrows of my brothers and sisters living in dreadful conditions throughout the history of the world. They too are being prepared for joys as unspeakable as their sufferings.) Faith is hope in Christ, while fantasy is hope in magic.

Jeff related what happened a few days after the self-discoveries I have been summarizing here:

> I was working in my garden and I started to think again about my blessings and what I've learned over the past few weeks. I love the Lord's Spirit, and the feelings of cleanness and understanding that come with it. It hit me with great force that I don't want anything different from just the way it is. I do love what God has entrusted to me, and so I can put my whole heart into the present moment. I can do the work that needs to be done. I can choose exactly what's right without worrying about anything else. I want to live all my life like this, in the faith that only if I live this way do I accept my challenges, afflictions and trials as being exactly what I have needed to help me to progress to this point. Everything is just the way it should be, and I wouldn't trade it.

Recall the severe persecutions suffered by the people of Alma the Elder under the occupational army of Amulon. They were driven to cry incessantly to God, first aloud and then, when threatened with death, in their hearts.

> And it came to pass that the voice of the Lord came to them in their afflictions, saying: Lift up your heads and be of good comfort. . . .
>
> And I will also ease the burdens which are put upon your shoulders, that even you cannot feel them upon your backs, even while you are in bondage; and this will I do that ye may stand as witnesses for me hereafter, and that ye may know of a surety that I, the Lord God, do visit my people in their afflictions.
>
> And now it came to pass that the burdens which were laid upon Alma and his brethren were made light; yea, the Lord did strengthen them that they could bear up their burdens with ease, and they did submit cheerfully and with patience to all the will of the Lord. (Mosiah 24:13–15.)

Near the end of his story, Jeff wrote:

> For a while I thought my trial meant I would have to live with what
> I called "the sweet thorn in my heart." But as I discovered the Savior's
> love and accepted my lot willingly and joyfully, I slowly started to see
> that the thorn wasn't a thorn at all, but a bud that had remained en-
> closed in rigid leaves because I had withheld my heart from those who
> depended on me. Now the leaves have opened. Linda has never been
> more dear to me. I thank God for this difficult but blessed time of learn-
> ing. With Paul I pray that nothing will separate me from the love of
> God which I have tasted. It is, as Nephi said, delicious to the soul and
> desirable above all other things.

Intriguing corroborations of what Jeff learned can be found
throughout the scriptures. I offer two examples. In Deuteronomy 1,
Moses recounted that the children of Israel feared to claim the inheritance the Lord intended for them; they murmured because they were
sure the present inhabitants, "greater and taller" than they, in cities
"great and walled up to heaven," would destroy them, and they feared
this in spite of the Lord's having delivered them out of Egypt, led
them in the wilderness, and promised to give them the land. On the
other hand, the Lord needed to warn them not to take a fancy to certain lands through which they would pass, including those held by
the children of Esau, Moab, and Ammon. "Take ye good heed unto
yourselves . . . meddle not with them; for I will not give you of their
land, no, not so much as a foot breadth; because I have given [it] unto
[them]" (Deuteronomy 2:4–5; see also 2:9, 19). Bountifully did the
Lord bless them; he intended to prosper them and expected them to
enjoy their inheritance. But he forbade them to take what he had not
given them.

King David, on the other hand, took what the Lord had forbidden, an inheritance that had been given to another. This he did even
though he had been as abundantly endowed as anyone ever has. How
crushing to him must have been the words of the prophet Nathan:

> Thus saith the Lord God of Israel, I anointed thee king over Israel, and I
> delivered thee out of the hand of Saul;
>     And I gave thee thy master's house, and thy master's wives into thy
> bosom, and gave thee the house of Israel and of Judah; and if that had
> been too little, I would moreover have given unto thee such and such
> things.

Wherefore hast thou despised the commandment of the Lord, to do evil in his sight? thou hast killed Uriah the Hittite with the sword, and hast taken his wife to be thy wife, and hast slain him with the sword of the children of Ammon.

Now therefore the sword shall never depart from thine house; because thou has despised me, and hast taken the wife of Uriah the Hittite to be thy wife.

Thus saith the Lord, Behold, I will raise up evil against thee out of thine own house, and I will take thy wives before thine eyes, and give them unto thy neighbour, and he shall lie with thy wives in the sight of this sun. (2 Samuel 12:7–11.)

Now, some may object that Jeff's situation and mine were not nearly as severe as many, where, for example, individuals have been victims of profound rejection or abuse. Their unhappiness is the product of horrible experiences, the objectors will say, not a failure of their faith in Christ's redemption. So we cannot apply Jeff's solution to them. Recovering faith may avail nothing in their situation; in fact, they may be too engulfed in pain to muster faith.

This objection confuses the issue. I have not suggested that every affliction will or even should be healed. I have suggested instead that we can be redeemed *in* our afflictions, and even *because* of them, if we are humble and faithful. "All things work together for good to them that love God" (Romans 8:28). To me this means that recovering faith will always avail much, whether or not our outward circumstances, including physical and emotional debilities, are changed. I know, for example, a number of people who have worked faithfully through severe depression, enjoying remarkable spiritual experiences and receiving assurances in the process. Still they suffer relapses, and during those times life is truly hard. But between these souls who are exercising all their faith and those who have given way to hopelessness, there is an enormous difference. In the lives of the faithful the Lord is working his redemption.

There may be cases of debility so severe that faith itself is impossible; of this I am not sure. But I suggest that we not too hastily assume that any particular case is of this type. That means we should never despair of trying the remedy of faith. It would be faithless not to.

But the question of whether some may in this life be incapable of faith is a question different from the one we are considering, which concerns the remedy for unhappiness available to all who *can* have faith, even if they or others happen to believe they can't. And that remedy consists in no longer thinking we must ignore or challenge or rectify or compensate for our circumstances in order to be happy, but in learning instead the way of acceptance and patience and trust in Christ.

The young Joseph Smith encountered verses in James which enjoined him, because he lacked wisdom, to ask of him who giveth liberally and upbraideth not. Just prior to these verses come two which express my point succinctly: "My brethren, count it all joy when ye fall into divers temptations; knowing this, that the trying of your faith worketh patience" (James 1:2–3). Much more likely than the possibility that we will find faith itself limited is the possibility that we will find that we have not exercised it enough.

More than twenty years of studying the amazing properties of self-deception have convinced me that much that we take to be afflictions imposed upon us by circumstance are in fact our own doing; we manage to deceive ourselves and others about who is responsible for these hardships. When we accept our circumstance and tend to it faithfully, we cease to project responsibility elsewhere, cease to live the lie that we are victimized beyond redemption, and let go of our resentment and our fantasies. Suddenly all is transformed. Of this I have heard many others testify, and I testify of it myself.

Amulek described this transformation: "Come forth," he said to the oppressed, whom he might have pitied and indulged, "and bring fruit unto repentance. Yea, I would that ye would come forth and harden not your hearts any longer . . . and . . . if ye will repent and harden not your hearts, immediately shall the great plan of redemption be brought about unto you." (Alma 34:30–31.)

Notice that Jeff's story says nothing of any transformation in his wife. Would it have invalidated his testimony if she had not changed in response to him? No, and this is a primary point: Joy in Christ does not depend upon circumstance; the Christlike feelings Jeff experienced did not depend upon change in Linda, just as Christ's own feelings do not depend on change in others.[1] And this point answers the question with which this article began: What if you are in the situation of the

---

1. If Jeff had tried to change in *order* to change his spouse, then his effort would have been manipulative rather than repentant; he would not have come unto Christ.

woman I described there, and your marriage partner provides no emotional sustenance? You don't know how much fault for this is yours.
But this you can know: If you accept your situation and bring yourself
to Christ, you will find in him the power to love your partner anyway.
You will be able to trust that in his exquisite timetable your spouse's
hour of repentance opportunity will come—and that your hour is
here already. You will see for yourself how, in the change of your
heart, the Lord redeems even this vale of sorrow and turns it into joy.
Can anyone having a testimony of his kindly power doubt this
promise? "In the world ye shall have tribulation: but be of good cheer;
I have overcome the world" (John 16:33).

This decidedly does not imply that we should suffer all abuse
whatsoever without attempting, in a righteous way, to stop it or to
leave. Whether and when to take either of these steps is an individual
decision for which we can receive inspiration. All that we can infer
from what has been said here is that, if we would proceed in righteousness, we must harbor no recrimination in our hearts—whether
we stay in the situation or leave. And this means that our decision
will not be guided by the fantasy that our chance for happiness lies in
relocating ourselves.

Assailed in the work of his ministry by afflictions and tribulations
of many kinds, the apostle Paul wrote: "For I have learned, in whatsoever state I am, therewith to be content. I know both how to be
abased, and I know how to abound: every where and in all things I am
instructed both to be full and to be hungry, both to abound and to suffer need. I can do all things through Christ which strengtheneth me."
(Philippians 4:11–13.)

And "all things" includes waiting for one's redemption with a lamp
full of oil, keeping vigil through the coldest nights, while the world
fills the landscape with fantasies for which they abandon the Lord and
his promises: "For they shall not be ashamed that wait for me" (Isaiah
49:23). The jewels that ultimately will sparkle in our crowns will be
found in the soil of the lot God has given us to cultivate.

**C. Terry Warner** *is a professor of philosophy and the chairman and founder of
The Arbinger Company, a group devoted to helping couples, families, and organi-
zations. He received his Ph.D. in philosophy from Yale University, and has taught*

at the university level for twenty-seven years. He has been a visiting senior member of Linacre College, Oxford University, and the dean of the College of General Studies at Brigham Young University. His area of focus is moral and social philosophy, and his ideas about human relationships have been adopted and propagated by business consultants, family therapists, social psychologists, counselors, and medical doctors.

# 15

## MARRIAGE:
## AN ADVENTURE
## IN LIVING AND GROWING
### Marilyn Jeppson Choules

*T*he summer that I was seven, I had the first hiking experience I can remember. On a cool June morning near Banff, I gazed over the clear surface of Lake Louise, letting my eyes continue on up to view the glacier above. Then my father spoke: "That's where we're going today." The glacier looked like a tiny patch of white on the high mountain slope.

Later, after walking through the brush around the lake, we began our ascent. I remember the air growing cooler and my legs beginning to feel tired when the glacier was just barely in view. As the mountainside grew steeper I feared I would fall. I remember wishing I was back in the tent under warm blankets. I had never imagined that this walk to the beautiful glacier would be so hard and cold and scary. I had not known I could feel so tired. But my father and mother encouraged us onward with rests and raisins and hiking songs.

I will never forget the moment my father said, "There it is." I looked up. In front of me I saw the gigantic white expanse. Just as we approached its edge, my mother said, "Oh, look down at the lake." It was now so small. My heart was singing. I had done it! I had climbed the whole way. Even though the trek up had been hard and cold and I had wanted to quit many times, the view was worth it. Up there, I saw what I could never have seen from the tent below.

The very nature of an adventure lies in overcoming obstacles and anticipating things unexpected. We can never know at the beginning what the end holds in store. Like my trek to the glacier as a seven-year-old, marriage is an adventure, complete with obstacles and rewards. Too often for couples, the wedding becomes the end goal when it is actually the beginning of the hike together. The trek may feel steep and difficult and even lonely at times. However, searching the scriptures, communing with God through prayer, and keeping an eye to the eternal perspective can be those nurturing stops along the way where we rest, eat raisins, and sing songs.

## A Common Pitfall

In marriage, we sometimes view each other's behavior as selfish. This behavior may actually stem from feelings such as fear, insecurity, loneliness, or confusion. When we have any of these feelings, without the ability to relieve them, we become angry and needy, which leaves us insensitive to the rights and needs of our partner.

## An Eternal Perspective

Vanessa[1] was expecting her third child. Her husband, Tim, was several years into a business venture. She was supportive of the enterprise, even helping with small deliveries, errands, and book work. The issue troubling their marriage was Vanessa's behavior towards Tim. His description of the situation was this: she acted as if he had to account for every minute and his time spent away from home was a personal affront to her. Vanessa described feeling rejected and unloved when he wasn't with her.

Tim related his memories of her in their dating days. At that time, he said, she was confident, involved in work, school, and a variety of activities she enjoyed. Now he felt trapped and exhausted trying to meet her needs. For her part, Vanessa said she felt unloved and unappreciated. She stated that she knew she was demanding but felt that because she was giving everything she had and didn't take time for herself, Tim should act in the same way. Whenever he wanted to watch a basketball game or go on an outing with his Boy Scout troop, Vanessa felt this meant he didn't love her.

---

1. All names have been changed.

It was evident that Tim and Vanessa loved each other and were committed to their marriage, but they were both in great pain and could not continue as they were.

In Vanessa's efforts to be a good wife and mother, it appeared that she had lost her sense of self and measured her worth by how much time Tim spent with her at home. It seemed she didn't feel valued unless Tim was right there, doing what she wanted, or expressing recognition and appreciation for every little thing she did.

We continued to sort through this problem and look for solutions. After a few sessions with them, I made a suggestion. "Vanessa," I said, "you need to realize who you are as a daughter of God and be more in tune with your spiritual self and your potential. I would like the two of you to arrange to be apart for twenty-four hours. This time is for you, Vanessa, to spend thinking and praying, letting your heart and mind be open to who you are, to get a sense of your earthly mission, the nature of your eternal spirit, and what you want to do with your life. I want you to tap into that intelligence which God organized a long time ago; that spirit in you destined to learn, grow, and develop into an adult woman; the same spirit cherished by God; the same spirit excited about coming to earth and obtaining a beautiful body." I stressed the importance of her being alone and praying for inspiration in seeking direction in her life. As they left my office that day, I did not know what would happen. I ached for their pain. I knew how hard they were trying. I hoped for a breakthrough.

When Tim and Vanessa returned the following week, I saw from the glow on their faces that something had changed, something had vastly improved. Vanessa was eager to share her feelings. She said, "I feel so peaceful. It was given to me to understand my potential." The extent of what she experienced was personal and sacred to her and remained private. But through her experience she awakened to a much greater awareness of who she was and what her Father in Heaven expected of her. She now had an eternal perspective. With this heightened awareness she no longer needed to have Tim validate her worth by his presence or his constant expressions of appreciation for all she was doing.

Tim was as excited as she was. "This is the Vanessa I remember: confident, energetic, and excited about life, experiencing things, growing and developing." Vanessa still had work to do in changing old patterns and habits. Tim needed to learn what his role was in supporting her in these changes and helping her develop in ways not limited to being the business and family servant.

Though not everyone in troubled marriages experiences as dramatic a change as Vanessa did, some similar elements must be in place if progress is to be made. These elements are: a desire to take responsibility for one's own life and a willingness to learn new things and grow in ways that will stretch the heart and mind. I also believe that we must understand our origin and destiny, our potential as God's children, and the purpose of this mortal life. Likewise, we must be consistent in our prayers and study of the scriptures if we are to grow spiritually.

The scriptures are filled with references to the eternal nature of our beings. One of my favorites is found in the Doctrine and Covenants: "Even before [we] were born, [we] with many others, received [our] first lessons in the world of spirits and were prepared to come forth in the due time of the Lord to labor in his vineyard for the salvation of the souls of men" (D&C 138:56).

Earlier in time, Abraham was privileged to see the intelligences, or spirits that were organized, in the premortal life. He relates: "Now the Lord had shown unto me, Abraham, the intelligences that were organized before the world was; and among all these there were many of the noble and great ones" (Abraham 3:22).

Part of understanding our eternal nature involves an appreciation of who we are and what our potential can be. We are the children of God. This message is repeated numerous times. The Lord said, "I have said, Ye are gods; and all of you are children of the most High" (Psalm 82:6). In Paul's teachings to the Romans, he observed, "The Spirit itself beareth witness with our spirit, that we are the children of God" (Romans 8:16).

With this understanding of our potential as God's children, we can gain a sense of worth and a vision of our possibilities. Sometimes, however, this belief in our potential is limited to a mortal perspective as a result of the influences of the world. I will illustrate with another example. A young man named Ed came to see me one day. He had told some of his friends that he did not want to live anymore. Their concern for Ed led him to me. His second wife had just told him that she wanted a divorce. He described feeling utterly rejected, hopeless, and devastated. As we explored together the recent events of his life, he shared similar feelings of rejection he had had earlier in his life. He remembered a scene from his boyhood in which his father was yelling at his mother while packing a suitcase to leave. "I can't stand it any longer," his father shouted. "You and that kid are pigs, stupid pigs; I'm not going to be saddled with this mess any longer." Ed described how he stood there watching as his father left the house. He told me: "I felt so awful; I knew it was my fault; I was no good. If I had been a good boy, he would have been able to love me enough to stay."

I asked Ed, "And what do you believe now?"

He hung his head and said: "I'm kind of ugly; I'm dumb. I guess I'm not very good either—neither of my wives have wanted me."

My heart went out to him. What a harsh example of how we are sometimes blind to our divine potential! Here was a married man still living with severe trauma that began in his youth. He certainly didn't believe that he could ever possess enough goodness or intelligence to become like his Heavenly Father. Such a notion seemed impossible to his mind. Yet his friend Dave, the one who made the appointment for him, had told me: "He's the best friend I've ever had. He is so good and so loyal. He would do anything for me."

As I worked with Ed in the following weeks, I came to know that Dave spoke the truth. Ed was kind, thoughtful, and responsible. He had a delightful sense of humor. Sadly, he did not see those things in himself. He was still seeing the little boy whose dad had walked out saying he was a "stupid pig." As a child, Ed did not have an opportunity in his home to learn who he really was with respect to his divine nature and potential. However, as he became acquainted with the gospel and was loved by caring friends, he began to heal and to feel his spiritual worth as a son of God. Such knowledge and application of true principles can allow a person to transform his life, even to achieve ultimate perfection. This we are told in Doctrine and Covenants 132:20: "Then shall they be gods, because they have no end; therefore shall they be from everlasting to everlasting, because they continue; then shall they be above all, because all things are subject unto them. Then shall they be gods, because they have all power, and the angels are subject unto them."

I say to couples: Seek to gain a clear vision of yourselves as sons and daughters of God. Come to appreciate your divine potential to become exalted beings.

## Individual Abilities and Talents

As we endeavor to understand our potential, it is helpful to recognize that we are each a unique combination of talent and ability. We are individuals with the capacity to think, ponder, and exert control over our destiny. As we look at the many different personalities around us that make up the Lord's kingdoms, it appears that perfection does not mean we are to become clones of others. "For all have not every gift given unto them; for there are many gifts, and to every man is given a gift by the Spirit of God. To some is given one, and to some is given another, that all may be profited thereby." (D&C 46:11–12.) The remainder of this revelation identifies different gifts that people may receive. Verse 26 affirms the reason for spiritual gifts: "And all these gifts come from God, for the benefit of the children of God."

Each of us needs to accept individual differences. We need to avoid comparison with others. We need to avoid seeing our own talent or ability as inferior or less valuable than that of another. We need to recognize our own gifts, talents, and intelligence and then nurture and develop them as Christ urged us to do in the parable of the talents. In doing so, we can have the same report: "His lord said unto him, Well done, thou good and faithful servant: thou hast been faithful over a few things, I will make thee ruler over many things: enter thou into the joy of thy lord" (Matthew 25:21).

I say to couples: Value your individual talents and abilities.

## Marital Differences

I remember talking with a couple about some of the challenges of being single. The husband, Brad, said: "We are both strong in our views and opinions, but I am grateful that Felicia sometimes says to me, 'Wait a minute, there is another side to that,' or 'I have another thought that perhaps we need to consider.' I have a brother who isn't married. Sometimes he tends to go off on a tangent. I realize that he doesn't have a wife to lovingly bring him back when his thinking gets a bit distorted."

Often couples come into my office with this complaint: "We are just too different. We are so far apart." And without fail, each expresses great loneliness despite the fact that they are married. Most often it isn't differences that cause problems as much as it is the inability of both to respect and value the differences that do exist.

I remember a classic case. Erik loved sports, especially football. He appreciated the finer points of the game. Ellen disdained what she called that "rough and animal-like behavior." She, on the other hand, loved the refinement of a graceful and romantic ballet. Erik was neat and meticulous about the organization of things—tools, appointments, and schedules. Ellen was not that way. She was spontaneous and casual about the way things got done. Erik was goal oriented and anxious to finish the task. Ellen loved to visit, to laugh, and to enjoy a task or activity without worrying about its completion date. Even if it never got finished, she seemed to enjoy herself, and others enjoyed being around her.

One can see how these differences could lead to conflict—and they did. By the time I met this couple, they were contemplating divorce. Both were hurt and angry. Ellen believed Erik saw her as a lazy, disorganized, and incompetent woman. Erik believed that Ellen thought he was critical, bossy, always needing to be right. As the three of us worked together, two factors seemed to come into play. First, they had a hard time seeing their differences as *assets* in the relationship. Second, their system of communication, as a way to resolve these differences, was not working.

In time, however, they came to see and appreciate their individual strengths. Erik came to value Ellen's ability to make tasks enjoyable, and Ellen could see that Erik's ability to organize was an important asset in some areas of their marriage. Their differences actually gave balance to their living. When they could see it this way, they were able to enjoy living their lives without leaving things undone. They felt good about their individual contribution to the marriage and yet could see value in the strengths of their partner.

I was happy to see them learn that advantages come from two approaches to many of life's situations. There were times when Ellen enjoyed an activity separate from Erik while he talked to his friends about the ins and outs of sports. And yet they could come together and enjoy joint activities as well. Ellen learned to value the teamwork that was essential for winning at football, and Erik learned to appreciate the grace and beauty of ballet. Each was enriched to a greater degree as they learned to value their differences.

I say to couples: Rejoice in your differences. The opportunity to hear a different viewpoint and gain a fresh perspective can broaden and balance us, and we can thus lead more meaningful and interesting lives.

## Cleaving

Women have the unique potential to bear children. Sometimes there is frustration and misunderstanding over the interpretation of this difference for women. This is illustrated in the marriage of a young couple. The wife, Jeannie, was pregnant with her third child. Greg was in the second year of a career he loved. As yet his salary was meager. Jeannie was working full-time to supplement their basic needs. Greg's pattern in the family was to relax on the sofa, in front of the television, while he issued attacking criticisms and demands to Jeannie and the two toddlers. Greg had grown up in a home where for a husband this was the model he had learned. When they came to see me, Jeannie was exhausted. She needed help and appreciation.

In the book of Moses we read: "Adam began to till the earth, and to have dominion over all the beasts of the field, and to eat his bread by the sweat of his brow, as I the Lord had commanded him. And Eve, also, his wife, did labor with him. And Adam knew his wife, and she bare unto him sons and daughters, and they began to multiply and to replenish the earth." (Moses 5:1–2.) The Lord commanded Adam to labor for his sustenance. He also indicated a partnership with Eve, in that she labored "with him." The next verse gives attention to the children Eve bore. As a woman, I feel attuned to the need for all women to feel sustained by their husbands as they bear children. When a husband can share in the responsibility of his wife's pregnancy—i.e., sharing housework, child care, shopping—she will be better able to care for her health and that of the unborn child and endure the stress of childbearing in general.

I love the dramatic use of the word *cleave* in Matthew 19:5: "For this cause shall a man leave father and mother, and shall cleave to his wife: and they twain shall be one flesh." There are several meanings for the word *cleave*. One meaning is "to adhere, cling, or stick fast." Another meaning is "to be faithful." These meanings seem to indicate that part of the husband's role is to be trustworthy, to protect, and to support his wife in an emotional way. President Ezra Taft Benson gave this counsel to LDS husbands: "What does it mean to 'cleave unto her'? It means to stay close to her, to be loyal and faithful to her, to communicate with her, and to express your love for her. Love means being sensitive to her feelings and needs . . . putting her welfare and self-esteem as a high priority in your life." ("To the Fathers in Israel," *Ensign*, November 1987, p. 50.) Men have been given the responsibility of the priesthood. And it would seem that cleaving to his wife—with the full meaning given by the prophet—is one of an LDS husband's most important responsibilities.

I remember a beautiful example of this principle. A young couple in their early thirties with several children came to see me. Penny found herself immobilized. Her husband, Greg, indicated that there didn't seem to be anything physically wrong with her. As I met with Penny over the next few months, she unfolded a history of much childhood abuse of every kind. My work with Penny required a great amount of time. Going back to her past through therapy was an ongoing emotional struggle for her. However, in order to heal, Penny now needed to expand this great amount of energy. Greg still came to sessions with her. He took notes. His role was to be supportive.

When children are abused, their young minds draw inaccurate conclusions about the meaning of what they experience. Their inaccurate beliefs govern much of what they feel, how they behave, and the way in which they view the world. As we examined and struggled to remake Penny's belief system, Greg was attentive. Many times she would become discouraged and feel overwhelmed with it all. Greg would put his arms around her and assure her that she could do this and that he was there to help her. Over several years as Penny struggled, sometimes feeling suicidal, Greg was consistent in his supportive role.

Greg's work was often affected, due to interruptions: a desperate phone call or the need to shuffle the children between baby-sitters. Sometimes there was nothing to do except stay at home to keep Penny safe and to care for the children. Of course Greg's career suffered. He went through several jobs. Sometimes Penny felt so guilty, she wanted to be dead so "Greg and the children wouldn't be saddled with her and could move on with someone who could be a real wife and mother."

Greg and Penny continued working hard on changing old beliefs and thinking patterns. They worked on building new habits of behavior. It was a slow, painstaking process. They did it together. I have never seen a more beautiful picture of unconditional love. Although her healing process greatly affected their lives, Greg was consistent in his love and support of Penny. I stood in awe of his ability to deal with the impact of this stress in his life. In response to my concern about his well-being he said: "I love Penny. She is my eternal companion. Whatever it takes is not too much. We will be fine." Now, much later, their lives are healthier. Greg has blossomed in his career and recently opened his own business. Penny feels good more of the time and is developing her talents as she continues to be a wife and mother. Greg's example of unconditional love created an atmosphere in which Penny could heal. His behavior reinforced the belief patterns she was working to develop—that she was lovable and valuable.

We have been given clear counsel regarding the importance of love: "And above all these things put on charity, which is the bond of perfectness" (Colossians 3:14). "I am filled with charity, which is everlasting love" (Moroni 8:17). "Now abideth faith, hope, charity, these three; but the greatest of these is charity" (1 Corinthians 13:13).

Is it any wonder that Christ's teachings stressed the importance of love? When he was asked which was the greatest commandment, he replied, "Thou shalt love the Lord thy God with all thy heart, and with all thy soul, and with all thy mind. This is the first and great commandment. And the second is like unto it, Thou shalt love thy neighbour as thyself. On these two commandments hang all the law and the prophets." (Matthew 22:37–40.)

At the Last Supper, Christ again stressed this great principle: "A new commandment I give unto you, That ye love one another; as I have loved you, that ye also love one another" (John 13:34).

The need to feel loved and valued completely was strongly brought home to me during a session. I had been working with a delightful couple, Jay and Brooke. Each was talented and charming. Over time Brooke had been distancing herself from Jay in a number of ways, indicating that she had no positive feelings towards him. Jay acknowledged that he had been hot-tempered in the early years of their marriage but felt he had made a lot of improvement. As I worked with Brooke, she revealed that her older brother had molested her when she was a child. She was embarrassed about this and felt disgusted and ashamed. She had never told her husband or anyone else.

We did some work on it along with some other self-esteem issues, but their marriage did not improve. They came into a session one day obviously upset with each other. In disciplining the children, Jay had done something that angered Brooke. As we discussed things, the part that seemed to bother her the most was that what Jay had done was different from what they had agreed upon together. Being left out of the process also bothered her. Brooke said: "It felt like I didn't matter; that I wasn't important." She expressed more anger and hurt until she was in tears.

I asked her husband not to defend himself. I asked him to let her express her feelings. Finally, she turned to him with tears streaming down her face and said, "I just need to know that you love me whether I'm ugly or fat, whether or not we can have sex. I just want you to love me."

Brooke had felt that she could only be lovable if she was certain things to Jay. This had happened in most of her relationships in life. Himself in tears, Jay reached over to her and said, "Oh Brooke, I do love you. I didn't understand." What he hadn't understood before was that she needed to feel completely loved and accepted. In attempting to defend himself, Jay re-salted Brooke's wounds and her belief that she was unlovable and unacceptable.

Honoring the agency of a spouse is also part of unconditional love. Of course this is easier when we don't live with someone. A neighbor's choices won't affect our lives as closely as the choices of family members. Some time ago I had a conversation with a man in which the issue of his wife's not doing something he wanted her to do came up. I made the comment, "Why don't you tell her?" He said, "I've told her it matters to me, but I also believe that if and when she chooses to do it, it should be her choice." I was touched by his ability to honor the principle of agency in his wife's life, even though it was not the most comfortable thing for him.

One of the most moving examples of acceptance and love came when a woman wrote to me after she and her husband had abruptly terminated their counseling sessions. She wrote: "During the last session something hit me. He is trying as hard as he can. I haven't been willing to love him for the man that he is and the good things he does. I have only been determined that he change the things which were uncomfortable for me. I see that he can't change anymore right now. So I've decided to concentrate on the things about him I can love and just not worry about the others."

I say to couples: Strive to develop an unconditional love for your spouse.

## Forgiving

Another part of unconditional love is forgiveness. Forgiving and letting go of past wrongs and hurts is very difficult. However, the scriptures give some very specific directions: "But if ye forgive not men their trespasses, neither will your Father forgive your trespasses" (Matthew 6:15). "I, the Lord, will forgive whom I will forgive, but of you it is required to forgive all men" (D&C 64:10).

The need to forgive is plainly stated by the Lord. As I work with people who feel greatly wronged, I often hear: "I know I need to forgive; I want to; but I still feel so angry." Here is the key. Anger is usually some kind of defense, frequently born out of the attempt to protect ourselves from the fear of possible future pain or hurt—similar to an animal which feels threatened and fights back. Sometimes the anger is an effort to get restitution for a past wrong which hasn't been or cannot be mended. Animals do not have the intelligence to do anything except react. Men and women, however, especially disciples of Christ, must develop a more intelligent, loving, and kindly response.

Some suggestions that might help:

1. Avoid getting into similar situations in the future.
2. Learn to change the way your mind interprets the other's behavior as hurtful to you. Many times the assault is not personal but rather something the other individual says out of his sense of inadequacy.

While I was working with a marriage in which the husband had committed adultery, he said to me: "I love Nena [his wife]. I know I've been critical of her and unfair. I turned to someone else. It isn't her fault. It's my insecurity. It's my problem." It *was* his problem, but as long as Nena internalized—believed that she was inadequate and unlovable—and took responsibility for *his* behavior, she was unable to let go of her "defensive" anger. As she came to recognize that her husband's choices of behavior were his responsibility, she was able to avoid taking it personally and begin the process of forgiving.

I say to couples: Endeavor to be forgiving and look for other more productive ways to deal with pain and fear.

## The Importance of Communication

"And the Lord God said, It is not good that man should be alone; I will make him an help meet for him" (Genesis 2:18). It is meant for men and women to desire companionship with each other. God himself said that Adam and Eve should share in a "help meet" relationship.

As I talk to single people, in either a professional or a personal conversation, I continually hear: "I'm lonely. I want to share my life with someone. I want to plan, work, and build with someone." Our spirit yearns to share intimate thoughts, ideas, and feelings with a confidant. From that familiar relationship, an individual finds his or her worth as the spouse listens, shares, and counsels. Such intimacy is a chief purpose in marriage.

The process of sharing and connecting in a companionship takes place on several levels. Verbal communication includes the *content* of what we verbalize. It also includes the tone of our voice and its inflection. Body language includes our facial expression and other physical indications of openness, closeness, warmth, or distance, all read in the way we move and position our body. We all give and receive communications at both verbal and nonverbal levels. Many times we are not fully aware of the total message we send to others. Or, others may misinterpret our real intent. Most of us have witnessed someone loudly defending themselves with, "I'm not angry! What makes you think I'm angry?"

Because of individual life experiences and perceptions, not everyone gives or receives messages in the same way. Therefore, it is important to develop a checking system between companions to make sure that the message we intend to give is, in fact, the message received.

I remember receiving a call one day from a client named Virginia. She was excited about the progress in her marriage. Her husband, Sid, had been reluctant to learn and work on some new communication patterns. But, surprising her that morning before leaving for work, he checked out her message. "You mean," he said with excitement in his voice, "when you said you wanted to get a baby-sitter for the children, that what you really meant was that you wanted to spend the evening alone with me?" She concurred. Proverbs 2:2 gives us a simple guide to listening: "Incline thine ear unto wisdom, and apply thine heart to understanding."

I say to couples: Develop ways to communicate effectively. Seek to understand each other's feelings, thoughts, and views.

## The Importance of Commitment

Every partnership in marriage needs to be based on commitment. When an eternal commitment has been made and problems arise, our attitude becomes one of, "How do we work it out?" rather than, "If we can work it out." I remember Harley and Pauline. At first only Harley came to see me. Each week he was in a different place because his wife, Pauline, went back and forth about staying in the marriage. He said, "We can't plan a vacation, decide to remodel the house, or anything else." Even short-term planning is difficult without the assurance of a long-term commitment.

Joint planning helps clarify not only what your mutual goals are but also how you will achieve them. If we are willing to hear each other's desires, ideas, and needs, the planning process can be a wonderful bonding experience.

I enjoyed watching a couple complete this process one day in my office after a few efforts to practice together. Maureen had found a piano she wanted to buy. It was going to cost more money than Barry thought necessary. He wanted to buy a second-hand instrument at a fraction of the cost from a friend. Maureen was concerned with tone and style. Barry's philosophy was this: "A piano is a piano as long as the keys make a noise when the children plunk them." However, Maureen persisted. She expressed her feelings. She explained her need that the piano have good tone and that it match their decor. Barry listened to her with new patience. Then she said, "I can see that you are concerned about the cost. I am too. What can we do?" He suggested they check out a few more new pianos and a few more used ones. They decided to spend the next two weeks looking and then talk about it at a specific time. They grinned as they looked at each other. Then they turned to me and asked, "How did we do?"

"How do you feel?"

"Great," they replied.

"Then I think you have just graduated."

Short-term planning is easier when eternal goals are clarified. Barry and Maureen had already decided that adding music through a piano to their family life would assist them in developing their family's appreciation of gospel principles through hymns.

I say to couples: Commit to each other completely. Plan your earthly and eternal lives together in order to accomplish what you both want to achieve.

## Including the Spirit of the Lord in Your Marriage

The foundation of a marriage needs to include faith in the Lord and in his plan for us. When individuals within a marriage feel the Lord's love for them they, in turn, will feel lovable and confident in growing together. Remember the case of Vanessa. When she came to feel that God loved her, she felt valuable. She gained a knowledge of her abilities and her potential. Once she felt this, she could move forward in her marriage relationship.

Seeking God's guidance helps a couple reinforce their partnership of marriage and, most important, opens hearts for mutual understanding. Seeking the Lord in prayer invites him to give us guidance beyond our own knowledge and experience. Embracing the blessings of the atonement of Jesus Christ helps in the healing of past or present pain and wounds. Christ's words are: "Come unto me, all ye that labour and are heavy laden, and I will give you rest. Take my yoke upon you, and learn of me; for I am meek and lowly in heart; and ye shall find rest unto your souls. For my yoke is easy and my burden is light." (Matthew 11:28–30.)

I say to couples: Enjoy the strength and power of God in your marriage. He wants you to succeed.

## Summary

Like a long adventure, marriage is an ongoing process. Sometimes we expect a "happily ever after" marriage. We feel disappointed and frustrated when there are problems. We forget that obstacles, which are problems to be solved, are inherent in the journey. Our task, however, is to learn to overcome these obstacles together. As you set foot to the path, you will begin to feel the joy the Lord has promised. Remember the words of the Preacher in Ecclesiastes 9:9: "Live joyfully with the wife [husband] whom thou lovest."


**Marilyn Jeppson Choules** *was born in Albany, California, and grew up in Riverside, California. She received a B.S. degree from Brigham Young University in 1962, two master's degrees (M.Ed. and M.C.) from Arizona State University in 1980 and 1981, and a Ph.D. from Brigham Young University in 1989. She has worked as a counselor for the past fifteen years. She has served as president, counselor, or teacher in ward and stake auxiliaries as well as stake camp director. She married Albert Choules Jr. in 1987. Combined they have six living children and fifteen grandchildren.*

# INDEX